P9-CQN-601

DATE DUE			
FEB 14'83			

Toward
a Science of
Consciousness

Toward a Science of Consciousness

Kenneth R. Pelletier

Published in
association with Robert Briggs

 DELACORTE
PRESS / NEW YORK

Published by
Delacorte Press
1 Dag Hammarskjold Plaza
New York, N.Y. 10017

Manufactured in the United States of America
First printing
Designed by MaryJane DiMassi

LIBRARY OF CONGRESS CATALOGING IN PUBLICATION DATA

Pelletier, Kenneth R
    Toward a science of consciousness.

    Bibliography: p. 260
    1. Consciousness.   I.   Title.
BF311.P33   153   78-15290

ISBN 0-440-08972-7
ISBN 0-440-58640-2 (pbk.)

To Arthur M. Young
teacher, guide, and friend

Acknowledgments

Throughout the development of the ideas presented in this book, there were many individuals who were a great influence and help. Actually this book would not have been realized at all if it were not for the involvement of the late Janet Kafka who envisioned this book as early as 1974. Most of all I wish to thank Joan Lynne Schleicher and Robert Briggs, two friends who shared this vision and have given their unwaning support and encouragement. Among the many other people who were so important, I wish to thank Gregory Bateson, Robert O. Becker, Doug Boyd, David E. Bresler, Fritjof Capra, Geoffrey Chu, James Fadiman, Jerome Frank, Daniel Goleman, Elmer E. Green, Alyce Green, Joe Kamiya, Gay Luce, Charles Muses, Erik Peper, Karl H. Pribham, Hal Puthoff, Theodore Roszak, Jack S. Saloma, Jack Schwarz, C. Norman

Shealy, Saul-Paul Siraq, Huston Smith, Tarthang Tulku Rinpoche, Norman S. Tresser, Charles Yaeger, and R. James Yandell. Research and manuscript preparation are always essential parts of any writing and those individuals who provided invaluable assistance are Peter Dreyer, Dolly Gattozzi, Christopher J. Kuppig, Lee Peake, Francis Wilcox, and Celia Zaentz.

Contents

An Age in Transition

chapter 1

*T*HROUGHOUT the last decade, apocalyptic visions
have abounded in response to the increasing fragmentation of knowledge, dehumanization of the individual, and generalized disruption that has occurred
throughout the world. Despite this apparent chaos of rapid
social, ecological, and individual change, there is another
strongly enunciated perspective that views the upheaval as
symptomatic of a profound evolutionary transformation of
human consciousness. Dismal prophecies of our future society as totally dominated by group orientation with little
or no freedom for individual expression are based upon the
assumption that interdependency creates less need for individual initiative and creativity rather than for more. Population analysts forecast that a population glut might create
further stress upon limited living and working space. This

projection is based totally upon external geographic spaces and ignores the factor that such external limitations of expansion may very well provide the impetus for an unprecedented mapping of internal, psychological realms not limited by geographic boundaries. Rather than seeing the present state of disruption as a linear progression toward self-destruction, it is possible to view these events as an inevitable process marking the end of an outmoded conception of the individual and his most fundamental beliefs.

Contemporary Western societies are characterized by a frantic proliferation of material goods, ecological exploitation, and a fragmentation of knowledge into highly specialized compartments. Innumerable dichotomies are presented to individuals each day: inner and outer reality; science and religion; Eastern meditative techniques and Western technology and medicine; order and chaos; and life and death. Despite an increased awareness of the world about them, many people have experienced an overwhelming sense of confusion and disorientation because they do not have a conceptual framework in which to fit all the information they encounter. There is a pressing need for an integration and comprehension of these complex phenomena. Despite the apparent fragmentation of knowledge, dissolution of the nuclear family, and the disruption of contemporary society, there is also a movement toward increased integration and enlightened interdependency. One immediate lesson to be gained from the ecological crises of the recent years is that man and his environment are interdependent systems (Kahn and Weiner, 1967). Air pollution does not adhere to geographic boundaries and a depletion of oil in remote locations on the earth has a profound impact upon every individual in the smallest town in the United States. It is extremely difficult if not impossible to resolve these difficulties by focusing upon one isolated factor of the problem. Air contamination is not resolved simply by enforcing pollution standards on a few factories. What is needed is a multifaceted approach which considers the impact of the automobile, waste disposal, commuting patterns, mass transit, and numerous other factors. Ultimately the issue of air pollution involves the question of reorienting the lifestyles of the industrialized nations which have been accustomed to function on the concept of infinite supply and infinite disposability of material goods.

Environmental pollution is a graphic form of feedback to the individuals of the industrial nations indicating a fundamental shortcoming in the psychological outlook of the people who assume that unlimited consumption of raw material, land, energy, and the environment will not lead to severe consequences. Recent shortages and crises are symptomatic of the fact that overexploitation of any one environmental resource has unforeseen, often dramatic consequences. One message being fed back is that any part is an integral aspect of the whole. Furthermore, the part can only be fully understood by an overview of the purpose and function of the whole (Young, 1976a and 1976b; Whitehead, 1961). Such is the case with environments, societies, and individuals. Out of the chaotic conditions of modern man has come a pressing need and an earnest quest for meaning and life goals beyond material saturation. Perhaps only when a certain stage of material glut has been achieved can the pendulum begin its move toward higher values and aspirations.

Emphasis in the newly emerging fields of science is upon interdependent systems and holistic orientations which seek to understand the relationship of the part to the whole and the whole to its parts. This deceptively simple principle is at the core of a comprehensive, integrated, holistic, acausal view of phenomena. This point of view sharply differs from a specialized, compartmentalized, linear, cause-and-effect approach to the same phenomena. However, it is very important to note that, as with all seemingly opposing perspectives, neither position yields a totally adequate view. Mapped out in the following chapters is an overview of how the superficial oppositions of these systems can be reconciled. Involved is a fundamental reorientation of modern man's *Weltanschauung,* or "world view," which is shifting to a view of himself and his planet as one interdependent organism rather than as a fragmented cosmic machine. This is the vision now emerging in modern medicine, psychology, and physics, as eloquently stated by physicist Werner Heisenberg in *Across the Frontiers:*

> A feeling will gradually grow up that life on earth represents a unity, that damage at one point can have effects everywhere else, that we are jointly responsible for the ordering of life upon this our earth. From the cosmic distances to which man can penetrate by the means of modern technology, we see perhaps more clearly than from earth itself the unitary laws whereby all life on our planet is ordered (p. 68).

When statements such as these begin to appear in the works of Nobel Prize-winning physicists and when arcane doctrines such as the Tibetan *Book of the Dead* and the *Abhidharma* are available in paperback in many bookstores, there are indications of the dawning of a new age, an age characterized by a humanization of science and technology, increased emphasis upon philosophical and spiritual values, and a major revision of man's view of himself and his universe.

Recently scientists and laymen have addressed themselves to these concerns by turning toward the study of consciousness, that is, inquiring into the nature of the mind that perceives, evaluates, and comprehends the events taking place in the world as well as perceptions formed within the mind itself. An immediate observation concerning the study of consciousness is that no dichotomous perspective—inner versus outer, material versus psychological, mind versus body—can provide an adequate description of the present state of knowledge. Any comprehensive definition of human consciousness can only be expressed as a reconciliation and integration of these and all other such oppositions. People of all times, geographic locations, and cultures have known the intricacies of consciousness but have expressed that knowledge in different metaphors. By juxtaposing these divergent glimpses of the nature of the mind, it is possible to sense and determine the common ground shared by all individuals who have explored both inner and outer reality. Yet today, many adherents of humanistic and religious disciplines dismiss science as inappropriate to their questions while the natural scientists tend to dismiss orthodox religion and the poetry of the humanities with equal disdain. These polarities are also noted by Heisenberg. One fundamental theme throughout this book is that the most important outcomes of physics, as modern man's most sophisticated science, are its philosophical implications. Addressing himself to the concepts of science and mysticism, Heisenberg notes:

> One extreme is the idea of an objective world, pursuing its regular course in space and time, independently of any kind of observing subject; this has been the guiding image from modern science. At the other extreme is the idea of a sub-

ject, mystically experiencing the unity of the world and no longer confronted by an object or by any objective world; this has been the guiding image of Asian mysticism. Our thinking moves somewhere in the middle, between these two limiting conceptions; we should maintain the tension resulting from these opposites (p. 227).

All too often man's concepts of himself and the universe oscillate between strident materialism and rampant occultism. These oscillations between polar opposites were observed by Martin Luther, who compared the beliefs of society to a drunken peasant who tries to climb on his donkey only to fall over on the other side; then he repeats the same process from the opposite direction in a never-ending cycle. Both the purely scientific/materialist and the mystical/spiritual views can be theoretically and experimentally justified to varying degrees, yet neither has demonstrated its adequacy in resolving the critical issues of man's quest to know himself and his world to the fullest. It is far more productive to consider both the humanistic and scientific perspectives than to dismiss either, for insight springs from unexpected sources—and syntheses.

Change and transformation are fundamental processes of any living system, and change seems to be inevitably linked with the partial or total destruction of what has gone before. In 1950, anthropologist Anthony F. C. Wallace proposed a theory of individual and cultural change that is particularly appropriate to the emerging study of consciousness. All individuals maintain an explicit or implicit world view, or set of beliefs and opinions concerning how the environment, culture, government, and other people function. Wallace conceptualizes that world view as a "mazeway":

It is . . . functionally necessary for every person in society to maintain a mental image of the society and its culture, as well as of his own body and its regularities, in order to act in ways which reduce stress at all levels of the system. The person does, in fact, maintain such an image. This mental image I have called "mazeway". . . . The "mazeway" is nature, society, culture, personality, and body image, as seen by one person (p. 264).

Due to social and environmental changes, the mazeway is never sufficiently comprehensive to interpret incoming data for the individual. When an overload of data occurs, the world view of that person must undergo a marked transformation, which Wallace terms "revitalization." Although the disruption of the old mazeway may occur over a prolonged period of time, the process of revitalization is seen as "usually occurring as a moment of insight, a brief period of realization of relationships and opportunities. The reformulation also seems normally to occur in its initial form in the mind of a single person rather than to grow directly out of group deliberations" (p. 270). As these fragments of individual insight begin to coalesce, a new order emerges in place of the old. Very often this new order is ushered in by the visionary experience of one individual who embodies the highest aspirations of the new culture. A striking example of such an individual was Black Elk, whose visions inspired an entire Indian nation, as narrated in *Black Elk Speaks* by John G. Neihardt. As in the instance of Black Elk, the prophet may not be welcomed and his effort may end in failure. But despite his personal downfall, the critical issue is the revitalization of a cultural order. Inherent in this new order is a sorting, integrating, and restructuring of elements from the old views into new ones. In modern times, components from psychology, physics, and mysticism have begun to coalesce and form the fundamental framework for a unified theory of consciousness.

Throughout the twentieth century, the attention given to the concept of altered states of consciousness was generated by the fact that influential thinkers—and, in the sixties, large numbers of individuals—experienced states of mind that were different from their normal mode of functioning. Through psychedelic drugs, fasting, chanting, sensory deprivation, and various meditative systems, and even reading Carlos Casteneda's series of books, people experienced other structures of reality. Upon returning to their usual state of consciousness, they realized that such experiences were precisely those ordinarily thought of as pathological, escapist, regressive, deviant, and subject to a whole host of other derogatory descriptions. As a consequence, much of the literature—as early as the writings of William James and Aldous Huxley—focused upon redefining these different perceptual states as having positive value for the individual and society as a whole (Tart, 1969; Pelletier and Garfield, 1976). Although the issue is far from being resolved, it seems unequivocal that various altered states can provide the occasion for unique creative insights into the nature of self, culture, and that shared construction termed reality. They may be thought of as tools of revitalization.

At the present time, a second aspect of research into and experience of altered-states consciousness is emerging. Many who left their normal societal roles to explore inner states have returned to their everyday pursuits with transformed perspectives on the questions that they had attempted to resolve. Perceiving themselves and the world about them in a markedly different way, they realized that the insights gleaned from these altered states have pragmatic applications and can serve as guides for innovation. Seeing the world in a different way made it possible for them to conceive of new ways to resolve old issues such as the nature of mind-body interaction and the basis of disease and healing. In later sections of this book, the details and implications of these innovations are explicated more fully. It seems that the knowledge gained from viewing old problems from new perspectives can have a profound effect upon the formulation of innovative solutions. Concepts derived from mystical reverie, dreams, or other altered states can have very pragmatic applications. Some individuals may dismiss the upsurge of interest in altered states of consciousness as a transient phenomenon. Others may choose to abandon the trappings of Western culture in favor of one of the numerous Asian traditions. On the one hand is denial, on the other is conversion, and either means will readily alleviate the conflict involved in the reorganization of an individual's *Weltanschauung*. Most important, it is necessary to reconcile Western technology with Eastern mystical and meditative traditions in order to bring about mutual enrichment rather than continued antagonism.

Material science and technology have been most extensively developed in the West, while the exploration of states of consciousness have been the province of the East. Science is defined as logical, rational, inductive, and dealing only with observable phenomena. On the other hand, mysticism is considered to be intuitive, holistic, deductive, and focused upon the unobservable phenomena of internal states. This compartmentalization of science and mysticism has persisted despite such recent syntheses as (1) the equation of the two hemispheres of the brain with two modes of consciousness—one logical and rational, the other intuitive and holistic; (2) demonstrations of voluntary control of the autonomic nervous system by means of biofeedback training; (3) discoveries of similarities of concepts in quantum physics and Buddhism; (4) applications of meditative techniques in the alleviation of physical disorders including cancer; (5) the phenomenon of twentieth-century astronauts experiencing transcendent states described in ancient religious texts; (6) studies of humanistic Indian traditions by Carlos Castaneda and Doug Boyd; (7) profound reformulations of the limits of scientific inquiry in Arthur M. Young's *The Reflexive Universe* and Thomas Kuhn's *The Structure of Scientific Revolutions;* as well as other striking examples of the integrations of scientific and mystical knowledge. In essence, both science and mysticism share a mutual goal, to know the nature of reality, and have even come to share a common vocabulary. Both attempt to formulate a paradigm, or model, of the universe that would be agreed upon by all individuals who are adequately skilled in that method of inquiry. Although these two approaches superficially appear mutually exclusive or even antagonistic, a great deal of modern research reveals that they share a common ground. This book explores the features of that common ground.

One brief anecdote helps to convey the sense of this convergence between these two ways of knowing. During the prolonged NASA lunar-space flights, the astronauts experienced a number of unpleasant side effects such as enlargement of the heart, decreased peripheral blood flow, irregularity of heart rate and blood pressure, and other physiological and psychological alterations. It would have been difficult to rectify these disorders by relying on pharmaceuticals since the drugs would have to be tested for their effects under zero gravity. Such testing was not possible and an alternative means of regulating these physiological changes was sought. One group of researchers submitted a proposal based upon the observation that many of these physiological disturbances were occurring in bodily systems that could be controlled by means of meditative practices or through the application of biofeedback. In theory, the astronauts could be capable of self-regulating their peripheral blood flow, heart rate, and blood pressure through meditative techniques, which would avoid the problem of drug effects. That proposal was termed "Neurophysiological Autoregulation During Prolonged Weightlessness," but what was more revealing was its subtitle: "Electric Zen in Outer Space." As facetious as that subtitle might appear, it does embody the essence of the emerging holistic sciences. Those few words epitomize the recent convergences of meditation and technology, ancient Buddhist practices and modern space flight, and inner and outer space. It is a poetic expression of the observation that creative insights and applications arise out of the synthesis of such unlikely oppositions.

As surprising as this synthesis might appear, it seems to have accurately anticipated subsequent events. In December 1972, *Time* magazine reported, in an article entitled "The Greening of the Astronauts," that many astronauts had experienced altered states of consciousness during prolonged space flight. Either during the flight or after their return to earth, they experienced profound personal changes in attitudes and life styles. Under conditions of zero gravity, many had experiences that they described in words that could have been drawn from the mystical utterances of the most ancient Eastern teachers. During his lunar mission on Apollo XII, astronaut Edgar Mitchell experienced a unity with all inhabitants of earth and sensed the delicacy of a small, blue planet suspended in infinite blackness. These astronauts were men trained to command some of the most sophisticated technology of the twentieth century, clearly not given to flights of unrestrained fantasy. Their survival depended upon the ability to respond immediately to complex orders and to attend to the very pragmatic task of piloting a space vehicle. Despite these demands upon their time and attention, they experienced the sense of humility, awe, and inspiration usually found in the esoteric tomes of Eastern mysticism. Captain Mitchell expressed his experience most aptly with, "You develop an instant global consciousness, a people orientation, an intense dissatisfaction with the state of the world and a compulsion to do something about it" (*Time,* 1972). Once back on earth, many astronauts followed the dictates of their unique experience. Astronaut Jim Irwin became a lay preacher in the Southern Baptist church, Rusty Schweikert became interested in Transcendental Meditation, and Edgar Mitchell founded the Institute for Noetic Sciences for the purpose of exploring the nature of consciousness.

In his autobiography, *Carrying the Fire,* astronaut Michael Collins offers insight into his own alteration in consciousness resulting from his two space flights. Like Prometheus, who dared to give man the gift of fire from the gods, Collins offers modern man just as significant a gift when he states,

> I can now lift my mind out into space and look back at a midget earth, I can see it hanging there surrounded by blackness, turning slowly in the relentless sunlight. When things are not going well here on earth . . . I can gain a bit of solace and perspective by making this mental trip.

Throughout Collins's book is a sense of serenity induced by his vision of the fragile nature of this planet when perceived from the barren surface of the moon, a clear example of the integration of the inner space of mind and the outer space of lunar flight. Such a perspective is the Promethean gift of twentieth-century man. To be sure, all astronauts did not follow the same path. Some accepted positions in universities and business, but the one common factor appears to be that they all experienced some alteration in their usual mode of consciousness and adjusted their lifestyles accordingly. Astronauts are not unique in having experienced a more holistic concept of the earth as a finite planet and a sense of the interdependency of that planet and its inhabitants. It is important to note that other individuals have experienced similar insights in the midst of more mundane activity, or perhaps due to special circumstances such as a meditative practice, intensive biofeedback training, or a near-death experience. Yet it has been technology, as epitomized in the space program, that has forced science to consider the nature of the mind in a new perspective.

Only twenty years ago, science was the basis of man's most fundamental belief system. Orthodox religion had been successfully challenged once the scientific discoveries of Copernicus, Kepler, and Galileo were accepted. Their tangible discoveries concerning the nature of the solar system proved to be refreshing disruptions of the oppressive dogmatism of the Judeo-Christian religions (Koestler, 1968, 1972). Science offered man visible, testable, and observable proof rather than faith, dogma, and an oppressive liturgical hierarchy. Over the centuries science came to displace religious dogma as the basis of a comprehensive and compelling belief system. It was a "religion" that preached the doctrine that the universe was a rational system of logical laws and that these laws were knowable and, once discovered, could be used for the betterment of the human race.

During the early 1950s, it became evident that this structure was limited. Faced with results of experiments conducted in previously unexplored areas of research utilizing new technological means of inquiry—such as radioastronomy—scientists began to question the ultimately "logical" nature of the universe. In order to address the anomalies of their research, they postulated the existence of such phenomena as "black holes" in space and a subatomic level of activity involving unobservable entities to which they gave the name "quarks." Innovative theories in physics, attempting to deal with these phenomena, postulated an "uncertainty principle" at the heart of quantum mechanics (Heisenberg, 1958, 1971), thereby challenging the very nature of the traditional scientific method. Thus physicists led the way in acknowledging that the matter-and-energy universe was infinitely more complex than an aggregate of "billiard-ball" atoms colliding with each other in a logical, rational manner. Science had usurped man's naive belief in a god residing in the heavens but had so far failed to provide an alternative explanation for man's deepest questions about the nature of life, relationships with others, and, ultimately, about his own conscious awareness. Most individuals were reasonably content with the technological luxuries produced from scientific discoveries, yet a fundamental philosophical dissatisfaction persisted.

That uneasiness derives from the growing recognition that science and the technological applications of science are not synonymous. Technological innovation is a matter of engineering whereas scientific inquiry is more a matter of paradigms of belief systems and philosophy. Conveniences, luxury, and material well-being have been gained through technology, acquired by assuming a particular philosophical stance termed the scientific method. It is extremely important to note that the scientific method is valuable only to the point of acknowledging its limitations as well as its applications. Unfortunately, the science enterprise has become increasingly dogmatized, prescribing such limits upon the nature of inquiry that it has come to exclude more than it includes. Each day, researchers make new discoveries, but some of these are rejected because they point to interactions that are considered unacceptable under the dominant scientific paradigms. Examples of these anomalies are the role of psychological factors in disease, interactions between physicists and fundamental particles of their experiments, and evidence of genuine parapsychological phenomena. As more of this "unacceptable" data arises from reliable research laboratories, it becomes evident that there is a substantial body of data that modern science does not consider because the phenomena do not lend themselves to systematic scrutiny by traditional methods. At some point, and it seems near at hand, the decision arises whether to adhere to a particular model of science and continue to exclude those phenomena or to amend the scientific method so as to consider them.

Many laymen and professionals mistook the tangible successes of technology to represent the absolute certainty of the philosophy of scientific inquiry that made them possible. This great misconception of the physical scientific method has had a major effect upon the social sciences, ranging from psychology to medicine, which rapidly evolved to their contemporary forms during the apex of scientific innovation (Coulter, 1975; DeRopp, 1972). People looked to the human sciences for consideration of experiential factors such as values, purpose, emotions, and meaning. Yet this kind of data was inadmissible in objective scientific inquiry. From the social sciences came no respite since psychology was rejecting the unscientific theories of James, Freud, and Jung in favor of more simplistic, behavioristic models of man. Revision and change entail resistance and turmoil whether in politics or science, and such a transition is not to be undertaken lightly.

Psychology has always been relegated to the status of a pseudo-science vis-à-vis the physical sciences, and its practitioners have compensated for that fact by attempting to parody the experimental approaches of the material sciences. Words such as "awareness" and "consciousness" were replaced by terms such as "stimulus" and "response," with the mind reduced to a "black box" mediating between the stimulus input and the response output. "Homo sapiens" as a biological computer or cybernetic system was the model of the individual based upon classical physics. Under this paradigm, man became an elaborate machine whose behavior could be predicted, altered, and controlled through an examination and manipulation of his component parts. It was assumed that a part of behavior could be isolated from the whole of the individual—a belief totally consistent with the prevailing scientific assumption that a minute part of a physical system could be observed without reference or disturbance to the larger system. The latter assumption indeed held true in the physical sciences and was extremely productive. By the same token, behaviorism as an objective scientific method has been an invaluable and creative system for understanding observable behavior. However, both classical physics and modern behaviorism have foundered seriously when faced with an ultimate inquiry into the nature of consciousness.

Today, the newest theories of quantum physics, the widespread use of psychedelic drugs, an influx of Eastern meditative and religious systems, the rise of human potential growth centers, and a renewed interest in the functions of the mind—all are conveying and necessitating the consideration of a new science, a science of consciousness. This science needs to draw upon divergent disciplines yet be based upon the fundamental processes of human perception, for perhaps the most basic issue facing contemporary science is the nature of observation itself. The role of psychology in formulating such a science is noted by Eugene P. Wigner in *Symmetries and Reflections:*

> That a higher integration of science is needed is perhaps best demonstrated by the observation that the basic entities of intuitionistic mathematics are the physical objects, that the basic concept in the epistemological structure of physics is the concept of observation, and that psychology is not yet ready for providing concepts and idealizations of such precision as are expected in mathematics or even physics. Thus this passing of responsibility from mathematics to physics, and hence to the science of cognition ends nowhere. This state of affairs should be remedied by a closer integration of the now separate disciplines.

Included in this emerging integrative science is the observation that *all* scientific inquiry involves highly subjective processes such as intuition, hunches, and emotions, although these have been systematically excluded from the final descriptions of scientific inquiry. This strident objectivity, at least in surface appearance, has created a science that is cold, dehumanized, aloof, valueless, and a potential danger to Western man insofar as the scientific view of reality has usurped all others.

According to one critic of science, Theodore Roszak, modern science provides information about the world but is devoid of meaning. In contrast to this perspective is that of "gnosis" which, according to Roszak, seeks the "meaningfulness of things which science has been unable to find as an objective feature of nature" (Wade, 1974). Gnosis is an intuitive mode which perceives the meaning of factual data. It was an integral part of the sixteenth- and seventeenth-century science created by scientist-mystics such as Copernicus, Kepler, and Newton. The quest for meaning is not antithetical to scientific inquiry, but that burden has typically been refused by science in the name of objectivity. Roszak elucidates the position of the modern scientist as tantamount to the ministry of earlier cultures:

> It is precisely at this point—where we turn to scientists for a clue to our destiny—that they have indeed a Promethean role to perform, as has every artist, sage, and seer. If people license the scientist's unrestricted pursuit of knowledge as a good in its own right, it is because they hope to see the scientists yet discharge that role; they hope to find gnosis in the scientist's knowledge. To the extent that scientists refuse that role, to the extent that their conception of what science is prevents them from seeking to join knowledge to wisdom, they are confessing that science is not gnosis, but something far less. And to that extent they forfeit—deservedly—the trust and allegiance of the society (*Daedalus*, Summer 1974).

Increased disillusionment with the products of the present technological thrust of scientific inquiry has underscored the weakness of research devoid of humanistic philosophical guidance. In *The Greening of America,* Charles Reich makes an eloquent appeal for the psychological factors in scientific inquiry to be given equal consideration in the process of investigation. Edward Shils, a University of Chicago sociologist, opposes this position and asserts that contemporary society holds a deep and inherent trust in the achievements of science and that this trust is "not likely to be dislodged by a decade of bitter criticism by academic humanists and journalists." This observation might hold true were it not for the marked disillusionment with purely materialistic paradigms that is now a major topic of debate among scientists themselves.

Most importantly, a strict adherence to classical science completely overlooks the proliferation of information concerning the pragmatic implications and applications of a more humanistic science. While most individuals depend, whether consciously or not, upon the fruits of scientific research for their comfort and well-being, the bankruptcy of material satisfaction in modern society indicates a desire for a different form of gratification than can be obtained from scientific discoveries. This latter goal, though inherently excluded from classical science, is the primary focus of a science of consciousness. Based upon the research and clinical applications of biofeedback and meditation, pragmatic solutions are being found for such very real issues as physical and psychological health, the psychogenesis of disease and its prevention, self-understanding, and a clearer comprehension of not only life but death itself. It is to these concerns that the emerging science of consciousness addresses itself. While the classical scientific method will not likely be discarded, it is probable that its paradigms will be significantly revised as researchers turn toward considerations of the interaction between mind and matter, the observer and the observed.

As a reaction to the sterility of material objectivity, many individuals in Western cultures have taken up Eastern meditative and spiritual disciplines, seeking a personal philosophy unavailable in science and absent from traditional Western religions as currently practiced. That turn is quite justified, but not to the extreme of abandoning, or more accurately, attempting to abandon, one's Western heritage for a veneer of Eastern lifestyle. Wholesale rejection of Western society and an uncritical acceptance of Eastern teachings resolves nothing. Integration of these two life perspectives is certainly a far more formidable and rigorous task but its rewards are commensurately great. A joining of the insights of Eastern meditative systems and Western technology yields valuable syntheses (Bateson, 1972; Capra, 1975; Goleman, 1975).

No one needs to be a prophet to predict that there will be many more Eastern teachers and gurus who will emerge from Asia and come to the West. Undoubtedly, there will be considerable wisdom and compassion in their teachings, but even more important is a meta-message that Westerners may not recognize. That meta-message is that there are an infinite number of means to attain inner knowing, serenity, and access to higher states of consciousness. Within Buddhism alone there are more than 624 sects, and each one prescribes a specific meditative procedure for attaining clarity of mind. There are meditations based upon walking and sensing the contact between the earth and feet, concentrating upon a visual image or mandala, reciting prayers out loud or silently repeating a mantra, engaging in prolonged sexual intercourse or embracing complete celibacy, as well as numerous other well-developed meditative systems. Whatever predisposition an individual has regarding what he believes his path or way to be, he will find a teacher who will affirm, reinforce, and amplify that predisposition.

Historically, people who share common ideals and values tend to gravitate to each other and reinforce their shared predispositions. In doing so, they too often lose sight of the fact that their perspective is one of many, and they tend to separate the world into those who believe and those who do not, those who are saved and those who are not, and the whole host of divisive barriers between "them" and "us." This can be the case no matter how idealistic is the intent and purpose of the organization of individuals. It is unfortunate when individuals lose sight of the fact that their own predispositions are being affirmed by the teachings of a master or the tenets of a group and mistake the external dogma as absolute truth. Such a situation leads nowhere; it is merely a self-fulfilling prophecy. Teachings require evaluation, not blind adherence. The individual always faces the question of whether to follow and imitate the teachings of a master or to follow his own path and fulfill his own potential to the degree that the teacher has fulfilled his. In the medieval church the issue was to imitate Christ, *imitatio Christi,* or for each Christian to pursue his individual path. That essential question still remains open today with no definitive answer because it is entirely a matter of individual decision to follow inner values in the midst of social or peer pressure. Ultimately, the task of each individual is to learn and be open to what is offered and to find and define one's own way.

Among the most productive approaches to the study of

consciousness has been the use of neurophysiological instrumentation such as the electroencephalogram, for detecting electrical activity of the brain, to determine the observable correlates of subtle mental states. In approaching such research, one caution must be kept clearly in mind: to resist confining all the phenomena of human consciousness to electrical activity recorded from the brain—even in a purely physical approach to the study of the nature of consciousness. There is increasing evidence that the brain is a center of consciousness but that the entire nervous system of the body is responsible for various aspects of conscious awareness. An example of reductionism can be taken from Frank Waters's *Book of the Hopi*. According to their tradition, the Hopi "knew" that consciousness resided in the heart and they thought white men were foolish because they believed that they thought with their heads. Were a Hopi researcher approaching the problem of the neurophysiological basis of consciousness, he would elect to make a detailed analysis of the electrical activity of the heart rather than the brain. His primary concern would be to correlate various fluctuations in heart behavior with variations in levels of awareness. Since he knew that consciousness resided in the heart, he would either not attempt to detect such activity in the brain or would treat such patterns as artifacts to be discarded or filtered out rather than seriously addressed. Today, Western researchers are in danger of becoming equally provincial.

Our present science and common sense support the concept that awareness resides predominantly at a point behind the eyes, between the ears, and above the neck. In contrast to this naive belief stands a vast array of information, ranging from Vedantic texts to laboratory research results, that supports the concept that the entire body is an instrument of consciousness. One particular component of awareness resides in the brain, while other physiological systems of the body seem more attuned to other aspects of awareness. Thus, our language is laden with expressions indicating that the seat of the emotions lies within the heart and cardiovascular system. Common phrases such as "her heart goes out to you," "her heart is not in it," "his heart is broken," "their blood ran cold," appear to have a validity beyond the simple aphorism. Through the use of electronic instrumentation it has become possible to demonstrate that in certain states of consciousness various systems of the body are differentially affected. That aspects of consciousness are distributed in the body musculature, cardiovascular system, internal organs, and brain has been recognized in all meditative systems and has been the cornerstone of a wide range of body-oriented therapies such as Reichian analysis and Rolfing. Recognition of the interconnections between states of consciousness and variations in neurophysiological activity supports an expanded concept of awareness that contends that the entire organism is an expression of consciousness and various components of an individual's total consciousness are located throughout the body.

Also of increasing importance is the field of contemporary psychological and physical healing. Some of the most innovative approaches to the integration of science and humanism have evolved from the healing professions. By the very nature of their work, therapists must create pragmatic applications of abstract, conceptual knowledge concerning the interaction of mind and body. This interface of theory and practice has given rise to a number of creative systems for the translation of insights into creative approaches to disorders ranging from migraine headaches to cancer (Benson, Beary, and Carol, 1974; Simonton and Simonton, 1975).

In Western culture, man has been conceptualized as having a separate body, mind, and spirit. This body-mind-spirit division is readily evidenced in the structure of the healing professions. Physicians are dedicated to the treatment of the body; psychiatrists and psychologists are concerned with treating the mind; and yet a third group, the clergy, is attendant to the soul, or to spiritual healing. These areas of specialization tend to be discrete and antagonistic. Yet fragmentation and divisiveness among healing perspectives is not inherent in any of them. In contrast to the currently accepted Western mode of increasing specialization, "primitive" societies have tended to create healing rituals that involve the whole person, his family, his society, and environmental factors as an integral part of the entire continuum ranging from health maintenance to disease and death. In effect, primitive cultures practice a prototype of holistic medicine.

Within the healing professions a new holistic trend is emerging, which emphasizes the prevention of illness as well as treatment of the whole person when illness is manifest. Treatment is geared toward helping an individual to formulate a more positive lifestyle in order to prevent the onset of illness, or to view symptoms as self-signals that some aspect of his present lifestyle requires rectification. Specific symptoms and manifestations of an illness obviously must be treated, but in that process an individual can learn a great deal about himself and the psychological factors that created or aggravated his disorder. This model of holistic healing focuses upon the psychogenic factors in the onset of disease and the role of psychological attitudes in promoting self-healing. Most important, an equal emphasis is placed upon the maintenance of psychological and spiritual health. In this approach to healing, rituals of meditation and modern technology come together in a new way, and in the process both are changed.

Throughout the evolution of the contemporary healing professions two polarities have been clearly evident. On the one hand is a philosophical and clinical orientation that essentially dismisses all psychological factors in disorders and considers both disease and health maintenance to be based upon purely physical considerations. In contrast is an equally extreme point of view that maintains that all physical illness is the result of a psychological deficit on the part of the individual (Coulter, 1975). All too frequently, a simple cold or a minor illness is interpreted to mean that the person has made himself ill because of a sufficient lack of awareness. A misconception common to both these orientations is the separation of mind and body. Neither view is sufficient to create a comprehensive schemata of the origin of disease or health. If the prevention of pathology is the ultimate goal of the healing professions, then health practitioners and laymen need to consider the whole person physically, psychologically, and spiritually. The method is to gain as much understanding as possible about the person's relationship with his total environment. This includes family, peers, job, living situation, and—most critically—his concept of himself, which is the keystone of the person's personal view of his universe. Perhaps the most essential aspect of the movement toward holistic systems of healing is that this perspective requires a profound alteration in an individual's belief system, or personal paradigm. In modern sciences ranging from the neurophysiology of consciousness to quantum physics, it is evident that the structure of an individual's personal belief system concerning the self and the universe governs that person's experience. Inherent in any belief system is the self-fulfilling prophecy that what is expected will be observed and what is observed confirms the expectations. Experience occurring outside this cultural, social, and individual matrix, if it reaches awareness, is considered to be anomalous and is dismissed. An immediate implication of this circumstance is that it is possible for an individual, by reformulating his belief system, to become aware of a vast realm of new possibilities.

The pressing need for a more comprehensive interpretation of man and his universe is evident in the sorcery of Castaneda's Don Juan, the metaphysical implications of quantum physics and consciousness research, and in applications of meditation and biofeedback in the healing professions. Each day it is clear that medical researchers and practitioners need to abandon artificial distinctions between mind, body, and environment. This necessity was noted by Nikolas Tinbergen, 1973 Nobel Laureate in Physiology and Medicine, who stated:

> The more that is being discovered about psychosomatic diseases, and in general about the extremely two-way traffic between the brain and the rest of the body, the more obvious it has become that too rigid a distinction between mind and body is of only limited use to medical science, in fact can be a hindrance to its advance (1974, p. 26).

Convergences of the ancient and modern, the psyche and soma, the East and West, and mysticism and science have occurred over the last decade. Out of these confluences have come many of the innovations in theory and practice that are discussed in later chapters. At present, most therapy systems wait until a person becomes ill before treatment or intervention is initiated. Preventive or prophylactic measures are seldom considered despite the very substantial and persuasive body of evidence showing that certain psychological, environmental, or dietary conditions have a strong probability of promoting the development of severe disorders. Preventive care approaches are based upon the hypothesis that all disorders are psychosomatic in the sense that both mind and body are involved in their etiology. In traditional Western medicine, psychosomatic became synonymous with imaginary when symptoms persisted in the absence of clearly diagnosed organic pathology. However, psychosomatic factors such as lifestyle, Type A behavior, and stress can be changed in a positive manner before physical disorders become evident. This change in perspective permits a profound alteration in the practice of health care away from the correction of pathology and toward the preservation of health.

Another innovation, akin to the reappraisal of psychosomatic disorders, considers both physical and psychological illness as potentially regenerative rather than necessarily degenerative. Symptoms may be an indication of the individual's attempt to undergo a self-healing process. From the work of Jungian psychiatrist John Perry (1962) comes recognition of the possibility that certain forms of psychosis may be usefully left to run their course, rather than be sedated, because the person may be engaged in a deep, personal transformation. From the evidence of clinical biofeedback comes the idea that a patient's migraine headache may be the least drastic symptom that could be expected given the individual's life situation. In both these instances, the symptom is a manifestation of the person's attempt to resolve a personal crisis; a sedative masking or alleviation of the symptom may have no effect upon the more fundamental disorder. A pharmacological panacea for all disorders is increasingly unlikely, and it is important to acknowledge the limitations as well as the applications of a purely pharmacological approach to health.

It is far too easy to replace one set of beliefs with another set equally restrictive. There are many instances in which traditional healing practices are a necessity and their advances are unquestionable. However, it is also clear that a new class of "pathogens" has emerged, in that stress disorders such as cardiovascular disease, ulcers, headaches, and respiratory problems have replaced the infectious diseases as the major health afflictions of the post-industrial nations. These afflictions of contemporary civilization require a holistic approach that recognizes and mobilizes the individual as well as environmental factors implicated in disease. This approach maximizes prevention and frees existing systems to better handle the great burden of standard surgical and pharmaceutical treatment when it is required. There is a host of disorders that do not require acute care; they are largely due to stress or are symptoms of prolonged stress upon an individual. Stress and stress-related disorders can be alleviated to a large degree by a holistic orientation employing a variety of existing methods such as clinical biofeedback, exercise programs, and dietary modifications. More severe pathology can be prevented (Brown, 1975; Dubos, 1965; Pelletier, 1977). Most systems of preventive therapy are holistic in orientation by necessity. If a therapist's role is to maintain health, then he needs to consider the fact that social, political, and economic pressures may place an individual under extreme stress. It is very likely that all political, economic, social, and philosophical systems create tension for a certain group of people in a given population. Preventive therapy needs to direct itself to answer the questions of which of these aspects are innately more beneficial or more stressful to the psychological health of the individual.

Consideration of the whole person, rather than his parts, places primary emphasis on the psychological factors in the healing process, on the maintenance of health, and on the prevention of illness. Holistic medicine also recognizes the inextricable connections between the whole person and his environment. Psychological and medical researchers have demonstrated that mind and body function as an integrated unit. Health exists when body and mind function in harmony, and illness can result when stress and conflict disrupt this process. It is clear that specific psychosomatic and psychosocial influences upon an individual predispose that person toward certain disorders.

Disorders ranging from migraine headaches to cancerous tumors can be alleviated by maximizing the patient's ability to exercise volition and choice regarding the course of his treatment. Out of this discovery has come increased emphasis upon the patient being an active and responsible participant in the healing process rather than a passive victim of either the disease or the treatment. Here, an extensive body of research supports the concept of pathogenic or disorder-prone personalities, such as the Type A individual who is predisposed toward cardiovascular disorders, and the carcinogenic person who is likely to develop cancer when subjected to extreme stress. The factors involved in these personality types are well-documented, but methods of altering their influences remain virtually unexplored. Recently, innovations such as environmental medicine, biological rhythms, electromagnetic induction of limb regeneration, and autonomic regulation are indications that holistic medicine is a viable approach. This concept of holistic, preventive health care is one of the most important innovations in modern theoretical medical research and its clinical applications.

Among the most fundamental challenges to present belief systems is the concept that consciousness is primary to matter. For modern science and most laymen, physical matter is considered to be primary and consciousness is viewed as an epiphenomenon that arises spontaneously at a certain stage of biological evolution. At best, this stance is an assumption, and at worst, it may be a misconception that impedes innovation. Consciousness is regarded as primary in all meditative systems, and the consideration of this perspective lends support to the healing potential of visualization, hypnosis, dreams, and meditative practices with physical and psychological disorders. From a purely materialistic, mechanistic stance, such phenomena are given little credence since these are subtle occurrences involving minute quanta of energy. By contrast, from an Eastern perspective the dynamics of consciousness are the forces governing the behavior of matter. It is most important to realize that these perspectives elicited by a holistic orientation are tentative hypotheses rather than dogmatic assertions. From the philosophical speculations of the critics of modern science to the pragmatic procedures of preventive medicine there is a clear message that one of the greatest challenges is the synthesis of a comprehensive overview of man and his environment. This new *Weltanschauung* needs to include such considerations as value, purpose, volition, and consciousness, since science has long usurped the adequacy of philosophy and religion to address itself to these critical concerns. From science, the study of consciousness gains rigor, and in turn science can return to the roots of its creativity in helping to resolve the pressing personal and philosophical issues confronting modern man.

It is of utmost importance to link the study of consciousness and meditative practice to the concept of improving social conditions. In the West, a deeply introspective and insular meditative practice is erroneously assumed to be escapist and self-indulgent in the face of the greater social ills of inadequate housing, food shortages, and crushing poverty. However, according to the Buddhist tradition, a person's first obligation is to free himself from "ignorance" (Guenther, 1975) and work toward enlightenment through meditation. An integral aspect of all meditative practice is to serve others out of the highest possible state of awareness that the practitioner can attain. But that meditator can only be as effective as the clarity of his mind allows him to be. Thus, the practitioner strives toward a state in which all his actions spring from a clear consciousness and are of the greatest benefit to all. Change begins with individuals becoming clear and ceasing to act out of misunderstanding and ignorance. This task of moving out of the bondage of individual anger, malice, greed, and self-service is the most formidable challenge of a lifetime. Nothing less than planetary survival hinges on the outcome.

Quantum Physics and Consciousness

chapter 2

*W*ITH the publication of Copernicus' *On the Revolution of the Heavenly Bodies* in the 16th century, Western science began to rely increasingly upon objective observation, experimentation, and empirical validation of hypotheses. This approach has been particularly well suited to the discovery and application of the laws governing the material universe, but it has had a major unforeseen consequence. Emphasis in the scientific method upon a particular model of scientific inquiry, one based upon observable phenomena, has had the result of systematically excluding the study of the mind and its subtle processes. Through the centuries, this empirical orientation of the scientific method has fostered natural and social sciences far more adept at dissecting natural phenomena into inanimate parts than studying organisms and systems as a whole.

Researchers did not anticipate a limit to this objective observation of inanimate matter until the early years of this century. The advent of quantum physics and the enunciation of Heisenberg's uncertainty principle, which implied that the observer is an integral part of the act of observation, marked the boundaries of the utility of the classical model of scientific inquiry. It was clear that theoretical constructs concerning the nature of the physical universe were to be qualified as statements of the observer's mental abstractions rather than regarded as facts about an absolute reality shared by all observers. With that principle, man was reinstated as an inseparable participant in the universe he sought to measure and define.

At the birth of science as we know it today, Aristotle divided all knowledge into two distinct categories dealing with the physical and the nonphysical aspects of reality, physics and metaphysics. Although numerous schools of thought concerned with the philosophy of scientific inquiry have sought to bridge the fundamental divisions, this dualism has persisted until the present day. The reality of human being lends itself to this view: The body is physical and the mind is not. In 1637 René Descartes formalized the mind and body duality into a formidable dogma with the *Discourse on Method*. His work subsequently had extensive influence upon the semantic analyses of the twentieth-century philosopher Wittgenstein, who emphasized the difference between the objective and communicable aspects of reality and the subjective or private aspects.

Purely materialist philosophers sought to dispose of this duality by postulating that mind and matter are identical and that mind has no existence independent of matter. A similar position had been advocated in Lucretius' *On the Nature of the Universe* as early as the first century B.C.

The contemporary behaviorist school of psychology formulated by John Watson and B. F. Skinner subscribes to it, as do the engineers of cybernetic models of the brain. As W. Ross Ashby notes in *Design for a Brain*, "Throughout the book, consciousness and its related subjective elements are not used for the simple reason that at no point have I found their introduction necessary." Mind-body dualism is exchanged for a brain-body concept in the cybernetic models, which presuppose that all mental functions are reducible to mechanistic programming techniques. Mind is considered an epiphenomenon that arises when a certain order of complexity has been established in the organization of organic material. Notwithstanding the efficiency of this model, its postulates do not really specify the conditions under which this spontaneous generation of mind will occur.

Opposed to the purely materialistic approaches to the nature of human being are the Western schools of idealistic philosophy, which assert that mind is the preeminent reality. Many variations on this position are to be found in the metaphysical idealism of Plato, Kant, and Hegel, and they extend to the extreme wherein direct knowledge of any material reality is doubted by Locke, Berkeley, and Hume. In their theories, material reality is an illusion or arbitrary construction, simply the epiphenomenon or byproduct of mind. Unfortunately, these monistic philosophies, which state that there is only one form of reality which can be either mind or matter, frequently are at odds with data derived by means of scientific experimentation and become dependent upon denial rather than explanation as their basis.

A third alternative proposes that mind and body are in interaction. As explicated by the modern philosophers Karl

Popper and C. D. Broad, Cartesian dualism is replaced by the equally tenable hypothesis that mind and body are engaged in inextricable interaction. Setting aside philosophical arguments, this position is highly viable as a pragmatic means of approaching such phenomena as psychosomatic disorders and in related areas of medicine wherein the negative effects of that putative interaction would seem to be vividly manifested.

Philosophical speculations upon the variations of these three basic positions are frequently overwrought and terminate in semantic quibbling. Without addressing themselves to the results of ongoing scientific research, philosophical debates upon the nature of the mind-body problem have not and will not resolve anything. The path of resolution requires that both the philosophical and the empirical aspects of that issue be addressed equally. In all discussions that follow, the parallels between quantum physics and the study of consciousness are intended to underscore the insights that researchers may garner in comparing one field with the other. Some of the data presented here suggest that there are direct correlates between experiments in physics and the neurophysiology of consciousness. Other data suggest comparisons that are more a matter of analogy. It is too early to determine whether such correlations are literal or metaphorical, but it is necessary to at least pose the questions.

Fortunately, contemporary thinkers are in an excellent position to undertake this task. In the light of recent discoveries in quantum physics, holography, and biofeedback, many key questions can be approached and answered in a manner that is satisfactory to both philosophical considerations and scientific pragmatisms. Ironical as it may seem, the way out of the morass of philosophical speculations on the mind-body problem has been prepared by a series of innovations in physics. Because science does not proceed in a vacuum, these innovations affect the biological, medical, and psychological disciplines. The discoveries illuminate fundamental issues concerning interactions between the material world of atoms and molecules and the invisible forces of energy governing their behavior. Classical physics asserted that force and matter were in interaction; this is expressed in Newton's definition of force as mass times acceleration. Today, modern physics, psychology, biology, and medicine affirm that mind and body—invisible forces and material substance—also exist in interaction. The immense task of defining the nature and limitations of that interaction lies immediately ahead in a future where material physics and the phenomenology of consciousness converge.

Specific links between quantum physics and the study of consciousness are enumerated in the latter sections of this chapter. However, at this point it is important to note that major scientific discoveries such as those of quantum physics have far-reaching effects with the potential of significantly altering man's view of himself and the universe of which he is a part. The next sections, which look into the nature and effects of paradigms, will indicate why this is so and will also illustrate the current need for revising theory and experimentation on the basis of a newly evolving model of scientific inquiry. It is necessary to examine the philosophical and logical basis of any proposed revisions in the concept of scientific inquiry. All too frequently, researchers and theoreticians proceed into new areas without first examining either their own biases and assumptions or the methods and insights of other disciplines. Such an examination will assure that the ensuing theory and research is well rooted and broad based rather than superficial and insular. Reviewing the interrelations among philosophies of science, formal logic, and data connecting quantum physics with phenomena of consciousness is both a means of grounding our proposed revisions and of adumbrating the practical implications.

Paradigms as Arbiters of Reality

According to Thomas S. Kuhn in *The Structure of Scientific Revolutions,* a scientific paradigm is a "super theory," a theoretical formulation embracing a wide diversity of existing data into a single internally consistent and coherent body of knowledge. Paradigms impose order upon basically random phenomena. A paradigm is a model of reality, and it gives rise to a philosophical predisposition that directs and interprets the scientific activity of its adherents. Its implicit judgments about the nature of reality include some and exclude other phenomena from scientific inquiry. Unfortunately, a paradigm tends to become increasingly inflexible. Rather than remaining a tentatively held theory of the nature and structure of one or another aspect of the universe, the paradigm usually becomes a dogma that defines rigid parameters within which researchers may conduct their inquiries.

One clear deficiency of such a dogma is that it becomes self-perpetuating: The paradigm dictates the essence of the questions to be raised and the means by which they are to be resolved. The paradigm itself is never questioned. In this sense, paradigms serve as prisms directing the attention of researchers only to those groupings and correlations of data that lend themselves to that particular kind of investigation. The results of such predetermined investigations implicitly verify the paradigm.

Paradigms serve as the foundations of the elaborate belief systems that permit man to interpret and comprehend his world with a degree of reliability and stability. Throughout history, the unknown or unexpected has been a source of fear more often than an occasion of joy in discovery and innovation. To many individuals and institutions the idea of change is extremely threatening. Irrational emotions of anxiety, fear, and resistance are elicited when people are confronted by the seemingly logical dictates of new discoveries. According to Kuhn:

> Novelty emerges only with difficulty, manifested by resistance against a background provided by expectation. Initially, only the anticipated and usual are experienced even under circumstances where anomaly is later to be observed. The later awareness of anomaly opens a period in which conceptual categories are adjusted until the initially anomalous has become the anticipated (p. 64).

Examples of earlier paradigms are Copernican astronomy, Newtonian physics, and Darwinian evolution. In each case, their acceptance necessitated the scientific community's rejection or radical modification of previously held theories—for example, Ptolemy's astronomy. History shows us that the adoption of each new paradigm produced a shift in the problems recognized as available for scientific scrutiny and in what constituted a valid problem solution. Furthermore, this shift in perspective transformed the scientific imagination, eventually resulting in a profound alteration of the *Weltanschauung* of all individuals who became aware of the implications of these new perspectives. Since culture and society are ultimately affected by the prevailing world views of their authorities, be they Nobel laureates or primitive shamans, alterations in the paradigms embraced by these key individuals hold the potential to radically restructure the world view of all members of that society.

Great confusion and unrest usually arise before a new paradigm emerges. It is inevitable that pervasive alterations in world perspective be met with resistance, despite the fact that certain demonstrable phenomena remain inexplicable in terms of the former paradigm. The new model is almost certain to be challenged, for it too may be incomplete in its initial enunciation and may not have been proved definitively. A new paradigm must explain all of the data contained in the previous model, as well as the data that had been identified as unexplainable. Ideally, the new paradigm would correctly predict new observations and the means for verifying them; but at the same time that the new model is gaining credibility, it is also likely to encounter data that it does not comprehend. Thus it will eventually give way to another paradigm. We see that paradigms are extremely potent arbiters of reality, and that all scientific disciplines are based upon paradigms, that is, upon shared sets of expectations, which, in turn, are accepted by society as the consensual validation of reality. From this state of consensus, shared by scientists and laymen alike, derives the concept of what constitutes an acceptable or proper question, method, and solution to any given inquiry.

An Inquiry into Objectivity

Let us consider now how paradigms actually shape the pursuit of knowledge. We begin by noting that scientific inquiry usually functions in a rather peculiar manner. A

problem is selected—e.g., "How do I move my arm?"
Actually the recognition and selection of the problem itself
is a function of the paradigm. The approach to answering
this question is determined by the academic training of the
scientist doing the asking. A biochemist will explore the
actin-myosin process in muscular contraction; a biophysi-
cist may use a scanning electron microscope to observe the
molecular and atomic structures involved in movement;
while a psychologist may seek the motivation for such an
act in terms of a response to a set of particular internal or
external stimuli. Whatever the case may be, each scientist
is trained to state and study the problem in terms of the
rules of evidence and methods of inquiry appropriate to his
training. Physicists seldom consider issues of "atomic motivation," anymore than psychologists consider "motivated
atoms." As evident as this may seem, it is worth under-
scoring the fact that each mode of inquiry employed by
various specialties operates from different premises and sets
certain methods of investigation in order to achieve some
desired degree of precision. If all modes of inquiry and
their possibilities were pursued simultaneously, all research would likely founder in contradictions and confusion.

Under most circumstances this convention functions extremely well. Unfortunately the scientific method of any
discipline can become inhibiting when the arbitrary constraints and limitations are treated as though they were
absolutes. "How do I move my arm?" is one example of a
question whose complete answer ranges from metaphysics
to molecular biology, with no one description being totally
adequate. At some point in the biochemical analysis of a
particular striate muscle, the biochemist will have to acknowledge a prior chain of events that led to the contrac-

tion of that particular muscle. Under the conditions and constraints of biochemical science, the next order of questions may not be answerable in strictly biochemical terms. At that point, the researcher may choose to continue his investigation within the strict confines of his scientific method and perhaps reach a point of diminishing returns, or he may choose to consider such nonbiochemical matters as motivation to take his study further. In any such process of scientific inquiry, it is readily evident that a great deal of the procedure is dependent upon the professional belief system of the researcher—the scientific paradigms to which he has pledged allegiance—rather than upon strictly logical dictates.

Moreover, personal paradigms also affect research. No matter how "objective" a scientific inquiry appears to be, any theory derived from objective observations is actually based upon very subjective factors such as insight, intuition, hunches, biases, beliefs, and interpretation. Each person subscribes to a personal paradigm or belief system, the mazeway discussed in Chapter 1. It is naive to assume that such a pervasive component of psychological functioning is, or can be, set aside as the person who is also a scientist crosses the threshold of his laboratory. Belief systems and their concomitant biases are integral to individual personality and usually operate below a person's normal level of conscious awareness. Though all well-trained researchers conscientiously attempt to eliminate biases from the experimental situation, subjectivity does enter into and does shape the results of the experimental research method.

To illustrate, let us consider one essential element of the scientific method—the isolation of relevant variables. The scientist takes an infinitely complex phenomenon, such as the ability of an individual to exercise control over his autonomic nervous system, then proceeds to isolate certain variables that he *believes* to be the most relevant in terms of the problem as stated. Then he chooses as many of the most suitable of these variables as it is possible for him to monitor and analyze simultaneously. All this appears to be commendably objective. It is usually overlooked, however, that this is an "as if" procedure; the researcher has acted *as if* these were the only or the most important variables related to the problem at hand. In fact, this may not be the case at all. It is equally possible that a variable to which he has paid no attention whatsoever is responsible for the phenomenon being studied. Therefore, the isolation of variables is a construct of the investigator's perceptions rather than an absolute determination of the factors responsible for a particular phenomenon.

In practice, a researcher isolates a small number of variables from the total realm of possibilities. He then evaluates the available means for measuring the specific attributes of the variables he has chosen to examine. Next, he performs the data reductions and analyses appropriate to those parameters and derives statistical data from his analyses. Finally, the researcher evaluates his hypothesis by means of these data (McCain and Segal, 1969). It should be evident that this process, essentially the mechanics of any scientific methodology, results in conclusions that are far removed from the initial dimensions of the phenomenon. They are, in fact, that researcher's personal and finite approximation of that phenomenon.

Another example of what we are discussing here is drawn from the field of quantum physics. As physicists probe into an invisible, subatomic universe where time is reversible and matter may be annihilated and created in billionths of a second, they find it no longer possible to adhere to their traditional conventions of objective research, for what is readily observable by anyone is highly tenuous. Physicists are required to focus their attention upon extremely ephemeral phenomena and to extrapolate theories based upon their observations of such transient, occasionally contradictory phenomena. Interestingly, there is a clear parallel between the orientation of quantum physics and the concept of projection in psychology. Projection, a pervasive term in psychology, is generally defined as an interpretation of events arising from the individual's own experiences and feelings. When a person engages in projection, he is generalizing his own idiosyncratic way of perceiving, yet he assumes that he is making an objective assessment of the external world. This dynamic underlines the most potent testing procedures in psychology, such as the Rorschach inkblot tests, sentence completions, and the Thematic Apperception Test(TAT)—in which a person is asked to make up a story about an ambiguous scene and to relate what went on before, during, and after the pictured image. There are no right or wrong answers; the very intent of the test is that the individual project or externalize his own fantasies, wishes, and unconscious processes. The essential feature of all projective methods is ambiguity. Each picture or inkblot is essentially quite neutral and does not dictate any particular type of response. As a person engages in evaluating and verbalizing about a series of these ambiguous stimuli, it becomes readily apparent that he is saying far more about his own perceptual processes than anything concerning the literal content of the ambiguous stimulus configurations. In short, by formulating a perception of these ambiguous pictures, the person reveals himself.

This situation is analogous to the plight of the quantum physicist who is faced with a bewildering Rorschach of subatomic phenomena: "virtual particles," "tracks in bubble chambers," "collapse of state vectors," "black holes," "vacuum fluctuations," "infinitely bootstrapped, geodelized hadrons," and the elusive "charmed quarks." Since the phenomena themselves do not inherently dictate any particular interpretations, he is free-—indeed obliged—to extrapolate as ingeniously as he is able within the limits of his observations. Such formulations are admittedly problematic, and given the high level of ambiguity in the stimulus configuration, it seems very likely that the physicist's theories reflect his own subjective perceptual system rather than any absolute qualities of material reality. The dynamic of projection is still quite alien to traditional physics, which has been accustomed to observing stable properties of matter. Consequently, it has been exceedingly difficult for physicists to reformulate their paradigms so as to take into account the effects of subjectivity. It is one matter to state a theoretical principle; it is quite another to introduce the ramifications of that principle into the body politic of the scientific method.

Further indications that quantum physics does project properties of mind upon matter reside in the very names and definitions of the processes under study. Although a number of properties have been subsumed under the rubric of "particles," in fact, no actual particles correspond to the labels. The quantum physicist's objects of study, the most fundamental interactions of matter and energy, are utterly invisible in their natural state. From such shadowy clues as his experiments provide, he postulates the existence of such entities as virtual particles, particles going backward in time, negative particles or antimatter. He resorts to descriptors such as "strangeness" and "charm" and proposes that the elementary particles may be composed of even more fundamental entities termed "quarks." It might be argued that the labels do not matter and that the real issue is the mathematical formalism to which the labels refer. However, as Sir Arthur Eddington pointed out in *The Philosophy of Physical Science,* if the scientist looks carefully at these formalisms, they appear to be descriptive of the structure of his own mind. At this level, ontology is equivalent to epistemology, since the reality that is detected is entirely dependent upon the means by which it is observed.

That bias and projection are pervasive in scientific inquiry is now acknowledged by most researchers. In psychology—whose inquiries concern living organisms and subtle, dynamic properties of mind—the effects of experimental bias and expectancy have been extensively documented, for example, by Robert Rosenthal in *Experimenter Effects in Behavioral Research.* Despite such studies as Rosenthal's, and although behavioral scientists are generally aware of the problem, behavioral psychology has persisted in its aspirations to become an "objective" science in the classical mode by adhering to a natural science methodology based on stringent controls and absolute noninteraction between experimenter and experiment.

Oddly enough, the subject of experimenter effect is of greater interest to contemporary physicists, the natural scientists par excellence, than to most psychologists. Physics has declared that statements about quantum-level phenomena are probabilistic, not absolute, and that seemingly contradictory results can be reconciled by adopting this orientation. According to Werner Heisenberg in *Across the Frontiers* (1975):

The seemingly contradictory pictures yielded in the interpretation of experiments in atomic physics initially had the effect of placing the concept of "possibility," of merely "potential reality," at the heart of the theoretical interpretation. The conflict between the material particles of Newtonian physics and the force field of the Faraday-Maxwell physics was thereby resolved; both are possible manifestations of the same physical reality. The opposition between force and matter had lost its essential meaning (p. 83).

Thus, as the level of analysis becomes increasingly subtle, as it is in quantum physics, molecular biology, and cognitive psychology, the method of inquiry and subsequent interpretations become more ambiguous and conclusions become probabilities rather than certainties.

The Limits of Logic

The foregoing critique of the classical scientific method is intended to expand its applicability rather than advocate its abandonment. It is important to realize that the rules of formal, scientific inquiry do not preclude the extension of the scientific method so as to accommodate subjective factors such as bias and belief in a rigorous manner. On the contrary, formal logic itself denies the viability of an inquiry based solely upon logical, empirical procedures. Kurt Gödel's Incompleteness Theorem elucidates this point. Using strictly formal methods Gödel demonstrated the incompleteness of logic. He proved that any finite set of consistent axioms is incapable of implying all the true theorems of the theory of numbers. That is, there would be true statements about arithmetic not deducible from that set of axioms. In effect, Gödel presented formal proof of a nonlogical component adhering to all logical systems. This proof, unrefuted to the present, stands athwart the hope of logicians to prove mathematics—and, by implication, all other sciences—totally logical.

In a corollary to this theorem, Gödel demonstrated that if one could deduce all the true statements of arithmetic from a set of axioms, that set of axioms would be inconsistent. That is, false statements could also be deduced from that set of axioms. From this it is clear that arithmetic has to be either incomplete or inconsistent in a formal proof. As a consequence, all formalized systems must eschew inconsistency and make do with incompleteness. It is still debatable, however, whether or not *all* systems are incomplete. With this one reservation in mind, it would seem that any comprehensive inquiry into the nature of consciousness must be incomplete if based purely upon logical inference.

Can it be proven from within a system of axioms that the system contains no inherent contradiction? The key word is "within"; given that condition, the answer is negative. According to Gödel, it is fundamentally impossible to know whether or not a set of postulates chosen in a logical system is in fact self-consistent. Only by the construction of another set of master postulates can the validity or the consistency of that first set be tested. However, with this second set of postulates the same question of logical consistency arises. It is evident that the problem's solution escapes into an infinite regress. This implies that the scientist who remains a pure logician has no real base from which he can reason with absolute assuredness. Adherence to a particular personal, scientific, or cultural paradigm is a function of belief or faith rather than a matter of necessity dictated by objective information.

A scientific paradigm may be thought of as an attempt to formalize a set of observations in order to deduce further observations. Gödel's Theorem is applicable: The paradigm will be either incomplete or inconsistent, if not both. In brief, there will always be more observations concerning man, the material world, and the universe than can be contained in any paradigm. In Shakespeare's terms: "There are more things in heaven and earth than are dreamt of in your philosophy." What was true in the sixteenth century is no less true today.

Among researchers, Gödel's Theorem is generally ignored because it seems to imply an ultimate futility about activities of scientific inquiry. However, the theorem imposes limitations upon only one particular type of inquiry, the type in which events are isolated, objective in the traditional sense, free of any readily observable interaction between the event and the observer, and presumed to occur in a strictly logical manner. The ideal corresponding to this type is, of course, mathematics. Yet, despite its profound philosophical implications, in actual practice Gödel's Theorem does not impose consequential limits upon most areas of scientific inquiry.

Beyond Determinism

In the classical model of scientific inquiry, nonphysical or nonobservable factors are systematically excluded. Scientific inquiry based upon observable phenomena must conform to two requirements. First, any observations must be performed with an accuracy appropriate to the claims of the theory being tested. In principle, these measurements could be made as precisely as one wished. Second, from these observations the scientist should be able to predict the occurrence of other similar phenomena. The discoveries of quantum physics have created serious problems for modern science regarding the fulfillment of these criteria. As will be shown, exceptions to these classical principles of objective inquiry have profound implications for the study of consciousness.

Frequent reference has been made to the uncertainty principle formulated by Werner Heisenberg in 1927, one of the most important challenges to the classical concept of absolute objective observation. The principle states that the position and momentum of an atomic particle are complementary quantities that can only be approximated, not precisely known. As physicists attempt to measure one with greater precision, the value of the other variable becomes the more uncertain. Heisenberg has, moreover, conclusively demonstrated that this uncertainty is not simply a matter of the physical limitations of present instruments. He showed that the imprecision in one measurement multiplied by the imprecision in the other measurement can never be less than Planck's Constant $(\hbar)$. This infinitesimal degree of uncertainty $(\hbar - 6.77 \times 10^{-27})$ is considered to be negligible in all but atomic and subatomic instances. However, the philosophical implications of the uncertainty principle mark the limits of any and all strictly deterministic interpretations of the physical universe. A deterministic paradigm requires that an observer be capable of ascertaining the position and momentum of even the most elementary particles. Heisenberg demonstrated the impossibility of such observations and, in a manner analogous to Gödel, affirmed the necessity of acknowledging the nonobjective components of any comprehensive system of inquiry. This point is extended in *The Reflexive Universe,* by mathematician and inventor Arthur M. Young:

In order for determinists to prove the assumption of predictability, then it is necessary to observe the position and momentum of this fundamental particle. In order to observe this fundamental particle or photon, the observer must cast light on the particle. However, the wavelength of light (10^{-5} cm.) is a million times greater than the diameter of the observed particle. Thus it is impossible to make the requisite observation to affirm a deterministic paradigm (1972, p. 215).

That there is a limit to the objectivity of observation even within physics, the most stringent of the natural sciences, has profound implications. Since all other sciences are based upon models derived from the natural sciences, especially from physics, it implies that research into states of consciousness can no longer employ the paradigms of old. According to the assumptions of Newton and Galileo in prequantum physics, man was simply another mechanism. By applying the laws of classical physics regarding cause and effect, the causes of a man's actions could be traced to their source. From this root assumption the notion evolved that research on human behavior would ultimately lead to that behavior being totally predictable. Yet, according to the uncertainty principle, the very act of measurement or observation transmits sufficient energy to alter the system that is observed, thus precluding total predictability. This effect is an ontological property; it cannot be circumvented or resolved through the use of increasingly fine probes or more sophisticated instrumentation.

Another aspect of the uncertainty principle is the limit imposed on the accuracy of knowledge about individual entities. Only the average value of a great many single observations can be predicted with any degree of accuracy.

Quantum theory is essentially based upon averaging procedures performed on multiple events. Quantum mechanics describes systems in statistical terms that generate the probability but not the certainty of a particular outcome. For example, an atom in an excited state will return to its ground state by one of two means of emitting energy. Quantum statistics give the probability of one occurring over the other but cannot definitively predict which one will occur. All of modern science refers to probability theory, for it gives access to the phenomenon in which events that are individually unpredictable can lead to very stable, average performances when treated en masse.

The end of determinism is also signaled by the necessity among physicists of referring to subatomic, nonobservable entities. Descriptions of the properties of these invisible "particles" and of the processes governing them begin to sound more and more similar to the properties that psychology ascribes to the phenomena of consciousness. There is nothing inherent in any aspect of the natural sciences that precludes the concept of consciousness as a real but nonphysical entity. There are many instances wherein mathematical or theoretical constructs are acceptable despite the fact that there is no empirical method of proving their physical reality. Strictly speaking, no theory or construct can be proven purely by empirical methods. Indeed, an increasing number of nonphysical factors or quantities have been hypothesized in recent years in order to create coherent theories. If the hypothecation of such factors enables a researcher to comprehend a theory more adequately, to make more accurate predictions, or to generate novel hypotheses, then the factor is considered to have validity even though it is undetectable. Examples of such recent constructs in quantum physics are "virtual particles," "antimatter," "tachyons," and "quarks," all of which remain undetected. Although these factors cannot be demonstrated to be physically real because there are no means to perform measurements upon them, they are invaluable explanatory and predictive factors in quantum theory. By its bold use of hypothetical entities, quantum physics has proved to have a profound impact upon the study of consciousness, where such abstractions are necessary but had previously been dismissed as unscientific.

At the present time, physics considers four fundamental forces to account for all known phenomena. These are: **(1)** *gravity*—which accounts for interactions between very large bodies ranging from ordinary objects to solar systems and galaxies; **(2)** *electromagnetic forces*—which deal with medium-scale phenomena and are most applicable in addressing living organisms; **(3)** *weak nuclear force;* and **(4)** *strong nuclear force*—both of which account for phenomena at the infinitesimal levels of subatomic physics. Despite the considerable explanatory power of these four forces, quantum physics has increasingly pressed for the postulation of at least one further force to account for certain inexplicable phenomena occurring below the limits of instrumental observation. Perhaps this factor is that of consciousness, which would transform physics from the study of forces interacting with inert objects to a science considering the dynamic properties of living systems. According to recent speculations in quantum physics, consideration of this possibility seems less likely to be a matter of choice than of necessity.

From the formal logic of Gödel, from Heisenberg's uncertainty principle, and from probability theory comes the consistent conclusion that there is a fundamental, inviolable limit upon the classical mode of inquiring into certain aspects of reality. Those aspects concern individual events at an infinitesimal level of analysis. It is refreshing in this context to note that according to all meditative systems, fundamental reality is beyond conception by the logical mind. This perspective has always been considered mystical, yet we now begin to see that it is another way of pointing to the same ultimately indeterminate, elementary particles that are the constituents of quantum physics.

It is the hypothesis here that the level of reality beyond determinism is that of consciousness, which requires different methods of observation and dictates an extension of existing scientific paradigms. These extensions are explicated in later chapters. The point here is to ground a science of nonobjective phenomena within existing scientific theory. It is important to bear in mind that the limitations of the current natural science paradigms stem from a particular method of interpreting certain data; no inherent limitations are dictated by the data themselves, except that other data may not be recognized as such within the parameters of the prevailing paradigm.

"Wavicles," Body-Minds, and Space-Time

Niels Bohr stated a fundamental principle of quantum physics that is also of considerable importance in approaching a science of consciousness. It is the principle of complementarity. The model of the atom generally accepted among physicists prior to the advent of quantum physics described it as being composed of a solid nucleus of protons and neutrons with a number of beadlike electrons whirling about it in clearly defined orbits. In effect, the model is analogous to a miniature solar system with the sun as the nucleus and the electrons as the planets in constant orbiting attendance. The model was useful, but did not correspond to the growing body of experimental data about atomic interactions. For one, electrons appeared to jump from one orbit into a different one without seeming to pass through any intervening space. Second, the orbits themselves were not linear trajectories but appeared to be blurred or vague tracks. These inexplicable findings gave rise to the observation that the electron sometimes behaved as though it were a corpuscle or particle, and other times behaved as though it were a wave. The two possibilities—wave or particle—seemed to be mutually exclusive; yet both were needed to provide a comprehensive account of the phenomena observed at the subatomic level.

It was Bohr's inspired idea that the wave theory and the particle theory are complementary to one another. The principle of complementarity is demonstrable under experimental conditions by having a single photon or a single electron discharged toward a solid shield that has two holes in it. Sometimes the single particle emerges from one hole and at other times seems to pass through both holes simultaneously. When either a single photon or a single electron passes through a hole, the interference pattern can only be attributed to the interaction of two wave forms. Thus, whether a photon or electron is a particle, or a wave, or a "wavicle" (both) is determined by the particular experimental measurements that preordain which properties will be manifested. Niels Bohr concluded that the particle and wave were irreconcilable and complementary aspects of the whole (Pribram, 1974).

It seems quite evident that the complementarity of particles in waves is a striking parallel to mind-body complementarity. Wolfgang Pauli (1952) has noted this:

The general problem of the relationship between mind and body, between the inward and the outward, cannot be said to have been solved by the concept of psycho-physical parallelism postulated in the last century. Modern science has perhaps brought us nearer to a more satisfactory understanding of this relationship, by introducing the concept of complementarity into physics itself. It would be the more satisfactory solution if mind and body could be interpreted as complementary aspects of the same reality (p. 164).

Thus, quantum theory makes a radical departure from Cartesian dualism and postulates the unitive principle of complementarity as one that may govern the interplay between matter and energy. In modern psychology, by contrast, there is still a great deal of investment in the dualism of mind and body. From physics one derives the concept that an "either-or" position is untenable, since both mind and matter may be a special case of a more unitary, organizing principle. This, as hypothesized here, can be referred to as consciousness. The dualism in the wave versus corpuscular theory of light has been resolved in the mathematics of quantum theory: These are interchangeable states; whether wave or particle occurs is dependent largely upon the experimental procedures adopted. In an analogous manner, the apparent dualism of mind and matter can be resolved by considering it to be a matter of emphasis rather than the reflection of an ontological duality. This is a potent assumption whose very pragmatic implications can be readily seen in the mind-body interaction of psychosomatic disorders or in cases of spontaneous remission, wherein severe organic disorders are alleviated or eliminated by an alteration in the patient's psychological orientation.

In addition to the uncertainty principle and the principle

of complementarity, there is yet another discovery of contemporary physics that has implications for the study of consciousness. This is the nature of time. According to Einstein's Relativity Theory, the faster a clock moves, the slower it keeps time. In other words, as velocity increases, time slows down. At the level of macrocosmic systems, as in astronomy, and at the level of microcosmic systems, as in quantum physics, time is not an absolute. It is not the familiar one-way, linear sequence of precise intervals. On the macrocosmic level, astronomers pose the likelihood of antimatter galaxies where time flows backward from our point of view, and the existence of black holes in space where extremely strong gravitation wraps both time and space in ways that are virtually unimaginable. At the other extreme, at the infinitesimal level of subatomic particles, Richard Feynman of California Institute of Technology hypothesizes that particles of antimatter are actually particles of matter going backward in time. This theory is based upon the observation that in a bubble chamber, a positron looks just like an electron except that its track bends the wrong way in an electrical field because its charge is opposite to that of an electron. Thus, according to modern physicists, a positron is an antimatter electron. Feynman's means of representing this phenomenon are the famous Feynman Diagrams, in which one axis represents time, the other represents space, and particles can move forward and backward in time. These time reversals are necessarily extremely brief since matter and antimatter instantaneously annihilate one another. So it is that, at very large and very small magnitudes, time assumes plasticity according to contemporary physics.

According to Einstein's theory, time, mass, speed, momentum, and energy may be different for all observers.

Each observer possesses a unique internal, perceptual universe with his own concepts of space and time. All that remains constant for the separate observers are the relations between these factors. As Jacob Bronowski put it ("A Twentieth Century Image of Man," delivered at the Salk Institute, La Jolla, 1973): "Each of us rides his personal universe, his own traveling box of space and time, and what they have in common is the same structure or coherence; when we formalize our experiences they yield the same laws." Time becomes a tenuous construct in relativity theory; in quantum physics, space becomes an equally ambiguous construct. Indeed, the concepts of space and time have been replaced by the relativity theory construct of space–time, which denotes the inextricable interaction of these two factors. Again, there is an analogy to the interaction of mind and body.

One immediate implication of the space-time concept is that science as we know it is based upon the study of phenomena located in a particular set of space-time coordinates. Scientific observations ought to be qualified by the observer's particular state of consciousness—which, after all, is characterized by a particular space-time configuration—that places him in a particular relationship to the events observed. If the observer were in a different state of consciousness, it is very likely that he would observe other variables, other interactions, and formulate different hypotheses about the events that have been observed. It is extremely important to note that there is nothing inherent in the scientific method which precludes the consideration of observations made in "altered" states of consciousness (Tart, 1975). A major criterion of science is that observers share the formal constructs of the information gained while in a particular, or ordinary, state of consciousness. That fundamental principle is not violated by postulating a specific science of consciousness wherein the observers share an extraordinary state and subsequently report their observations.

$$Et = \hbar$$

Perhaps the most important argument against equating properties of consciousness with properties of quantum events as described by contemporary physics is that the magnitude of these quantum events are too small to have any relevance for large living systems. A second reservation is that the uncertainty of quantum events may constitute only an infinitesimal and insignificant amount of random, background "noise" in the biological system. Both objections are based upon assumptions that may not hold true in the light of recent research evidence.

An assumption inherent in these reservations about the small size of quantum events is that large size is a necessary prerequisite for significant alteration in a large system. In 1935, in *New Pathways in Science,* Sir Arthur Eddington considered the possibility that consciousness, or mind, did interact with the physical brain within the limits defined by the uncertainty principle. He rejected the notion on the grounds that the range defined by this uncertainty would be too small to effect the larger changes noted in the neurons of the brain. However, since that time, the consideration of "triggering mechanisms" in cybernetic theory, the concept of the brain as a "cascade amplifier" in engineering, have graphically demonstrated that infinitesimally small units of energy can have an effect upon macro systems. In its most familiar application, the interruption of a beam of light is used to open a two-ton bank vault door. Recent theories concerning the neurophysiology of consciousness propose that similar processes occur in the brain.

A brief examination of a basic equation in quantum physics provides another avenue of approach to this question of altering macro systems through the action of micro events. In resolving one of the more difficult points of difference between classical and quantum physics, Albert Einstein formulated a theory stating that the photon, the most fundamental particle, contains an amount of energy proportional to its frequency, or rate of oscillation. The higher the frequency of the photon, the higher its state of energy. This is opposite to waves of sound or water, which require more energy as they become longer. The equation that expresses this relationship is: $Et = \hbar$, where energy (E) times time (t) is equal to Planck's constant ($\hbar$), which represents the fixed interaction between energy and time. The point is, given this equation we can deduce that infinite energy could be compacted in infinitely short wave lengths. Thus it becomes possible to hypothesize that there is sufficient energy even at small quantum magnitudes to affect a large system such as the brain. In sum, we can conclude that infinitesimal size is by no means a limitation on considering consciousness as interacting consequentially with matter at a quantum level.

There is a tendency in Western psychology to attribute no energy to thought other than in a metaphorical sense. In direct contrast to this point of view is the Tibetan Buddhist (Guenther, 1975) concept that thought is infinitely powerful and actually holds sway over matter. It seems that quantum physics lends credence to this concept in that infinite energy can be an attribute of an infinitely short wave length. In fact, a recent theory by physicist Evan Harris Walker, discussed in detail in Chapter 4, provides critical links between the orders of magnitude and energy operational at the level of the single brain neuron. At this point, it is sufficient to establish that energy can be inversely proportional to size and that the infinitesimal dimensions ascribed to thought processes may be an asset rather than a liability in approaching mind-body interactions.

Before considering the problem of the randomness of quantum events and the implication that they are therefore insignificant "noise" in organic systems, there is one further parallel between quantum events and the properties of consciousness that has an important bearing upon the consideration of the magnitudes of size and energy required for the interaction of consciousness and matter. This is the concept of angular momentum, which is represented by the formula: $A = mvL$, where angular momentum (A) is equal to mass (m) times velocity (v) times the radius of the turning object (L). While angular momentum is a mathematical concept it can be illustrated by comparing it to the actions of a figure skater. A figure skater starts to spin with his arms outspread; as he draws his arms in (decreasing his radius), he spins faster. The conservation of angular momentum demands that "A" remain constant; therefore, velocity must increase, for the amount of energy stored is directly proportional to the radius. In other words, an infinitely small radius can store infinite energy. Here again, smallness is a virtue rather than a limitation in considering quantum events.

Another way to understand angular momentum is to picture a string with a ball tied at either end. If the whole assembly were held by one of the balls and thrown into the air, it would rotate in an end-over-end circular fashion. If the string were made longer, the speed of the rotation of the balls would become slower. If the string were made shorter, the rate of rotation would become faster. Theoretically, the speed of rotation approaches infinity as the string is further shortened. At either extreme, the system supposes a theoretical state of infinite stability as it approaches infinite time or infinite energy (Capra, 1975). Concepts such as these are not readily amenable to verbal description, but it is paradoxically true that an infinitesimal amount of energy is required to perturb equilibrium when any system approaches this extreme stability. In the case of the angular momentum model, the balls are free to fly in any direction when the string is cut. The one infinitesimal factor governing the direction they take is the timing of the cut (Young, 1976). For the purpose of noting the connections between quantum physics and a science of consciousness, the most important point is that the descriptions used by the physicists in talking about angular momentum are precisely analogous to the terms used in psychology to refer to certain functions of attention. For example, the question of which direction the balls will fly is a matter of the orientation of the balls when the string is cut and, in psychological terms, orientation has a profound effect upon the direction of an individual's course when his energy is released in action. Similarly, the timing of any intervention is a singularly important factor whether one is considering neuron firings in the brain or psychotherapy. Of course, timing and orientation in the context of angular momentum is not the same as timing and orientation at the level of psychological events. Notwithstanding, events at the quantum level appear to foreshadow and may serve usefully as rudimentary prototypes for processes more clearly evidenced at higher levels of complexity. This concept of quantum events as prototypical of certain events at higher levels of organization is an integral aspect of the theories of psychiatrist Gordon G. Globus and mathematician Arthur M. Young, which are discussed more fully in Chapter 8.

Obviously, one objection to the equation of quantum and psychological events is that this is rampant anthropomorphism. To declare that a process is anthropomorphic is babble, not an explanation. Yet, as noted earlier, perhaps the reason for the abundance of concepts such as "attraction," "repulsion," "annihilation," "orientation," and innumerable others in quantum physics is precisely that the physicist, seeking order in an ambiguous field, has as ultimate reference little more than the structure of his own mind, delineated by perceptions, inspired by intuition.

Both psychology and physics can benefit from the convergence of these disciplines. As suggested above, for example, the psychological concept of attention can play a role in reinterpreting some of the classical laws of physics. Another example concerns one of the pillars of classical physics, the second law of thermodynamics, which states that the energy of a closed system tends to become uniformly distributed throughout that system. The measure of this capacity is termed entropy—exemplified by the tendency of stones to roll downhill and hot objects to grow cooler as they radiate heat. In other words, the total energy of a given system gradually becomes unavailable because it is distributed or averaged over a larger area. The second law of thermodynamics applied to the universe as a whole defines it as a gradually subsiding agitation of inanimate objects, what is popularly referred to as "the heat death of the universe." This law, based upon inorganic interactions and closed systems, does not hold true for living organisms, which are not closed systems and are involved in the building up of more complex systems from the energy they create. In effect, organic systems are examples of negatively entropic systems, systems that create order from chaos. As early as 1939, Eddington postulated the possibility of physics having to resolve the problem of individual particles behaving in a correlated and orderly manner. He hypothesized that such a state might occur when matter was in interaction with mind as in the negatively entropic state of living systems. Such ordered systems would stand in contrast to the usual uncorrelated or random behavior of the fundamental particles of contemporary physics.

The Confluence of Science and Religion

Support for the concept of a holistic approach to the study of consciousness may be derived from quantum physics, as has been discussed. Bohr propounded the principle of complementarity; Heisenberg has underscored the fact that the whole can be known only by taking into account the unitary system formed by the observer and the observed; both Gödel and, in 1932, von Neuman stated that within a positivist system based purely upon natural, observable phenomena reality becomes less and less knowable as observations become more refined. Scientists and researchers can no longer assume that their observations and measurements are true facts about the nature of reality, but must consider them to be ineluctable consequences of their experimental procedures. Both current quantum physics and research concerning the neurophysiological basis of consciousness have begun to formulate new models of man and universe. This trend is in keeping with the often-quoted statement of Sir James Jeans:

> Today there is a wide measure of agreement, which on the physical side of science approaches almost to unanimity, that the stream of knowledge is heading toward a non-mechanical reality; the universe begins to look more like a great thought than like a great machine (1937, p. 122).

It seems evident that the most sophisticated sciences of both matter and mind are turning from the atomistic reductionism of Aristotle toward the holistic, integrated assertions of Plato. An idealized symmetry or unity is the fundamental characteristic of a "unified field theory" in physics, which would unify such seemingly different fields as gravitational and electromagnetic forces. Both the science of quantum physics and states of consciousness are concerned with idealized conceptions of reality, which may or may not have an apparent correspondence to the immediate perception of normative reality.

One of the long-standing factors differentiating a science of matter from a science of consciousness stems from their methods of inquiry and discovery. Traditionally, an individual's inspired awareness of his own consciousness is considered to come about through revelation or transcendent inspiration. On the other hand, scientific knowledge is thought to be derived by logical deduction or through the accumulation of data, which are analyzed according to accepted methods and, on the basis of this analysis, drawn into generalizations, which are termed laws. However, such a description of the scientific method is highly idealized and in fact bears little resemblance to what actually takes place.

Scientific insights do not come about in a logically deductive manner but in a way closely akin to revelation. After the overview of formal logic, it should be clear that no *insight* could possibly come about through deduction; at best, deduction can sort out false conjectures that are internally inconsistent. In science, researchers often speak of a sudden insight, an odd intuition, a discovery made purely by accident, or a moment of truly transcendent inspiration. In any case, the actual moment of scientific insight begins to sound increasingly as though it were an instance of mystical revelation. Evidence of these occurrences may be found in a selection of quotations from "Mystics and Physicists: Similarities in World View" (LeShan, 1969a). Numerous examples abound in the biographies of scientists, ranging from Kekule's conceptualization of the benzine ring while sleeping before a fire to Crick and Watson's sudden insight into the structure of the DNA molecule.

Regarding the convergence of the sciences of matter and mind, physicist Charles H. Townes, who won the 1964 Nobel Prize in physics for his role in the development of the laser, wrote in an article entitled "The Convergence of Science and Religion":

> Finally, if science and religion are so broadly similar, and not arbitrarily limited in their domains, they should at some time clearly converge. I believe this confluence is inevitable. For they both represent man's efforts to understand his universe and must ultimately be dealing with the same substance. As we understand more in each realm, the two must grow together. . . . But converge they must, and through this should come new strength for both (pp. 10–19).

This convergence is the essence of a science of consciousness in which the observable and the unobservable meet and illuminate each other. In a sense, physics is the new revealed religion: There is a myriad of data which requires proper interpretation to reveal its meaning concerning the structure of the physical universe and human consciousness itself.

Despite this awareness on the part of many physicists and despite the great impetus that the rise of quantum physics has given to fields such as molecular biology, scientists are not yet able to understand the basic characteristics of living organisms. Drawing upon principles from quantum physics, a science of consciousness and living systems can ask what property of mind is being described in the physicist's vision of an invisible, unknowable, subatomic universe. This is an ontological problem that cannot be resolved by more sensitive instrumentation; it demands a quantum leap to another level of explanation and theory. That further and more subtle level of analysis can be reached in two ways. One is by examining the nature of quantum events in the brain as fundamental interactions between mind and matter. The other uses the finest probe ever conceived—the trained and focused attention of consciousness itself. These approaches go beyond theoretical speculation and can provide new understanding of the nature of the interaction between mind and body and can illuminate such pragmatic issues as psychosomatic disorders. Quantum events in the neurophysiological processes of the brain are considered in Chapter 4, and meditative disciplines as complementary to rigorous scientific inquiry is the subject of Chapter 5. Before the full import of the convergence between the material and consciousness sciences can be drawn out, however, it is necessary to examine the nature of the observer of these events and reformulate the arcane issue of mind-body interaction.

Between
Psyche and Soma

chapter 3

*D*URING the fifth century B.C., Hippocrates delivered one of the first statements on record of the nature of the relationship between brain and consciousness. This material was part of a lecture on the epileptic condition, but his words created the foundations for a great deal of contemporary thinking about the interaction between mind and brain. Hippocrates said, "To consciousness the brain is messenger," and this insight stands today as the basis of the most recent observations, which increasingly indicate that the phenomena of consciousness cannot be totally explained by the activity of the brain. In fact, it seems evident that the brain can be likened to a computer that must be programmed and operated by the independent agent of mind.

Throughout the evolution of the theories concerning the

relationship between brain function and mind are two basic positions with a host of various mixtures of the two between, usually combining the worst of both and resolving little. On one hand are the theorists who adopt the position that mind and brain are synonymous and that the electrical and biochemical activity of the brain gives rise to the phenomena of consciousness. On the other hand are those who assert that mind and brain are distinct, separate elements engaged in interaction. Most prominent among the proponents of this latter position are Sir John Eccles and, most recently, the renowned Canadian neurosurgeon Wilder Penfield. Based upon thirty years of clinical evidence and basic research in epilepsy and electrical stimulation of the brain, Penfield concluded in his controversial book, *The Mystery of the Mind,* that the physical brain is a necessary but insufficient condition to account for the phenomena of consciousness. He wrote that

> because it seems to me certain that it will always be quite impossible to explain the mind on the basis of neuronal action within the brain . . . if one chooses . . . the dualistic alternative, the mind must be viewed as a basic *element* in itself. One might, then, call it a *medium,* an *essence,* a *soma.* That is to say, it has a *continuing existence* (Penfield, 1976, pp. 80, 81).

There is a tendency among researchers either to focus upon the physical brain and dismiss concepts such as mind or to discuss properties of consciousness devoid of any knowledge of brain function. These positions are equally provincial; neither can resolve the critical issue of mind-brain interaction. An approach that synthesizes these perspectives would examine the properties of brain as objectively as possible in order to research the neurophysiological substrates of consciousness. To address questions to observable activity in the brain is necessary but the limitations of this line of inquiry need to be acknowledged as well (Eccles, 1970; Penfield, 1976). Throughout this book, we have been surveying scientific literature that approaches properties of mind beginning with observable phenomena and leading to the level of quantum physical events. However, no matter how incisive this approach, a quantum distinction remains between brain functions and the phenomena of consciousness. When physical observation has reached its limits, then the subtle ability of mind to reflect upon its own processes comes into play in formulating a science of consciousness.

As researchers probe the synaptic clefts of single neurons in the brain for the definitive explanation of the biochemical processes involved in neurotransmitters, the same limitation is imposed upon their observation of this animate event as Heisenberg discovered about the observation of events occurring in inanimate matter. Thus far, all attempts to observe the fundamental processes of animate or inanimate matter by physical instrumentation appear to be abruptly limited by the magnitude defined by the Heisenberg uncertainty principle. As instrumented approaches to altered states of consciousness become increasingly sophisticated, the limits of that mode of inquiry become simultaneously evident. Rather than acknowledging defeat in the face of these limits, there is the possibility that researchers may adopt alternative methods of exploring the mind.

Information concerning the functions of the basic brain structures is very important in creating a conceptual model to understand such phenomena of consciousness as the voluntary control of internal states through meditation. A great deal is known about the mechanisms by which the brain operates but there are innumerable ways to interpret what those processes mean. Many disciplines claim to alter physiological and neurological functions through various forms of meditation, autogenic training, hypnosis, Jacobson's relaxation techniques, biofeedback, and others. Research evidence indicates that these methods do produce such alterations in consciousness and biological functioning but at present there is no adequate theory of how these changes occur. If future research is to become increasingly productive, a model is needed to test and to guide such inquiry.

Given certain characteristics of the brain, there are some aspects of the phenomena of consciousness that can be explicated satisfactorily, yet other properties remain totally inexplicable on a purely neurophysiological basis. One major objective of any comprehensive theory of consciousness is to map the relationship between the electrical activity of the nervous system and such phenomena as thought, perception, feeing, and volition. This chapter will review a number of innovative theories concerning the evolution and functioning of the nervous system with regard to the neurological substrates of consciousness. Our consideration of this issue is not mere philosophical speculation, but an attempt to formulate a precise model of the interaction at the core of all psychosomatic disorders, meditation systems, and innovative methods of treatment such as clinical biofeedback and acupuncture.

The work of several researchers contributes to the psychosomatic model presented here. First to suggest such a model of psychosomatic interaction was Walter B. Cannon in his 1937 book, *The Wisdom of the Body*. Between 1937 and the present, researchers have refined and detailed Cannon's basic insights and have traced some of the precise neurological and psychological processes involved in the voluntary control of internal states. Among the contemporary researchers are Hans Selye at the University of Montreal, Gary Schwartz and Herbert Benson at Harvard University, and Elmer and Alyce Green of the Menninger Foundation. Details of their work are discussed in Chapters 5 and 6. But in order to discuss these innovative theories, it is first necessary to establish a basic outline of neurological and psychological interaction in the brain.

Structure of the Brain

For the following discussion of the neurological substrate of consciousness, we begin with a rudimentary outline of the functions of specific structures within the brain. Of course, there are no simple relationships among these functions, for all brain processes take place in the context of a delicately intermeshed matrix of checks, balances, and feedback loops whereby one system of the brain controls and is controlled by many other systems. Moreover, due to the diffuseness and poor differentiation of many of the cell masses of the human brain, the boundaries between systems have been established for explanatory convenience and do not necessarily represent definite distinctions. As is evident from any neurology textbook, major and minute structures of the brain are labeled in abundance, while relatively little is known about the neurophysiological functioning of these structures and systems. There is even less information about the relationships between neurophysiological events and the presence or absence of such psychological variables as attention, emotion, and other attributes of consciousness. Despite the many gaps in scientific understanding of this most sophisticated organ of the body, a great deal of the information in hand is pertinent to resolving the issue of the relationship between observable events in the brain and the actual phenomenology of consciousness.

Overall, the lower, or subcortical, areas of the brain are involved in regulating ongoing bodily activities of such systems as respiration, circulation, and digestion, while higher, cortical areas are concerned with abstract intellectual functions. The subcortex begins at the brain stem, which appears as a bulbous extension at the top of the spinal cord. There are three major structures: (**1**) the cerebellum, which serves as a coordinating center for all voluntary movements and smooth muscle, or involuntary, activity; (**2**) the medulla oblongata, which contains the centers regulating such basic processes as heartbeat, respiration rate, and blood-vessel diameter; and (**3**) the pons, which plays a role in sleep-cycle regulation. The medulla oblongata is the main channel of communication between the brain and the rest of the body. Nerve tracts and fibers continue through the foramen magnum of the skull (L., great opening) without interruption from cord to medulla and thence to other portions of the brain.

Moving up from the brain stem the next major component is the diencephalon (Gr., between brain), or interbrain, which is made up of the basal ganglia, thalamus, and hypothalamus. Functions within the diencephalon regulate emotions such as fear, hate, passion, and euphoria. If control were not exercised over this area by higher centers in the cortex, individuals would tend to react in an incessant vacillation of emotional extremes.

The thalamus, the name derived from the Greek word

for an inner chamber, appears to be hollow and may be said to resemble an empty room. At the present time, its specific functions are not known. According to the observations of Ernest Gardner in his book *Fundamentals of Neurology,* "The only generalization possible is that both the thalamus and the postcentral gyrus (the primary receptive area for general tactile sensations) are concerned in the initial recognition of pain, temperature, touch, pressure, and position sense" (Gardner, 1968, p. 188). Of greater interest is the smaller hypothalamus, which connects the brain stem to the cerebral cortex and is known to play a vital role in the regulation of the pituitary gland, considered to be the master gland of the entire body.

In 1954, James Olds and Peter Milner discovered that the hypothalamus is a strong "pleasure center." Olds implanted electrodes in the hypothalamus of laboratory rats and allowed the rats to deliver one-volt electrical charges to that area of the brain by pressing a lever. It turned out that the electrical stimulation was so pleasurable that the rats ignored food and water and continued pressing the lever until sheer exhaustion stopped them. Such pleasure centers of the brain are termed "positive reinforcement areas," signifying that stimulation there will induce the subject to repeat the action that preceded the stimulation. Further research with cats, dolphins, monkeys, and humans has affirmed the existence of both pleasure and pain centers associated with the hypothalamus. While about 60 percent of the brain does not respond to stimulation, 35 percent responds pleasurably and produces positive reinforcement, and only 5 percent produces negative reinforcement, or pain. Electrical stimulation of brain pleasure centers, a research strategy of considerable controversy, may be an analog of certain meditation exercises.

Evidence suggests it may be possible to self-induce significant physiological and psychological states; this self-stimulation of pleasure centers may serve as a neurological explanation for some of the pleasurable sensations induced by various forms of meditation.

Higher up from the diencephalon in the hierarchy of the brain is the limbic system (L., border), which is more complex than the diencephalon but interconnected with it. The limbic system, also referred to as the visceral brain, consists of the hippocampus, cingulate gyrus, certain parts of the temporal and frontal cortex, certain thalamic and hypothalamic nuclei, and parts of the basal ganglia and amygdaloid bodies (Gardner, 1968, p. 335). It is concerned with various aspects of emotion and behavior, especially with many outward expressions of emotion. It has been possible with experimental animals and with human patients to implant electrodes in this area of the brain. Most research has focused upon the interconnection of the limbic system and the temporal lobes, which are the primary receptive areas for hearing. Surgical intervention in temporal lobe areas indicates that these lobes mediate sexual behavior and the presence or absence of emotional expression. Lesions in these areas produce "hallucinations, disordered recognition and memory, disturbance of reality, dream states, clouding of consciousness, sensory fits, and psychomotor epilepsy" (Gardner, p. 336). From the severity of these disturbances, it is clear that there is a definite but as yet incompletely defined relationship between mood states and neurophysiological activity.

A part of the limbic system receiving increased attention is the hippocampus. This part of the brain is also termed the rhinencephalon (L., nose brain) since it was originally thought to be concerned primarily with smell. It is comprised of a primitive type of cortex or archicortex. Electrical stimulation of this area causes widespread disruptive activity in the higher cerebral hemispheres. Researchers have noted the potential of certain smells to evoke vivid imagery. Perhaps the hippocampus's extensive impact upon higher brain centers is responsible for this phenomenon. Just as surgical intervention in the brain produces alterations in psychological functioning, the feedback structure of the brain strongly implies that psychological factors ranging from extreme emotional states to subtle meditation exercises also affect brain structures and modify their function. However, the critical issue is to determine whether or not the phenomena of consciousness are limited to nervous activities.

Finally, at the apex of the brain hierarchy is the cerebral cortex, or gray matter, of the brain, which governs all high-order abstract functions such as language, memory, judgment, and other intellectual activities. From the cerebral cortex, control is initiated over the more primitive areas of the brain. Voluntary muscular movement is also initiated from the cortical zone—the sensorimotor cortex can be visualized as an imaginary band, one inch wide, passing over the top of the head from one ear to the other. Impulses for movement originate in this sensorimotor area and travel down pathways to the base of the cortex and then through the midbrain to the opposite side of the brain before descending to the spinal column for transmission to the appropriate body muscles. Therefore, muscular activity on either side of the body requires the mutual cooperation of the sensorimotor cortex areas on both sides of the brain. Research by Barry Sterman at the University of California in Los Angeles (1976) has demonstrated that individuals with sensorimotor seizures can learn to control their seizure activity by means of biofeedback. After a period of training, these individuals can learn to recognize when their sensorimotor rhythm is becoming abnormal and then initiate a procedure to correct the rhythm to its normal range of activity. Such ability is a clear indication of a psychosomatic interaction, where a disciplined mental focus can intervene to correct a severe disorder.

Here at the cortex, the highest center regulating brain activity, lies the opportunity to observe the closest relationship between detectable neurological activity and the phenomena of consciousness. Two important areas of research have direct bearing on this inquiry: **(1)** studies of the reticular activating system (RAS) as a link between cortical and subcortical processes, and **(2)** studies of the cerebral hemispheres in which unique properties of consciousness are relegated to each hemisphere. Observations of reticular activity bear importantly on issues of conscious and unconscious mental processes. Links between this activity and the phenomena of consciousness, discussed in an earlier book, *Consciousness: East and West* (Pelletier and Garfield, 1976), are highly relevant to a comprehensive neuropsychological model of mental functions. For our purposes in this chapter, the emphasis will be upon the RAS as the vertical communication link between the brain and body, as the channel by which impressions do or do not reach the cerebral cortex for intellectual interpretation. Dual hemisphere research, discussed later in this chapter, has equally important implications for penetrating the interrelationship of higher-order cognitive processes. Hemisphere research also provides us with a model for comprehending brain function along a horizontal axis.

Vertical Unity

Neurological channels between cortical and subcortical areas of the brain comprise an elaborate system of interdependent feedback loops. Information enters the feedback loops by means of the afferent nerve tracts, which conduct impulses directly to the cerebral cortex, and also by way of collateral nerves that divert into the brain stem and become intermingled with the network of nerves described earlier as the reticular activating system, or RAS.

This observation of neuroanatomy is intended to point out that psychological theories propounded prior to the major work on the RAS, which began in the early 1950s, have either explicitly or implicitly subscribed to a model of the brain based upon gross anatomical evidence of a dichotomy between cortical and subcortical brain functions. As noted earlier in discussing early distinctions made between the autonomic and central nervous systems, such evidence was used to support psychological theories of an essentially dualistic brain in which the main problem was to determine the conditions under which the "higher" or the "lower" brain function would dominate behavior. However, recent research on the reticular activation system has resulted in a communication model of continual information exchange between the subcortical sectors of the brain that is supplanting the dualistic model. The neurological evidence suggests a dialogue between autonomic and cortical processes in contrast to an incessant all-or-nothing struggle between these processes vying for dominance. In short, rather than viewing man as being either dominated or liberated by his lower, subcortical process, the communication model provides the basis for postulating a harmonious integration of the cortical and subcortical functions.

A model embracing the possibility of a balance between higher and lower functions, the conscious and unconscious, is a radical departure from theories that view human behavior as a constant struggle of intellect to subdue animal instincts. The former is a model of mediative harmony while the latter—from which Western man is only beginning to emerge—is based on conquest and subjugation. Neurological theory may seem far removed from everyday reality, but it is quite easy to see projections of the latter intrapsychic models onto our culture. There are "wars on poverty"; medicine is exhorted to "conquer disease"; and almost everyone believes in the biblical mandate that "man shall have dominion over nature." In sharp contrast, Eastern and Western meditation disciplines emphasize interdependence, harmony, and cooperation. We see this perspective reflected in the recent interest in the interdependence of ecological systems. Structurally, the reticular activating system is a "column of cells occupying the central portions of the medulla, pons, and midbrain and extending upwards through the subthalamus into the ventromedial parts of the thalamus" (Prince, 1971, p. 117). Note, however, that the RAS crosses many conventional anatomical boundaries and is at present conceived as a functional unity rather than a structural one.

Physiologically, the RAS serves two basic functions: (1) It arouses and activates the cortex to become receptive to visceral stimulation; and (2) it transmits impulses from the cortex to the musculature and the autonomic nervous system (Rothballer, 1956). These two inseparable functions are termed "tonic activation" when the ascending RAS serves its arousal function, and "phasic activation" when the descending RAS serves its directive function. According to the research of Sharpless and Jasper (1956):

> The tonic component of the reticular system is capable only of crude differentiation between stimuli and produces long-lasting, persistent changes in reactivity that must occur in response to highly specific stimuli.

It is brief reactivity that characterizes phasic activation, which occurs when an individual consciously reacts to a stimulus and initiates an action.

Descending, or phasic, RAS functions have been demonstrated to be closely concerned with the psychological process of selective attention. In pioneering research, R. Hernandez-Peon (1963) recorded electrical activity from the cochlear nucleus, the essential organ of hearing in the inner ear, of an unanesthetized cat. Prominent electrical potentials were evoked from this nucleus when the relaxed or drowsing cat was exposed to click stimuli. However, these evoked potentials were markedly attenuated or absent when the cat's attention was distracted by the sight of mice in a beaker or by the odor of fish. In accounting for this phenomenon, Hernandez-Peon hypothesized that the descending RAS determines the threshold of sensory stimulation to sensory organs. In light of similar findings in research performed earlier (Galambos, 1956; Granit, 1955) Hernandez-Peon's work indicates that an RAS descending function is the narrowing and focusing of attention, resulting in the selective alteration of information at the first synapse or even at the receptor organ itself.

These conclusions recognized the RAS as serving the important function of selecting and screening stimuli from the autonomic nervous system prior to their registration in the cortical, or more conscious, areas of the brain. Stimuli barred from conscious consideration are nevertheless registered—subliminally, or out of conscious awareness—where they may and do affect an individual's behavior. This evidence concurs with a communication model of the brain even though it points to a psychological differentiation between consciously and unconsciously registered information; the evidence is contrary to a dualistic conflict model of conscious control versus unconscious impulses.

Concerning this last critical point, a communication model of the brain proposes that the psychological distinction between conscious and unconscious processes is a matter of differences in the quantity and quality of available information rather than an inherent, conflicting duality between conscious, or socially controlled, and unconscious instincts. This distinction will be more fully explicated below in the review of research on subliminal perception. At this point it is important to note that the model suggests a continuum of consciousness and defines the RAS as mediating conscious awareness along that continuum. This model does not include an equation of unconscious psychological processes with autonomic neurological processes; the former, in any case, are symbolic while the latter are electrical. The difference between them is irreconcilable and constitutes the essence of the quantum distinction between mind and brain. Notwithstanding, because the functioning of psychological and neurological systems are inextricably intertwined, the insights gained in one system may significantly illuminate the problems of the other.

Neurologists have tended to conceptualize the nervous system as a collection of more or less separate circuits, each performing a particular task. Yet there is increasing evidence that these circuits are in fact an integrated, holistic system and that the reticular activating system serves the integrative function. UCLA neurosurgeon, J. D. French, has stated this view succinctly:

> It [the RAS] awakens the brain to consciousness and keeps it alert; it directs the traffic of messages in the nervous system; it monitors the myriad of stimuli that beat upon our senses, accepting what we need to perceive and rejecting what is irrelevant; it tempers and refines our muscular activity and bodily movements. We can even go further and say that it contributes in an important way to the highest mental processes—the focusing of attention, introspection and doubtless all forms of reasoning (French, 1957, p. 38).

The exact nature of the link between neurological and psychological processes remains a speculative area of theory, research, and application. Significantly, there is a growing trend among consciousness researchers to move beyond the electrical and biochemical bases of brain activity to the atomic and subatomic levels of action. With a new precision and refinement of both theory and instrumentation, physicists and neuropsychologists have approached the problem of consciousness from divergent perspectives to arrive at strikingly similar conclusions. Chapter 4 discusses these most recent speculations about the interaction of mind and brain.

Subliminal Perception

Research on subliminal perception provides another important line of evidence that supports a communication model of neuropsychological functioning, validating the neurological observation that important stimuli that affect behavior are registered out of awareness. The classic study in this area was conducted in 1917 by O. Poetzl, who exposed tachistoscopic, or rapidly shown, pictures to research subjects for $1/100$ of a second. Poetzl had his subjects report fully on what they had perceived, then he demonstrated that elements of the pictures which had *not* been described or drawn in the subjects' reports appeared in the manifest content of the dreams that the subjects reported the next morning. More recent research by C. Fisher (1954, 1957) and L. Luborsky and H. Shevrin (1956), using much the same procedure, has confirmed this phenomenon. Additionally, Fisher (1956, 1957) has demonstrated that aspects of subliminally perceived pictures may subsequently appear in conscious imagery, free association, and hallucinations, as well as in dreams. Drawing upon these findings it can be hypothesized that a large amount of visual material is subliminally registered in extremely brief intervals, such as $1/100$ or $1/200$ of a second, and that although such perceptions are largely debarred from conscious registration as a function of selective attention, they do affect psychological processes such as dreams, spontaneous imagery, and free association. Of further interest, especially to research on altered states of consciousness, is the fact that although the previously unreported elements may be reproduced with photographic accuracy, the dreams and images more often demonstrate that numerous transformations and distortions have occurred (Fisher, 1957). This finding defines a major task of consciousness research, which is to understand the symbolic transformations of physical stimuli, past perceptions, ongoing fantasies, and images.

Experimental work on subliminal stimulation goes back to well before the turn of the century, but it was not until Charles Fisher undertook to replicate Poetzl's little-known tachistoscopic experiments in the early 1950s that investigations of subliminal perception were made relevant to modern psychology. Over the ensuing twenty years many more studies have steadily accumulated and the phenomenon of subliminal perception has emerged as a new scientific fact. This conclusion was first reached by Bevan, an experimental psychologist, who based his opinion on a landmark review in 1964 of over eighty studies on the subject. A more recent comprehensive overview and analysis of research on subliminal perception was undertaken by Dixon in 1971. He concluded that the existence of subliminal perception has been demonstrated in at least eight different categories: dreams, memory, adaptation level, conscious perception, verbal behavior, emotional responses, drive-related behavior, and perceptual thresholds. Following Dixon's work, the center of interest shifted from demonstrating the existence of subliminal perception to exploring its nature and implications.

Most prominent among the contemporary researchers in this area is Howard Shevrin of the University of Michigan. In 1973, Shevrin reported his series of experiments using subliminal stimuli and observed variations in cortical-evoked responses to explore the neurophysiological correlates of this mode of perception. A cortical-evoked response shows up on an electroencephalogram as the reflection of an individual's processing of information. Shevrin looked at the variations in this response in his subjects in order to discover whether cortical-evoked responses would discriminate consciously perceived information from unconsciously perceived information.

In his extensive series of experiments he demonstrated a relationship between the electrical activity of the brain in response to a stimulus and to unconscious thought processes involving attention, perception, primary process thinking, and repression. His aim was to investigate the conditions under which a subliminal input would undergo primary—or unconscious—transformations or distortions involving defenses, and secondary—or more conscious and intellectual—transformations in the association process.

Shevrin's experimental subjects were twelve pairs of fraternal twins, ranging in age from thirteen to nineteen. Each pair of twins was rated as respressive or nonrepressive, and one twin was identified as being more likely to repress a subliminal input (1973). Each twin was then given three tasks to perform: (1) free association, (2) selective attention, and (3) mental arithmetic. As each of them performed these jobs both the amplitude (or size of the electrical discharge) and the latency (or delay time between seeing and registering the stimuli) of their EEG activity were recorded simultaneously. The fact that the average evoked response (or average level of electrical discharge) is associated with attention provided Shevrin with a means for testing his theoretical construct concerning unconscious attention. If the hypothesized difference between primary and secondary processing of information actually existed, the average evoked response should show an increase in the amplitude associated with attention whenever a subliminal stimulus had been attended to unconsciously. After an extensive series of experiments presenting numerous subliminal inputs to these sets of twins, Shevrin examined the differential response between the repressive and the nonrepressive twin. It became clear to

Shevrin that the twins were in fact responding differentially. His conclusion to his series of experiments was:

> Apparently, the same subliminal input may be "processed" in a rational, veridical way and in an irrational, unrealistic way. High amplitude of evoked responses in a component occurring within the first two hundred and sixty milliseconds post-stimulus is associated with conceptual-level effects, whereas bursts of alpha occurring at 1.5 seconds post-stimulus are associated with clang and rebus effects (p. 84).

Both "clang" and "rebus effects" are the results of unconscious defense mechanisms of repression. This degree of rapidity and a differential response to input was suggested by Fisher in 1956 with his early work on subliminal perception.

In the experiments Shevrin found it was indeed possible to differentiate between the average evoked response of an individual who responded to information indicative of repression as opposed to an individual who responded to an input of information in an open and nonrepressive manner. In each experimental situation the repressive subject showed a greater amplitude of response in the early stages of the AER than did the nonrepressive control. Shevrin inferred from these data that the repressive individual would recognize the disturbing or potentially emotional stimulus, such as the picture of a burning house, and then quickly cover over this transient or brief reactivity to that response via repression, and the subsequent activity in the EEG would be dampened or lessened. In addition to the concrete findings made, Shevrin's work is important because it is a demonstration that subtle psychological processes can be researched in an empirical manner.

A Communication Model of the Brain

Another researcher, George S. Klein (1959), has suggested that the subliminal perception research data as a whole would profit from a distinction between "registration" and "conscious perception," such that registration denotes the general reception of all incoming stimuli by one aspect of the nervous system and conscious perception denotes the process whereby certain stimuli gain dominance over less immediately important stimuli and thus enter into conscious awareness at the cortical level. Similar distinctions are in use by neurologists in order to differentiate between the tonic and phasic functions of the reticular activating system. Again, this convergence of neurological and psychological theory supports a communication model of the brain in which all internal and external information is potentially available for conscious scrutiny. However, it is attended to differentially both in terms of RAS and cortical activation and in terms of selective attention. In this model, it is hypothesized that an individual has been processing psychological and physiological stimuli throughout his life in his own individualistic manner. Some stimuli have typically been processed consciously and other stimuli have been processed beyond awareness, or unconsciously.

In the communication model of neuropsychological functioning, the innate animal instincts of the conflict model are replaced by influences that are relatively inaccessible to conscious mentation. Thereby, differences between conscious and unconscious processes or social and instinctual processes are conceptualized not as conflict but as a matter of difficulty in gaining access to all the influences upon behavior. Although this reformulation of intra-individual and inter-individual information processing is moderate, it provides the basis for a model of psychological functioning in which unconscious processes are simply held out of immediate awareness, rather than emphasizing a qualitative, categorical, dualistic distinction between conscious-unconscious and voluntary-autonomic. Metaphorically, it is quite different to consider an individual as one engaged in sorting out complex information rather than as one attempting to subordinate an inner animal instinct in order to conform to the external demands of the social order.

This parallelism between neurological and psychological processes does not resolve the philosophical issue of mind and body duality but it does provide a scheme for conceptualizing the interaction of mind and body. Interaction is the key word. It is an indisputable fact from everyday experience and is readily observable in psychosomatic disorders, in which mental states have a profound effect upon the individual's physical body. All that really remains of this duality of mind and body issue is to define the exact process by which an intangible mental event interacts with the material system of the brain and body. As formidable as that task appears to be, a good beginning has already been made by tracing the rudimentary channels through which information from the bodily senses reaches the centers of higher awareness. The model outlined above has a great deal to offer in terms of explaining many of the findings of recent research in meditation, psychosomatic medicine, altered states of consciousness, imagery-based psychotherapies, and clinical biofeedback.

More, it offers a means of conceptualizing the etiology

of, and pragmatic treatments for, a wide range of psycho-somatic disorders. Various Eastern and Western meditation systems, biofeedback training, relaxation therapy, psychosynthesis, and numerous similar approaches offer the potential for an individual to clarify the relationships between his physiological and psychological states with unprecedented accuracy and thereby to reduce intra-organismic, psychosomatic stress and the accompanying disorders. Through a manipulation of imagery, sensations, or biofeedback indices, an individual could establish a clear communication between his higher-order cortical processes and subcortical physical processes in order to induce a more harmonious integration of these functions. He could learn the nonverbal language that his muscles, organs, and limbs use to communicate with his higher functions. By learning this "language" he can adjust dysfunctional physical processes. In effect, an individual needs to learn to ask the unconscious for directions in a manner consistent with the arcane dictum of "know thyself." Research strategies to test such hypotheses would involve biochemical, neuro-humoral, and psychophysiological indices; actually, such an approach would probe into the ultimate question of mind-body interaction.

Horizontal Unity

At the apex of the brain is the cortex, comprised of two distinct hemispheres. In relating properties of consciousness to brain function and structure, the hemispheres provide a model of the horizontal exchange of information between two specialized components of the brain. Neurophysiologist Roger Sperry, working at the California

Institute of Technology, made critical discoveries concerning the horizontal organization of brain functions and consciousness. His early research was devoted to extensive experimentation on brain functioning in laboratory animals such as the rhesus monkey; he was particularly interested in the connection between the two hemispheres of the brain. Drawing upon this animal research, in 1961 he began a series of experiments with animals and later with human subjects that led to the observation that each cerebral hemisphere performs unique psychological functions. Briefly, the left hemisphere was found to be predominantly analytical, logical, and intellectual, concerned primarily with verbal and mathematical abstractions. This hemisphere processes information sequentially in a linear, orderly fashion. On the other side, the right hemisphere is specialized in holistic, intuitive, and spatial tasks, concentrating upon phenomena such as musical perception, the recognition of faces, and orientation in space. It appears to process information more diffusely, to integrate material in a simultaneous, holistic fashion. These basic observations have given rise to some of the most innovative theories and research studies on the neurophysiology of consciousness.

On a purely neurophysiological basis the left hemisphere governs the functions of the right side of the body and the right hemisphere regulates the left side of the body, which is termed a contralateral crossover. The left hemisphere is dominant in most right-handed people and in about half of all left-handed people. The left hemisphere is termed dominant because damage to the left side appears to cause more severe impairments in functioning than damage to the right hemisphere. This distinction is probably more culturally determined than based upon objective observation. In a highly verbal and literate society, verbal and written communication is greatly valued. These functions are most impaired by damage to the left hemisphere where the speech centers are located for virtually all individuals. Comparable damage to the right or nonverbal hemisphere does not usually impair verbal communications for most patients.

Differences between the left and right hemispheres of the brain were first noted in 1836 by Dax, who ascribed language to the left hemisphere. This observation was based upon the fact that language and speech impairment, the condition termed aphasia, was much more likely with left-hemisphere lesions than with right-hemisphere lesions of comparable size, nature, and location. Several years later the French brain surgeon Paul Broca demonstrated that aphasia was associated with lesions in the third frontal convolution of the left hemisphere. Another early recognition of hemispheric asymmetry occurred in the 1860's when John Huwlings Jackson, the pioneering English brain surgeon, noted that human brains seemed to operate as though on "two brains," (Taylor, 1932, p. 130) one located in the left cerebral hemisphere, which is used for analytical functions, and one located in the right hemisphere, which is used for intuitive reasoning.

Now, as then, most of the knowledge of left and right-hemisphere specialization is based upon the clinical assessment of brain-damaged patients. In recent years, an important source of subjects for such clinical assessment has been people whose chronic epilepsy is treated by means of the radical neurosurgery termed cerebral commissurotomy by Bogen (1969, 1973). A complete commissurotomy involves severing the entire corpus callosum, the fibrous tract which links the two hemispheres and the anterior and hippocampal commissures; in some cases the massa intermedia is sectioned as well. Commissurotomies provide significant relief of chronic epilepsy. Prior to the development of the epilepsy operation, the patients of Joseph Bogen, from the White Memorial Medical Center in Los Angeles, had suffered from increasingly more frequent and severe seizures. These seizures were especially aggravated during the daytime, could not be controlled by any medication, and developed frequently into a status epilepticus. The so-called split-brain operation dramatically improved their conditions. Following a postoperative phase of symptoms reminiscent of organic brain damage, the patients apparently regained their levels of functioning prior to the onset of the disease. However, special tests, which had been developed in animal experiments, revealed that a wide variety of defects of integration between the two cerebral hemispheres could be elicited. It appeared that each of the separated hemispheres registered specific sensations, perceptions, mental associations, and ideas; each had its own learning processes and its own separate chain of memories, all of which seemed to be largely inaccessible to the other hemisphere.

Hemispheric asymmetry is a complex subject. Let us begin our discussion simply, by enumerating a few of the generally accepted findings. (1) Right-handed men exhibit the most asymmetrical distribution, the greatest degree of lateral specialization. (2) Women in general and left-handed individuals of both sexes may have reversed or more diffuse specialization, and women generally demonstrate a more bisymmetrical distribution of functions. (3) Hemisphere specialization evolves from infancy to adulthood. (4) Memory seems to be located asymmetrically; thus, short-term memory is affected when surgeons stimulate certain areas of the left hemisphere, but memory is not affected at all when corresponding locations on the right side are stimulated. (5) These distinctions are not rigid and dualistic but are more a matter of a specialized division of labor, with some overlap, between the two hemispheres. The last point is the most difficult to grasp. There has been an increasing tendency toward an overly simplistic model of the left-right duality of human consciousness by laymen and researchers alike. Despite the popular clichés, the data on hemispheric asymmetry ultimately lend more support to a unitary than to a dualistic view of consciousness.

Two Modes of Mental Operation

Differences in the functions of the two hemispheres in man were first studied systematically by Roger Sperry and Michael Gazzaniga. A forty-eight-year-old veteran of World War II who suffered from intractable epileptic seizures due to a head injury underwent what was at the time (1961) an experimental operation in order to control the seizures. Drs. Philip Vogel and Joseph Bogen of the White Memorial Medical Center in Los Angeles performed the surgery: severing the corpus callosum, the massive fiber tract— approximately 3½ inches long and a quarter-inch thick— that connects the two hemispheres of the brain. The rationale for the procedure is that the severing of the interhemispheric bridge prevents the spread of seizure from one hemisphere to the other, leaving the uninvolved hemisphere available to maintain bodily control. After the surgery, the patient appeared to function normally, just as Roger Sperry had observed to be the case with his laboratory animals. Regarding the apparent lack of disruption in this case, Sperry has noted:

The discrepancy between the large size, strategic position, and apparent importance of the corpus callosum on the one hand, and the lack of functional disturbance after its section on the other, posed for many years one of the more intriguing and challenging enigmas of brain function (Sperry, 1968, p. 83).

Under Sperry's direction, graduate student Michael Gazzaniga, later author of *The Bisected Brain,* ran the patient through an extensive series of tests. Eventually, the researchers were led to conclude that the sides of the man's brain operated differently and independently when the line of communication between them was severed. Among their observations: **(1)** The patient could only carry out verbal commands with the right hand and the right side of his body, which is the side controlled by the left brain; **(2)** by contrast, he could only perform tactile and visual tasks, such as piling up blocks or drawing a picture, with his left hand, which is controlled by the right brain hemisphere; and, most interesting of all, **(3)** there were instances where his left hand would act at odds with his right hand, such as when "he threatened his wife with his left hand while his right hand tried to come to his wife's rescue and bring the belligerent hand under control" (Pines, 1977). In brief, it seemed that the man had two distinct modes of functioning, residing separately, each in its own hemisphere, with little contact between them.

It is unlikely that hemispheric specialization is due to neurological differences between the two hemispheres, since the morphological differences are negligible. It is the psychological differences that are quite marked, and these would appear to be largely a matter of different cognitive styles, or a difference in the processing of information. It is conceivable that in the absence of the mediator (i.e., an intact corpus callosum), the left and right cognitive styles could generate behavior that may be curious by its antagonism with itself—as in the case of the split-brain patient mentioned above. In a recent paper by Drs. Levy, Trevarlen, and Sperry, this cognitive difference is described most succinctly:

> Recent commissurotomy studies have shown that the two disconnected hemispheres, working on the same tasks, may process the same sensory information in distinctly different ways, and that the two modes of mental operation involving spatial synthesis for the right and temporal analysis for the left show indications of mutual antagonism (Levy, 1970). The propensity of the language hemisphere to note analytical details in a way that facilitates their description in language seems to interfere with the perception of an over-all Gestalt, leaving the left hemisphere "unable to see the wood for the trees." This interference effect suggested a rationale for the evolution of lateral specialization . . . (Levy et al., 1972).

Division of labor between the two hemispheres seems to be more a matter of psychological efficiency than neurological necessity. As a whole, the brain is an adaptive pattern recognizer. It must perform vast numbers of fine discriminations and determine the commonalities underlying a large amount of information. In accordance with principles of economy, all raw stimuli are not permanently encoded and stored. Only the essential features of stimuli are retained in the form of an engram, whereby access to them can be gained quickly and reliably (Meyer, 1972). Thus, it appears that the left hemisphere builds up schemata that consists of a hierarchy of categories, to which stimuli are assigned according to their relative importance. These schemata as a whole must yield an effective and reliable representation of external reality. The categories allow an individual to anticipate and comprehend a vast array of problem situations that may be encountered. Furthermore, these schemata, amounting to an individual's unique representation of reality, give him a means of transmitting his experience to other individuals. By virtue of its specialization, the division of labor ascribed to the left hemisphere is the making of categorical distinctions; it names, identifies, classifies, analyzes, describes, explains, and reasons.

By contrast, right hemisphere functioning is more fluid and diffuse. Its properties are more analogous to raw experience itself. However, this very lack of specificity enables it to function in a holistic capacity with a much more free-floating format of comprehension. One of its functions seems to be to juxtapose dissimilar stimuli for creative comparison as in "horseless-carriage" or "wireless-telegraph." It thereby provides a basis for matching similar concepts, relative comparisons, such as between subtleties of word definitions, and similarity judgments between disparate elements of experience, such as reactions to authority figures. The right hemisphere makes its most important contributions in developing analogs of spatial topography, as in sorting the figure from the ground in a painting, or of an unfamiliar, uncategorized sensory configuration.

No doubt the left hemisphere has some holistic capacity and the right has some ability to categorize. The division of asymmetrical functions is dependent upon a number of variables, the most obvious being age, sex, handedness, culture, and, to a degree, one's training in a vocation or profession. Thus, it is much too simplistic to confine psychological functions exclusively to the left or right hemispheres. Rather, there seem to be numerous functions stored in both the left and right hemispheres that are deployed in a flexible manner and adapted to the needs at hand. The perception of music provides an interesting illustration of this flexibility. For a long time one of the enigmas of hemispheric asymmetry was that the recognition of music could not be adequately traced exclusively to one side or the other of the brain. In other words, it could not be ascertained whether music appreciation was an analytical left-brain function or an intuitive right-brain function. Within the last year, two psychologists from Columbia University, Thomas Bever and Robert Chiarello, discovered that music perception is a function of both hemispheres. However, there is a difference between musicians and nonmusicians in terms of left-right deployment in musical appreciation. Musicians tended to use the left hemisphere, or their analytical side, when attending to music. By contrast, those who were not musically trained used the right side of their brain for more intuitive perceptions in the appreciation of music. This conclusion was reached after the researchers channelled music individually into the left ears of subjects and then into the right. They discovered that musically naive people recognized melodies best in their left ear, which has its information processes in the right hemisphere. Musically trained subjects were much better at recognizing melodies when played in the right ear, which is transmitted to the left or analytical side of the brain (Bever and Chiarello, 1974).

It seems unequivocal, then, that the left and right modes of functioning are not independent in the intact brain. Rather, it is likely that hemispheric functions are highly integrated and the relative contributions of each side to a task are dependent upon the demands of the situation and the differential capacities of the hemispheres within a particular individual (Mountcastle, 1962). Indeed, recalling the material presented in Chapter 2, it is possible that much of what we detect about the differences between the left and right hemispheres may very well be artifacts of the testing situations or surgical procedures (Mountcastle, 1962). The analogy in physics is the case wherein the principle of complementarity comes into play. Depending upon the design of the experiment, a researcher will determine that light either is composed of particles or is a probability fog.

Sex Differences

As noted above, a great deal of the knowledge concerning the asymmetrical functions of the two hemispheres has been based upon testing and observation of people who have incurred brain damage. In the study of sixty-four men and women who underwent a temporal lobotomy, an accepted procedure in certain cases of intractable temporal lobe epilepsy, D. H. Lansdell of the National Institute of Neurological Diseases and Blindness made two interesting observations. First, the data suggest there is some neurophysiological mechanism underlying artistic appreciation since it appears to be affected by temporal lobe surgery. And second, the research indicates that there is a more homogeneous distribution of this particular hemispheric function in females than in males, who appear to have these functions more asymmetrically distributed. All of the patients were given the Graves Design Judgment Test, which is an indicator of "aptitude for the appreciation and production of art structure," before and after surgery (Lansdell, 1952). Following removal of the temporal lobe from the patient's dominant hemisphere, the men showed a decrease in artistic aptitude whereas the women showed an increase. In the instances in which temporal lobe removal was from the patient's subdominant hemisphere, the men showed a rise in artistic aptitude while the women's scores indicated a decrease. However, these results appeared to be only transient, for there were no differences in artistic aptitude among the forty-two men and women who were tested again a year or more after their operations. Part of the early results may have been due to the sudden effects of surgical intervention. The lack of permanent change indicates a plasticity of the brain in redistributing disturbed functions after partial brain removal or damage. Thus, although the immediate post-surgical tests indicated that the esthetic function may be differentially distributed in men and women, the follow-up tests revealed that these distributions are not necessarily fixed and invariate.

More recent studies concerning possible sex differences in hemispheric functions have been undertaken by testing normal individuals. Paul Bakan and his colleagues had subjects look at slide projections of right or left body parts and asked them to identify the body part as right or left (Bakan and Putnam, 1974). There were no significant differences between right- and left-handed subjects, but the performance of women was significantly less accurate than that of men, regardless of handedness. It has been suggested that the ability to discriminate right from left is dependent upon the development of functional hemispheric asymmetry in the brain. The researchers, therefore, suggested that the female deficit in right-left discrimination in particular and in visual-spatial skills in general may be due to a sex difference in the hemispheric organization of the brain. This implies that the female brain develops with a lesser degree of functional hemispheric asymmetry. This hypothesis joins a considerable body of evidence demonstrating that female and male brains differ with respect to lateral organization. Such observations are usually posed in terms of "deficits" in function, but this may reflect a sexist as well as a cultural stereotype, which presupposes that hemispheric asymmetry is necessarily a positive attribute. It may very well be that the lack of extreme hemispheric asymmetry is a positive value in and of itself, conferring increased flexibility on those who develop this way. In any case, there is increasing evidence that males and females differ with regard to hemispheric asymmetry, which lends credence to the concept that sexuality reflects complementary opposites with regard to perception—as in the yin-yang of Tao.

During another experiment, sex differences were noted in electroencephalogram (EEG) patterns of asymmetry among fourteen right-handed people, nine males and five females. There were three experimental conditions: **(1)** subjects whistled songs, recited lyrics, and sang; **(2)** they were requested to self-induce certain emotional responses; and **(3)** they were tested to see if one group could produce asymmetry for a longer percent-time during biofeedback of the EEG alpha frequency. Conditions were designed to feedback both symmetrical and asymmetrical activity from the left and right hemispheres (Davidson et al., 1975). For the first condition, females revealed greater asymmetry between whistle and talk conditions, the right hemisphere becoming quite active during the whistle task and the left being active while reciting. There were no observed differences for the males. In the second task involving emotional response, females showed greater right hemisphere activation during emotional versus nonemotional conditions. Again, males showed no differences. Lastly, females demonstrated greater ability to produce hemispheric asymmetry during feedback conditions. Overall, the female subjects manifested greater asymmetry than males during these self-generated tasks. Results such as these indicate not only that the hemispheres specialized in terms of function, but also that there are sex differences with regard to ability and level of activity in highly specific tasks. Perhaps acknowledging and exploring these differential abilities will provide a scientific basis for seeking the mutual interdependence of male and female free of the social stereotypes that have imprisoned each sex for so long.

Specialized, But Not Compartmentalized

Since Freud's early attempts, psychologists and neurophysiologists have attempted to relate the phenomenology of mind to specific anatomical or neurophysiological properties of the brain. Given the recent advances in neurophysiology, there is a revived interest in this area. In a scene from a now-famous movie made by Roger Sperry, a commissurotomy patient is shown in the midst of an experiment involving tachistoscopic pictures. Among a series of otherwise dull pictures, the patient is flashed a photograph of a nude woman, in the left half of the viewing field only. The split-brain subject, whose right hemisphere was thus stimulated, at first reported seeing nothing. Then she immediately flushed, alternately squirmed, smiled, and looked uncomfortable and confused. However, her left hemisphere was still unaware of what had caused the emotional turmoil in her body. What finally could be verbalized by the left hemisphere was only the comment, "Oh, Dr. Sperry, you have some machine!" This behavior of the split-brain patient has been interpreted as an indication of the unconscious nature of the emotional reaction, making it unavailable to her language apparatus. The two independent consciousnesses were at odds, as reflected in the patient's repression and denial of the disturbing image.

Psychiatrist David Galin, at the Langley Porter Neuropsychiatric Institute in San Francisco, has considered the implications of the neurophysiological substrates of unconscious mental processes. Galin postulates parallels between some aspects of the disconnected right hemisphere and some aspects of primary process thinking and repression. As the basis for this hypothesis, Galin used clinical and experimental observations concerning unconscious processes through somatic expression, dreaming, the denial of illness, the emotional reaction induced by intracarotid sodium amytal, and the therapeutic response to unilateral electroshock treatment for depression (Galin, 1974). As part of his research, Galin summarized a great volume of findings that support parallels between right hemisphere function and primary process thinking. One implication of his literature review was that the right hemisphere uses a primarily nonverbal mode of representation and that it reasons by a nonlinear mode of association rather than by syllogistic logic. It typically grasps the concept of the whole from just a part, and its solutions to problems are based on multiple converging determinants rather than a single causal chain. Second, the research literature indicates that the right hemisphere is less involved with perception of time and sequence than the left hemisphere. Most importantly, the right hemisphere possesses words, but these words are not organized for use in propositions and sentences, rather they reflect a holistic style. Also, the right hemisphere is particularly adept in the recognition of faces. Since the right hemisphere deals more effectively with complex patterns taken as a whole than with individual parts taken serially, its mode of expression is most often in the form of "word pictures" such as metaphors, puns, double entendres, and rebus. Elements of these verbal constructions do not have fixed definitions but depend on context, and can shift in meaning when seen as parts of a new pattern.

In relating these findings to the hypothesis that some unconscious processes may be localized in the right hemisphere, Galin discussed several conditions in which the two separate streams of consciousness could result in unconscious conflict. One condition would be a situation where a mother assures her child of her love, but her facial expression shows the opposite. Usually the verbal expression, perceived in the left hemisphere, would predominate. However, the child might sense anger if the right hemisphere perception of the negative facial expression was strong enough. Regardless of the child's external reaction, the ambivalent experience may persist as image and memory for him, and thus influence future feelings and behavior. Since the two hemsipheres do process information differentially, it is entirely possible to assume that separate channels of information may frequently conflict, creating the basis for anxiety and neurophysiological stress. Such conflicting information needs to be resolved, and it is possibly resolved in the intact brain by one hemisphere assuming temporary dominance over the other. This temporary override of one hemisphere by the other can be thought of as a functional commissurotomy and is perhaps the neurophysiological concomitant of repression. Despite the fact that this process might alleviate the temporary stress, all of the conflicting information is subliminally processed and may be reactivated at a later time. Thus, it may be premature to attempt to isolate most unconscious activity in the right hemisphere. There is a need for a more dynamic model involving a constant fluctuating feedback between the two hemsipheres, whereby discrepant information can be resolved.

The results of recent research indicate that the compartmentalization of brain function into left and right hemispheres is premature. Studies of how the brain processes visual information are confounded by the fact that information from both sides of the visual field is sent to both hemispheres. This makes it difficult to tell, even in split-brain subjects, which half of the brain is responding to which input. One means of getting around this problem is through the use of a "Z lens," developed by Eran Zaidel at the California Institute of Technology. First, one eye (the left, in language research) is covered by a patch, eliminating one source of information completely. Then the right eye is covered by an oversize contact lens, the middle of which is fitted with a tiny aluminum tube about the size of the pupil. The tube contains a lens to focus the incoming images and a floating half-screen, which moves with the eye to block out the left side of the retina, the part that normally feeds information to the left hemisphere. With the tube and eyepatch in place, only the right hemisphere "sees" whatever the person is shown.

Sperry and Zaidel have used this device to give various language tests to the right hemisphere of split-brain subjects. In a simple test, the examiner speaks a word such as "horse" and then shows the person a picture of four animals, including a horse. Both hemispheres hear the word, but only the right one sees the picture. Subjects were able to point to the horse only with their left hand, which is controlled by the right hemisphere. Using more complex words and sentences, the researchers found that the right hemisphere was only about two years behind the left in understanding vocabulary, and as capable as a five-year-old in handling syntax. These findings support the theory that the two hemispheres develop functions equally until about the age of five, when each starts to specialize. The right hemisphere's language potential offers hope for people who lose language facilities after their left hemisphere is damaged by a stroke or other trauma. If further research confirms Sperry's and Zaidel's work, the right hemisphere might be retrained to restore at least some of the lost abilities (Zaidel and Sperry, 1975). Again, this research indicates that when procedures that can begin to match the subtlety of brain function are used, the two hemispheres appear to be specialized but not compartmentalized in their functions.

Creativity and Unitive Consciousness

Perhaps one of the most intriguing bridges between neurophysiology and states of consciousness concerns the relationship between hemispheric functions and creativity. After observing numerous patients who had undergone a commissurotomy, Joseph Bogen noted that the patients had a quantitative as well as a qualitative paucity of dreams, fantasies, and symbolization (Bogen and Bogen, 1969). From these observations, Bogen has speculated that interhemispheric collaboration might be necessary for truly creative thinking. One of the essential capacities of the right hemisphere appears to be the storage of dissimilar bits of information. Its capacity to store and process dissimilar elements may very well be the neurophysiological element essential to creativity.

One of the most interesting discussions of this possible connection was written by Albert Rothenberg, a psychiatrist at the Yale University School of Medicine. In an article entitled "The Process of Janusian Thinking in Creativity" (1971), Rothenberg defined Janusian thinking as "the capacity to conceive and utilize two or more opposite or contradictory ideas, concepts, or images simultaneously." Janus was the Roman god with two faces who looked and apprehended in opposite directions simultaneously. In analyzing the property of creative insight to synthesize disparate elements of experience, Rothenberg's observations parallel the reports of Bogen, Galin, and other researchers concerning the dynamic interplay between the left and right hemispheres. This capacity is discussed in relation to its role in the creative process in art, literature, architecture, science, and mathematics. Essential to all the examples cited was the necessity for the individual both to perceive new interrelationships between data and to have the critical and expressive capacity to articulate those insights clearly. According to Rothenberg:

> The simultaneous presence of contradictory and conflictual elements in the creator's consciousness allows for new integrations and resolutions and the Janusian thought must be susceptible to such resolutions to be more than a logical absurdity (Rothenberg, 1971, p. 7).

One of the most outstanding quantum physicists, Eugene Wigner, also points out the necessity of maintaining oppositions as a prerequisite to creativity. Wigner's theory is known as the "conservation of parity." Essentially, it states that any object or process and its exact opposite are, at least theoretically, equally capable of existing. Perhaps such a conservation of parity exists as a prerequisite of creative insight, since such experiences frequently are characterized by the person recognizing the need for a higher order of reasoning when two apparently contradictory facts are both true. A graphic example of this principle in action can be drawn from the discovery of the double-helix structure of DNA, which is the basic molecule of genetic replication. DNA's structure, as determined by J. D. Watson and F. H. C. Crick, is composed of two similar but opposed spatial forms. Among the developments that led to this discovery was Watson's recognition of the fact that the identical chains ran in opposite directions. This insight occurred after a long period of in-depth analysis involving X-ray crystallography and detailed analytical assessment. However, the actual moment of insight is described by Watson in the followng manner.

> When I got to our still empty office the following morning, I quickly cleared away papers from my desktop so I would have a large, flat surface on which to form pairs of bases held together by hydrogen bonds. Though I initially went back to my like-with-like prejudices, I saw all too well that they led nowhere . . . then [I saw that] both pairs could be flipped flopped over and still have their glycosidic bonds facing in the same direction. This had the important consequence that a given chain could contain both purines and pyrimidines. At the same time, it strongly suggested that the backbones of the two chains run in opposite directions (Watson and Crick, 1974).

Thus, the actual breakthrough consisted of conceiving simultaneously of identical but spatially opposed forms. A further example, to be found in Rothenberg's previously cited article, is that of Arnold Schoenberg's creation of the twelve-tone scale, an important development leading to the so-called atonal movement in modern music. Schoenberg reported that he had arrived at this notion by means of the recognition that consonants and dissonants were equivalent. His comment that "dissonances are only the remote consonances" is a clear statement of the integration of two oppositional modes of perception.

Of course, it is extremely important to note that one prepares for the truly creative act by knowing a field well and knowing which widely held facts are important and susceptible to opposition or contradiction on some level. Conflict and opposition are not themselves the essence of creativity. Rather, creativity arises from the reordering of superficially disparate or disjunctive facts once those facts have been acquired in a logical, rational, and analytic manner. Creativity does not require the abandonment of the rational faculty, but it does involve some degree of humility in regard to the power of the intellect. One very amusing anecdote is cited by Bertrand Russell in his *History of Western Philosophy* (1945). Discussing the much-celebrated sudden glory of the spontaneous mystical insight that is experienced at the point of resolution of creative work, Russell cites a case example from William James who described a man who gained mystical experience from laughing gas. Whenever he was under its influence, he knew the secret of the universe, but when he came to, he had forgotten it. At last, with immense effort, he wrote down the secret before the vision had faded. When completely recovered, he rushed to see what he had written. It was: "A smell of petroleum prevails throughout." In other words, nonsense. It seems that the essence of creativity must entail a synthesis of left and right hemisphere functions.

Empirical evidence for this observation is offered by

Marie Malory Hall of the Veterans Hospital in Boston, Massachusetts. Hall and her colleagues conducted studies of forty-eight men and one woman patient, all right-handed, who were afflicted with a variety of left-hemisphere lesions ranging from tumors to vascular trauma such as a stroke. In describing the psychological differences between comparable left-brain, right-brain lesions, they note that an individual with a left-brain lesion appears ''limited, arid, unimaginative, and ruefully aware that this is so'' (Hall, Hall, and Lavoie, 1968). A damaged left hemisphere may be likened to a powerful judiciary body that is given more to censorship than to justice. It appears to be a rather pedantic critic who will not appear foolish yet lacks an imaginative capacity. On the other hand, patients with homologous lesions of the right hemisphere demonstrate an ease of perceptual organization and an expansiveness that may lead beyond the individual's capacity to handle them. Often, the individual's perceptions inappropriately combined parts into wholes and resulted in preposterous or bizarre figures rather than genuinely imaginative ones. Based upon interpretation of Rorschach test results of one such patient, the researchers concluded:

> His vigilance is diminished and he shows a lack of selective attention. He overextends his talents and expresses no awareness that there is a flaw in his performance. The tempering effects of self-criticism are too little in evidence; there is a want of prudence. This suggests that the normal right hemisphere may be the inventor, the innovator, the artist, which, when diseased, exceeds its powers and so disregards its left-sided critic that it falls repeatedly into ludicrous assertions (Hall, Hall, and Lavoie, 1968, p. 37).

It appears that the left hemisphere is the logician and the critic while the right is the innovator and the artist. When they function harmoniously there is creativity, but neither can adequately stand alone in this regard.

It is fairly evident that the findings concerning the hemispheres of the brain seem to support the concept of a duality of consciousness. Opposed to this viewpoint is our almost universal introspective experience of a unity of consciousness—a sense of a singular identity of "I." Perhaps that singular identity exists prior to the information elements stored in either the left or right hemisphere and has access to both under ideal circumstances. Dichotic listening experiments and visual half-field studies imply that one hemisphere is superior to the other with some materials. Special presentation methods can even demonstrate that both hemispheres working in some sense independently can increase overall capacity. Yet progress in understanding mind-brain interaction would falter if the concept of left-right hemisphere duality were to become an overly simplistic and dogmatic model. According to Marcel Kinsbourne:

> The vast evidence so far shows only that a given strategy is more efficiently implemented by one hemisphere than the other. Thus, the two hemispheres of man harbor not two consciousnesses, but different elements of the total human repertoire of problem solving strategies. It is probably best (most adaptive) not to commit oneself to those located on one side only, but to draw on each and all of them as the situation requires (Kinsbourne, 1970, p. 10).

It appears that in man each hemisphere can initiate the full range of human behavior, though to different levels of excellence. The inferior processor is suppressed and this suppression is mediated by the corpus callosum. There appears to be a mechanism, the nature of which is yet unknown, that channels mental capacity to the superior one of two alternative cerebral processes whenever the situation demands the processing in question.

Actually, exploring situations in which there is a call for increased cooperation between the hemispheres would seem to be an infinitely more fruitful line of inquiry than continuing with the isolation of increasingly minute variables into left and right pigeonholes. It is hypothesized that during unitive or transcendent experiences, as have been reported throughout time, the normally asynchronous activity of the hemispheres would become synchronous. Galin and Ornstein (1972) have speculated that the two hemispheres are in close communication when they exhibit the same brain waves. Under those conditions, the full potential of both hemispheres would be available to the individual; he would have simultaneous access to his analytic left hemisphere and to his synthetic, holistic right hemisphere. And under those conditions, researchers may discover the neurophysiological basis of higher states of consciousness. Such evidence would lend support to the hypothesis that increased synchrony between the two hemispheres could create the prerequisite conditions for a bilateral information exchange that would be subjectively reported as an ''aha'' experience, or one of significant insight and creativity. Perhaps a scientific inquiry into the mystical experience may not be an insoluble paradox as science approaches the most subtle properties of consciousness.

Holograms and Human Consciousness

*I*N THE preceding chapter we presented a communication model that organizes the brain and body along a vertical axis and reviewed the research and literature dealing with left-right hemisphere functions of the brain, which indicate a horizontal dimension to the neurophysiological basis of consciousness. Now we turn to one of the most significant new areas of scientific inquiry concerning the nature of the mind. This new area is a confluence of neurophysiology, psychology, states of consciousness, classical Newtonian physics, and contemporary quantum physics. It is essentiially holistic research that tests notions of multidimensional models of consciousness. This is the area providing holographic models of consciousness for our consideration. *Holograph* is derived from the two Greek roots *holo* meaning "whole" and *graph* meaning "to write." A *hologram* is an image in which the whole is written into each of the parts just as the genetic information for the entire body is encoded in each cell. This property and others of the hologram represent some of the most potent approaches ever mounted to probe the enigmas of mind-body relations.

Hologram theory was initially developed by the Nobel physicist Dennis Gabor in the late 1940s in an attempt to upgrade the quality of electron-microscope photography. The invention of the laser twenty years later made it possible actually to create a hologram, which is a three-dimensional image produced by wavefront reconstruction. To explain the process briefly: Coherent light, or light of approximately the same frequency, is emitted from a laser and strikes a half-silvered mirror. Part of the coherent laser light, a "reference beam," passes directly through the partially silvered mirror and falls upon the photographic plate. Another part of the laser light is deflected toward a three-dimensional object to be photographed, such as a box. After the light is deflected to the box, it is then reflected off the box toward the photographic plate. Light reflected from the box creates an interference pattern with the laser light, which was projected directly through the partially silvered mirror. This resulting interference pattern is recorded on the photographic plate and ends the first stage of creating a hologram of a three-dimensional object. Up to this point, the procedures are a slight variation upon standard photography. However, the real significance of this interference pattern is evident in stage two when the photographic plate is illuminated with either ordinary or laser light. When light passes through the plate, a wavefront is created and, to the observer on the far side of the plate, the resulting image appears to be a full, three-dimensional representation of the original object.

As we will see, many aspects of this three-dimensional photography have profound implications for the holographic theory of the interaction between brain function and consciousness. Such a parallel may be found in a model of memory function. Two important properties of the hologram provide evidence for the similarity. If the laser light illuminates only one small portion of the hologram, the observer will still see the complete three-dimensional image, although its details will be less clear. If a small section of the photographic plate is cut out and a laser light projected through it, the observer will still see the entire three-dimensional object, although it will be diminished in intensity. We may apply these holographic properties usefully to instances in which stroke patients report complete but greatly dimmed memories. Furthermore, hologram research lends itself to considerations of such fundamental issues in neurophysiology as the degree to which brain function is isolated in specific anatomical areas and the extent to which all functions are diffused throughout the entire cerebral cortex. There are long-standing areas of debate regarding whether the functions of the brain are fixed in specific areas or organized more diffusely. A holographic model resolves this dilemma since it accounts for both localized functions as well as the fluidity of that specialized information being stored throughout other areas of the brain (Eccles, 1973). The hologram also serves as a neurophysiological model in which brain function is potentially distributed throughout each cell of the brain, although certain anatomical areas specialize and emphasize certain aspects while other potentials remain dormant in those areas. If this proves to be the case, then it may be possible to devise innovative methods of eliciting this dormant information in patients having suffered traumatic brain damage, so that they may regain at least some of their normal functions.

Applications of laser theory to brain function may also provide insight into the memory and associative processes. It seems that the brain's ability to associate one bit of information with another finds an analogy in the hologram produced by bouncing laser light off two different objects. In this procedure, the light reflected from each object becomes the reference wave for the other object. Then if either one of the original objects represented on the photographic plate is reilluminated with the same laser light at the same angle, the other object will also emerge, resulting in two distinct images. This interrelationship of holographic images may provide a useful model for conceptualizing the neuronal associative functions in the brain. Encoding information of the whole in each of its subordinate parts is analogous to the encoding noted earlier, where all DNA-to-RNA genetic information for the entire organism is contained in the nucleus of any single cell of that organism. Clues from the very nucleus of cellular structure can provide insight into such pragmatic clinical problems when intuition accompanies rigorous observation.

Holography's Roots in Psychophysics

Formulations of holographic models of the brain may be said to have begun with the research of Karl Lashley in the 1920s, which was reported in his monumental work on *Brain Mechanisms and Intelligence,* published in 1929.

The initial question addressed by Lashley concerned one of the most fundamental issues of neurophysiology: To what extent are particular psychological or physiological functions localized within specific areas of the brain? Experiments indicate that on a gross level, specific functions do appear to be localized in specific regions. However, other, equally valid data indicate that extensive damage to such localized areas often does not completely impair the functions associated with them. Focusing on the memory function of the brain, Lashley's experiments demonstrated that large portions of a laboratory rat's cerebral cortex could be excised and yet the rat's memory would remain intact, albeit dulled proportionately to the amount of tissue removed. From these experiments, Lashley deduced that every memory was stored in every part of the rat's cortex, and that the intensity of memory depended upon the total number of intact cortical cells. Memory appeared to vary along two parameters: localization and amount of redundancy in the information stored in that location.

Lashley also addressed the question of how the bioelectric signals of the brain could combine to create a stable visual perception. Lashley theorized on the basis of his research that of the innumerable overlapping waves created by the firing of billions of discontinuous neurons, some parts of the waves are cancelled out while others are reinforced; so-called interference patterns are generated. Stable interference patterns—diffused over the entire cerebral cortex—constitute the information of all perceptual systems and memory. He concluded that visual stability was produced by means of an interference pattern of the waves from the nerve signals and that visual perception functioned in a manner analogous to the photographic plate hologram that Gabor was to describe two decades later.

Missing from Lashley's theory was any means for retrieving specific elements from the intricate kaleidoscope of stored-information patterns. It was the physicist Gabor who worked out that in order to sort specific bits of information from a hologram, there needs to be a single constant, or reference wave form. This wave form must remain constant in both frequency and phase, such that it creates neither interference within itself nor becomes part of the random activity of interference patterns. This requirement kept hologram theory problematical until the invention of the laser beam in the 1960s. The invention of lasers provided researchers in physics with a tool for constructing the coherent, stable reference beam that Gabor had in mind, and their advent greatly strengthened the concept that a similar phenomenon could serve an organizing function in holographic theories of neuropsychology.

Holographic Models of Memory

Most recently, the hologram model of brain function is largely the work of Karl H. Pribram of Stanford University, who began his studies in the early 1950s. Pribram's early research focused on brain functions and largely favored use of experimental procedures involving surgery and electrophysiology. In particular, his studies explored the frontal cortex of primates, measured attention by means of eye movements, and determined the effect of food deprivation and pharmacological agents upon motivation. One of Pribram's major contributions to the development of a hologram theory of brain function was his recognition that holograms can be constructed in infinitesimal layers with each bit of specific information being retrievable. Thus, successive holographic images superimposed on a single, thick photographic plate would have the effect of storing billions of bits of information within a cubic centimeter. Pribram saw that this may be analogous to the brain's method of storing vast amounts of information within its relatively limited confines. In writing of the hologram theory Pribram notes that

> [holography] has many fascinating properties among which the facility for distributing and storing large amounts of information is paramount. These properties are just those needed to resolve the paradox posed by the demand for functional liability, the rapidly paced transients in the context of demonstrated anatomical constraints in neural input organization (Pribram, 1971, p. 141).

Always mindful of the limitations as well as the usefulness of applying analogies to the functions of biological brains, Pribram's research productively explores the areas common to cybernetics, holography, and the neurophysiology of brain processes. Proceeding on the basis of a model of the brain as an elaborate and sophisticated computer, Pribram provides a highly detailed analysis of how information-processing occurs in the brain in his book, *Language of the Brain: Experimental Paradoxes and Principles in Neuropsychology.* According to this research, the holograms offering the most potential for understanding brain functions are those which can be expressed in mathematical terms as Fourier transforms. Fourier transforms can be best understood by picturing a continuously oscillating wave—for example, any of the EEG frequencies considered in the next chapter. Fourier analysis is a means of breaking up such a compound wave into its constituent components and, conversely, a means of generating a compound wave form from its basic components. Such transforms, essential in assessing brain activity, are an integral aspect of hologram theory.

Fourier transforms have a unique attribute, since the identical equation convolves and devolves itself and "thus any process represented by the spatial Fourier transform can encode and subsequently decode simply by recurring at some second stage" (Pribram, 1971, p. 149). This principle points to the hologram property of storing the whole in each part, each part being capable of generating the whole. It is refreshing to note how similar this concept is to the mystical utterances of the poet William Blake who perceived "the universe in a grain of sand and eternity in an hour." Properties of space and time are completely elastic in the holographic models of the brain and are strikingly reminiscent of the recorded experiences of individuals undergoing altered states of consciousness.

Through the use of Fourier transforms and two concepts borrowed from laser physics, the perplexing problem of long-term memory storage and retrieval becomes resolvable. In Pribram's theory, memory functions in a two-step process. A stimulus such as a sound, smell, or an image triggers an individual's short-term memory, which then resonates through the infinite complexity of the brain's stored holograms until an association is triggered in long-term memory. This correspondence between an immediate sensory stimulus and a fragment of a stored memory initiates the retrieval of the entire stored memory. Remember, holographic theory states that the whole image is replicated in each of its component parts—i.e., there is total multi-level redundancy; therefore, any pattern or pattern-set of long-term memory can be elicited selectively from all others with infinite facility. Just as the memory was encoded within an infinitesimal space by means of a Fourier-like transform, that same memory can be decoded into a certain dimensional wholeness by a precise reversal of the same Fourier transform. Through these holographic transformations a highly complex, yet utterly discrete, memory can be retrieved quite readily from an infinite array of possibilities. It should be pointed out that this is, of course, a highly idealized conceptual model; variables such as age, sex, stimulus intensity, circumstances, environment, and more affect the process of memory recall in actual experience.

The unusual phenomenon of eidetic imagery, commonly known as photographic memory, may also be interpreted in the light of holographic theory. Those who possess the faculty of eidetic imagery have the ability to commit to memory large amounts of visual information in an extremely brief period of time. (The term applied to these individuals is Eidetiker, from the Greek word *eidetikos,* which means relating to image or knowledge.) Using an EEG and an electro-oculograph, or EOG, researchers Daniel Pollen and Michael Tractenberg tested an individual named Elizabeth (as it happened, an art professor at Harvard University [*Nature,* May 12, 1972]). According to these experiments, Elizabeth had normal vision and normal alpha blocking, or a shift into fast frequency EEG activity, when she was actively attending to the external world; during such periods she claimed to be building up an eidetic image when visually scanning an object or page. However, when involved in calling up the eidetic image with her eyes closed, and reproducing that information in a very detailed manner, Elizabeth's alpha rhythm became very prominent. Even when she "projected" an eidetic image of a page from Goethe's *Faust* onto a screen six meters away and then read it, her alpha rhythm was more prominent than when reading an ordinary page of print from the same distance, although the amplitude of the eyes-open alpha waves was only a third that of her eyes-closed alpha waves. The EOG measurements showed that she moved her eyes much less when reading an eidetic page than when reading a real page. Further, when asked to bring an eidetic image as close to her eyes as possible, her eyes turned inward while they were closed, just as if she was actually moving a real picture close to her eyes. Pollen and Tractenberg suggest a connection between these data and a holographic model of memory that Pollen has put forward. They note that although the entire scene stored in the memory hologram can be remembered from just one tiny bit of the hologram, but will be quite dim (just as our usual memory is quite dim), the image will be as vivid as the originally recorded scene if the entire hologram is processed. Perhaps Eidetikers somehow have access to very large regions of memory holograms. Continuing research may give an indication whether or not this is the case. Perhaps these individuals have developed a focused attention as in meditation that acts as a form of coherent, mental laser that can reconstruct detailed information with great accuracy.

Other evidence that helps to strengthen the position of a holographic model of the brain comes from the work of an Indiana zoologist, Paul Pietsch. Scores of neurophysiological studies of memory have utilized the method of ablating, or surgically removing, parts of the brain in animal subjects to determine what brain activities are impaired in consequence. The evidence of such experiments using laboratory rats has indicated that memory is retained intact if just one small segment of the brain remains intact. While suggestive, these data do not necessarily support a holographic model of brain functioning; they may mean, alternately, that the storage system of the brain is such that all information, including all metaprograms, is recoverable from any specific brain part. In contradistinction, the hologram model posits information encoded in a pattern system that is independent of specific brain tissue and/or localized functions. If this is the case, then it should be possible to disrupt the tissue completely (but not remove it) and yet not affect normal brain functioning.

Pietsch tested this hypothesis in a series of experiments on salamanders. Having an extraordinary capacity for self-regeneration, the salamander offers researchers a uniquely simple brain/body model to study. If a flesh wound is made or an amputation is inflicted upon a leg or tail, the salamander can heal itself or regenerate the severed part completely in a few days. Salamanders also exhibit marked feeding behavior and eat meat almost incessantly, especially tubiform worms. Since feeding behavior is believed to be governed by the pre-medullar portion of the brain, Pietsch chose this area for his ablation studies, reasoning that any alterations in brain function would have the readily observable behavioral result of an alteration in feeding behavior. In his experiments, Pietsch excised portions of the salamander's medulla, cut it into small pieces, minced up these pieces, and put this tissue back in the salamander's brain. After a few weeks of recovery, the salamanders were showing their normal feeding behavior. According to Pietsch (1972):

> In more than 700 operations, I rotated, reversed, added, subtracted, and scrambled the brain parts. I shuffled. I reshuffled. I sliced, lengthened, deviated, shortened, ap-

posed, transposed, juxtaposed, and flipped. I sliced front to back with lengths of spinal cord, of medulla, with other pieces of brain turned inside out. But nothing short of dispatching the brain to the slop bucket—nothing expunged feeding (p. 66).

Thus, despite ultra-radical intervention in brain tissues, brain functions remained intact. Pietsch asked what—other than a hologram model—could account for these results. One possibility was that the salamander's feeding behavior was governed from another part of the brain, spinal column, or even from another part of its anatomy. Pietsch next decided to determine whether the pre-medullar brain did control feeding behavior.

If the feeding program is due to a holographic structure in interaction with but not limited by brain tissue, and this behavior is unaffected by radical surgical intervention, then it can be altered only by replacing the entire brain with another brain bearing a different feeding program. Additionally, if the feeding-behavior program was located elsewhere in the salamander, then the insertion of another brain should have no effect on behavior. Again, the choice of the salamander was judicious since an aspect of its regeneration mechanism is an unusually great capacity for accepting foreign tissue. Pietsch selected the brain of a tadpole for this brain transplant since the tadpole, unlike the worm-eating salamander, is herbivorous. After the brain transplants, the salamanders with tadpole brains ate the algae from the surface of a tubiform worm but would not eat the worms, which, recall, are normally a staple in the salamander diet. Through this series of ingenious experiments, Pietsch demonstrated that feeding-behavior programs did reside within the brain and, furthermore, that they were encoded in the manner of a hologram. From these experiments, it seems that mental functions are governed by, but not inexorably determined by, brain tissue. Although one cannot extrapolate directly from the salamander to humans, when these results are considered in the context of the entire body of hologram literature, they seem to demonstrate a marked degree of autonomy between mind and brain.

Slow-wave Potentials

Karl Pribram's holographic model of neuropsychology includes a concept of neuronal functioning that differs from the conventional concept of how the nervous system operates. Some three decades ago Sir Charles Sherrington resolved a pressing issue in neurology research by proposing that nerve cells do not exist in a continuous net of interconnected "wiring," but rather are very slightly separated from each other; the point of almost-contact he termed the "synapse" (Sherrington, 1947). Electrical charges travel through the neuron, or nerve cell, up to the point of its termination at the synapse. When a sufficient amount of electrical activity accumulates, in graded increments, chemical mediators at the synapse are released into the "synaptic cleft." Thus, the electrical impulses of the nervous system are propagated by chemical molecules. When the neuron has discharged, it then turns off and remains in a dormant state until it is fired again. At any single moment very large numbers of neurons are firing simultaneously, generating a considerable electrical current that can be recorded as an electroencephalogram. This analysis should make it evident why an EEG recorded from the outside, or even from inside the skull, is a grossly average measure of

the actual activity of the nervous system. This highly simplistic version of the electrical activity of the nervous
system—the EEG record—has remained the dominant
model of electrochemical brain function to the present
time. Since the late 1940s, neurophysiologists have amply
documented the existence of the synapse through the use
of electron microscopes, and the image of electrical discharges jumping the gap between neurons in an all-or-none
binary fashion is considered to reflect an incontrovertible
fact.

However, this concept has been refined by more recent
research in physics and neurophysiology, the data of which
are incorporated in Pribram's holography model. Recent
experimentation has demonstrated that when the single
neuron is probed, rhythmic, slow-potential energy alterna-
tions can be detected within the cell even in the absence of
propagated nerve impulses. "Slow-wave potentials" are
small, short-wave length, slow impulses of electrical activity occurring between the synapses. Experimental evidence
indicates that the individual neurons do not function in a
binary manner but are rather in a continuous state of activity of varying intensity. Thus, current theory considers two
activities of the neuron: (1) nerve impulse unit discharges
occurring in a binary "on-off" fashion on an intracellular
basis; and (2) graded, slow-potential changes that wax and
wane continuously at the junctions between the neurons.
This second attribute of the nervous system contributes to
a key concept in Pribram's theorizing, for these continuously undulating, slow-wave potentials can be influenced
by infinitesimal amounts of energy. They thus provide a
model by means of which we can conceptualize how the
subtle phenomena of consciousness may interact with these
comparably subtle physical properties of the brain. Both

physicists and neurophysiologists have thought about the details of such a model (an innovative theory by physicist Evan Harris Walker will be outlined later in this chapter). For now it is sufficient to note that the hologram model describes a convergence of the functions of brain and consciousness in mutual interaction.

The evidence for slow-wave potentials of brain activity provides the neurophysiology of psychological processes with a conceptual alternative to the limited confines of the model of relatively gross activity associated with binary, conducted nerve impulses. Thus, the new level of subtlety that is observed in the neuron may be an adequate vehicle of the experiential subtleties of consciousness. Another implication of Pribram's model is that these slow-wave potentials, being exceedingly minute, are extremely sensitive to the chemical medium that surrounds nerve cells, and possibly to other electromagnetic frequencies from the larger environment as well (Adey, 1975). In other words, hologram theory provides a model for understanding how drugs or spontaneous biochemical imbalances affect behavior: By modifying, however slightly, the brain's chemical medium they alter the ongoing activity of slow-potential waves. It also provides raw material for allied theories that would relate environmental influences, such as circadian or natural biological rhythms based on the twenty-four hour day (Luce, 1971), as well as electrical field activity generated near power stations (Becker, 1973), to changes in the functioning of an individual's nervous system. Furthermore, these slow-potential waves may prove to be a link between central-nervous-system properties and meditation and biofeedback, since both meditation practice and biofeedback training have been associated with sustained slow-frequency brain-wave activity in ranges comparable to the range of the slow-potential wave found at neuronal junctures. Doubtless this sustained and coherent low-frequency activity of the brain profoundly affects nerve transmission, and perhaps these frequencies are intimately involved with the ensuing states of consciousness. All of this must remain highly speculative, but there is considerable research evidence in support of these observations.

Realities Enfolded and Unfolded

Hologram theory is significant for another reason which ranges beyond neurology, psychology, and studies of behavior *per se*. It seems that holographic models of the brain are consistent with and supported by the most innovative formulations of contemporary quantum physics. As research neurologists probe the synaptic cleft they have begun to deal with the same orders of magnitude as are addressed in modern physics. For the neurologist—as for the physicist and the philosopher—the certainty of objective observation of the physical dimensions of consciousness meets with the limitation expressed in the uncertainty principle: The observed and the observer are no longer separated by space or time. As Karl Pribram has noted:

> . . . we perceive a physical universe not much different in basic organization from the brain. . . . For science is of a piece, and full understanding cannot be restricted to the developments made possible by one discipline alone. This is especially true for perception—where perceiver meets the perceived and the perceived meets the perceiver (1974, p. 10).

In effect, the brain and its functions are an integral aspect of the environment that is observed. Nothing can be observed in isolation.

One means of talking about the perceiver-perceived interaction has been agreed upon by both Pribram and quantum physicist David Bohm with their use of the terms explicate and implicate. Each theorist notes that scientific analysis explicates extrinsic properties of the physical world—for example, the scientific laws of gravity. Juxtaposed to this way of knowing is implicate study, which seeks to understand intrinsic or subjective psychological properties. Each sphere is knowable according to its own rules of observation, and the interaction of the two governs the dynamics of an individual's perceptions. In other words, we cannot account for one's constructions of reality until both these ways of knowing are taken into account. Physics has attempted to deal with this realization by accounting not only for experimental observations but for every aspect of the total field, including the observer.

At the most fundamental level of mind and matter—that of synaptic function and quantum charges—the concept of a transcendent, unitary principle is clearly manifest. And here again, hologram theory provides a way of conceiving how the physical brain may participate in this understanding. Holography requires the existence in the brain of discrete events, such as the nerve impulses, as well as continuous events such as the pre-synaptic, post-synaptic, and dendritic slow-potential waves. This is precisely analogous to Niels Bohr's Complementarity Principle, which postulates the existence of *discrete* events (particle states) and *continuous* events (wave functions) to account for all the observed phenomena in quantum physics. Most importantly, in both the holographic models of consciousness and the quantum physics models of matter, these two qualities of discreteness and continuity are two special and interdependent cases of a more encompassing whole. Niels Bohr, aware of certain parallels between his formulations of physics and Chinese philosophy, chose the Chinese symbol of the *t'ai-chi* as the center of his coat of arms when he was knighted in 1947. A most graphic representation of this concept is the Chinese Taoist symbol of the yin and yang, a representation of both the discrete and the continuous, which are ". . . two complementary descriptions of the same reality, each of them being only partly correct and having a limited range of application. Each picture is needed to give a full description of the atomic reality, and both are to be applied within the limitations given by the uncertainty principle" (Capra, 1975). Since individual events at the quantum level are ultimately unobservable and unknowable by direct observation, physics has had to rely increasingly upon statistical and probabilistic constructions of physical reality. According to the "Copenhagen School" of interpretation, the wave equations of Schroedinger (1935) and de Broglie (1964) are the most adequate descriptions of the average probabilities of chance occurrences of particular singularities or events. Thus, natural science constructs a probabilistic rather than an absolute image of reality. In a parallel manner, the processes of an individual's brain are continuously constructing probabilistic—not absolute—external realities. "Reality" is a construction created by the interaction of the observer and the observed and both are discrete aspects of a larger whole.

In a more formal sense, reality is dependent upon probability rather than necessity. This can be illustrated most clearly in the mathematical terms of statistics. Statistics is based upon random distributions governed by overriding mathematical laws of order and form. When particular events are plotted and averaged over time, their occurrences tend to fall in the shape of a normal, or bell, curve with the most frequently occurring events represented in the middle and other, less frequently occurring events represented at the "tails" or edges of the bell curve. Mathematically, this configuration is referred to as a Gaussian distribution. An important factor to note is that an averaged aggregate of random events produces a symmetrical structure. Although little if anything can be determined about individual events, it is possible to determine certain tendencies and overall patterns from the distribution of the individual cases.

Quantum physics and virtually all science depends on the concept of certain underlying symmetries that order random events (Weinberg, 1974). This concept is fundamental to determining the basic laws governing the properties of matter and is a key concept in considering the properties of human consciousness that order information into an overall image of reality. Virtually all psychology supports the concept of a "constructional theory of perception" (Pribram, 1974), in which perception is the outcome of an interaction between the physical structure of the brain and a probability distribution of events in the external environment. Insofar as structures of perception within the brain are dependent upon the programming and distribution of holograms, then out of an infinitude of possible perceptions, certain outcomes are preselected by the specific holograms of an individual's brain. Perception of events in the tails of the bell curve of probability distribution is not impossible but simply unlikely. Our normal mode of functioning is consensual; thus individuals tend to perceive only the most frequently occurring set of events, which becomes consistent over time, reinforces itself, and rapidly becomes subjectively and socially institutionalized as the average state of consciousness. However, during an altered state of consciousness, the metaprograms of the individual's holograms are altered such that the probability of perceiving events in the tails of the curves greatly increases.

It is important to note that there is nothing in natural sciences, mathematics, or probability theory to preclude the concept of altered states of perception. In fact, the evidence seems to dictate the necessity of multiple constructions of reality. The biologist R. Thom has noted the necessity of considering the perception of these improbable events and has developed mathematics specifically for that purpose. In his book *Stabilité Structurelle et Morphogenese* (1972), he describes a type of transiently stable phenomenon emerging from a highly fluctuating field; these he terms "catastrophes." No matter how unstable or transient these "catastrophes" might be, they must be governed by certain mathematical symmetries that are yet to be discovered. These low-probability phenomena may provide the means for a fuller understanding of general biological and psychological processes. Research can no longer limit itself to looking at commonly occurring events just because they are the most readily observable ones. Despite the possible difficulties of observing less common occurrences, any comprehensive description of reality requires that they be taken into account. In the material sciences, physicist David Bohm notes that the best opportunities for observing the occurrence of unusual events may be in the interactions among high-frequency, high-energy particles of nuclear reactions or in the proximity of galactic black holes. In science it is usually the case that, for a comprehensive understanding of frequently observed phenomena, one must scrutinize the variations, aberrations, or alterations of those phenomena. Just as the data from subquantum levels serve to elucidate the laws of physics, so, too, the properties of altered states of consciousness can serve to amplify and elucidate the entire range of human consciousness.

One further observation concerning the uncertainty of particular events within a Gaussian distribution is also important to a science of consciousness. "Uncertainty" is usually interpreted to mean unpredictability, randomness, and chance with a negative connotation. In science "chance" or "indeterminacy" is a nemesis because any purely indeterminant process is ultimately unknowable and cannot be formulated into fixed scientific laws. However, it is also true that the indeterminacy inherent in scientific inquiry has a highly positive aspect, for it is uncertainty that provides space for all innovation and creativity. It is from the unexpected, the chance occurrence, or the juxtaposition of unlikely factors, that profound insight and discovery arises. In short, chance or unpredictable occurrences in the midst of fixed laws imply the opportunity for innovation and freedom. If the concept of mind is eliminated from science, then uncertainty is understandably negative since it means that man is a passive observer in a universe ultimately beyond his reason. On the other hand, if the universe is a constructed interaction between the observer and the observed, then uncertainty becomes the very factor that allows man to exert his consciousness as an active participant in the universe as a whole. According to Lincoln Barnett in *The Universe and Dr. Einstein* (1947) nature appears to operate on orderly mathematical principles.

Einstein had more poetically observed that "God does not play dice with the universe."

It appears that probability distributions of events in the physical world interact with the perceptual holographic programs of the observer's brain to produce a construction termed "reality." Such a definition of reality requires that all such constructions are tenuous, transient, and illusory to a degree. It is interesting that mathematics should point to an attribute of reality that corresponds to the ephemeral contents of personal consciousness—collectively termed *maya* (Sanskrit, illusion)—described in all meditation systems. Perhaps the ultimate symmetrical functions sought by mathematicians beyond the uncertainty principle are descriptive of such experiences of human consciousness as volition and intention (Staal, 1975). The world's library of mystical literature contains much information relevant to model-building in this area.

Quantum Psychophysics

Holographic models of human consciousness require neurophysiologists to take into account events at the same order of magnitude as is addressed in quantum physics. As noted previously in these pages, there is nothing inherent in any aspect of the natural sciences that excludes the consideration of the interface between neurophysiology and the phenomenology of consciousness. Quite the opposite, it seems increasingly necessary to postulate the presence of such nonphysical entities in the most advanced areas of science, including mathematics, physics, and neurology. Those researchers who have attempted to penetrate the ultimate mystery of mind in interaction with matter have focused upon quantum events occurring in and among the neurons of the brain.

Early in the development of quantum mechanical theory it was recognized that the Heisenberg uncertainty principle had a direct bearing on the philosophical problem of free will. Niels Bohr suggested that certain key points in the regulatory mechanisms of the brain might be so sensitive and delicately balanced that they should properly be regarded as quantum mechanical in nature and could be considered to be the physical mechanisms by which an individual exerts will or volition (Bohr, 1934). Another physicist, Sir Arthur Eddington, examined the possibility that mind controlled the brain within the limits allowed by the Heisenberg principle, although he eventually discarded the idea since he considered the range of influence to be too small to affect the physical brain (Eddington, 1935). Speculating in the context of neurological knowledge of the mid-1930s, Eddington addressed his thinking to an object as large as the neuron or the nerve cell.

Nerve cells are treelike in appearance with one branch of the cell body usually longer than the others. This is the axon, which carries electrical current from the cell body to its terminal point or "end foot," that is in close proximity to other cells. If the adjacent cell is another neuron, then this zone of interaction is a synapse, the space between the two neurons being the synaptic cleft. Quite importantly, the synaptic cleft is on the order of 200 to 300 A° or Angstroms (one Angstrom $= \frac{1}{100,000,000}$ of a centimeter), which is a magnitude in the range considered by quantum physics. In the current understanding, the transmission of nerve impulses across this cleft is initiated by a nerve impulse arriving at the end foot and causing the release of "packets" of chemical neurotransmitters, which are infinitesimally smaller than 200 A°, from the synaptic vesicles, or sacs, which are part of the presynaptic terminal. Actually, the precise process is not yet understood, for the delicately poised, highly volatile synaptic activity is only now beginning to be studied in terms of quantum physics. Graded, slow-potential changes wax and wane continuously at the junctions between neurons. These potentials can be influenced by infinitesimal amounts of energy on the order of quantum events. Interestingly, in the earliest explorations of the cortex by electron microscopy, researchers expected to find something unique about synaptic organization in areas concerned with higher functions. It was assumed that those cells would bear some property that would not be found, for one example, in cells of the spinal column. However, in recent years they have concluded that the basic nature of the synapse is constant throughout the nervous system. In fact, all synapses are alike in their essential features and in their mode of chemical transmission. There appears to be no essential differences between the parts of the nervous system that, like the spinal column, are associated with autonomic activity and those that, like the cortex, are associated with mentation, imagery, and other such "higher order" phenomena of consciousness.

Commenting on the convergence between quantum physics and innovations in neurophysiological measurement, the neurologist John C. Eccles has pointed out that the synaptic vesicle, embedded in the prosynaptic terminal, is an approximately spherical structure of 400 A° diameter, and that Eddington thought the uncertainty principle was applicable to an object of this size, having calculated the uncertainty of the position of such an object to be about 50 A° in one millisecond. This value is extremely significant because 50 A° might be the order of magnitude in which consciousness might operate in interaction with the neurophysiological mechanisms of the brain, within the limits allowed by uncertainty. According to Eccles, "It is therefore possible that the permitted range of behavior of a synaptic vesicle may be adequate to allow for the effective operation of the postulated 'mind influences' on the active cerebral cortex" (p. 125). Neurophysiologists and physicists are now familiar with many details of cell life. Many consider synaptic vesicles, slow wave potentials, and Fourier transforms to be the key principles by which mind is operational. Experimental research by Eccles and other neurologists has yielded data permitting great refinement of the concept of ephemeral mind acting upon static matter. Theirs is a model of ineffably subtle interactions among infinitesimal energy fields occurring in quantum space.

Advanced thinking about brain function no longer employs hardware metaphors of the brain as a machine or even a sophisticated computer. Rather, the brain is thought to function by virtue of "spatio-temporal fields of influence." Again as Eccles has noted:

> . . . These spatio-temporal fields of influence are exerted by the mind on the brain in willed action. If one uses the expressive terminology of Ryle (1949), the "ghost" operates a "machine," not of ropes and pulleys, valves and pipes, but of microscopic spatio-temporal patterns of activity in the neuronal net woven by the synaptic connections of ten thousand million neurons, and even then only by operating on neurons that are momentarily poised close to a just-threshold level of excitability. It would appear that it is the sort of machine a "ghost" could operate, if by ghost we mean in the first place an "agent" whose action has es-

caped detection even by the most delicate physical instruments (Eccles, 1970).

A "ghost" that has escaped and might elude detection by physical instrumentation within the limits of the uncertainty principle would certainly be a cause for despair if inquiry into the nature of consciousness were to be limited to physical observation of events in the brain. Fortunately, the mind is able to reflect upon itself and thus to transcend this limit and provide another approach through the systematic study of the phenomenology of consciousness.

A case in point is the theory of quantum physicist Evan Harris Walker at the NASA Electronics Research Center in Cambridge, Massachusetts. Writing in "Mathematical Biosciences," Walker purports to demonstrate the mathematics by which quantum events in the brain operate in the synaptic cleft and give rise to conscious perception. His basic thesis is that it is possible for neurophysiological and consciousness states to interact within the limits of certain basic mathematical constraints. For example, with reference to the precise mechanism of neurotransmitters, Walker cites a phenomenon in physics whereby an electron can "tunnel through" a barrier, such as is found in the presynaptic membrane of the synaptic cleft, and initiate a large flow of electrons once the delicate electrical potential has been altered. According to Walker, "In fact, under the conditions existing at the synaptic cleft in which electric impulses apparently propagate to within a mere 200 A°, it would be surprising if quantum mechanical tunneling did not occur" (1970, p. 159). Furthermore, Walker postulates that these "short-range tunneling processes" act in accord with "long-range tunneling" that propagates over distances in the brain as great as several centimeters.

He derives equations for differential speeds of data-processing for three states of consciousness—a rate for subconscious activity, an average data-processing rate for the active brain, and a decision rate during which he postulates that attention sorts among alternatives and exercises choice.

Walker's theory is expressed in complex mathematical formulations not readily translatable into verbal metaphors; the version presented here can hardly do it justice. His major conclusions, however, can be stated succinctly: **(1)** consciousness is both real and nonphysical; **(2)** consciousness is coupled to the physical brain by means of quantum mechanical wave function; **(3)** the brain is a logical instrument that employs a certain physical process for some of its data management, a process that can be properly described only by quantum physics; and, most important, **(4)** events in the brain are governed by a higher order, what is termed a "hidden variable" in physics, and these hidden variables are synonymous with consciousness. Clearly, it is not possible to evaluate Walker's theory at the present time. Notwithstanding, it is a remarkably incisive attempt to apply the principles of mathematics and quantum physics to the phenomena of consciousness. Walker's work stands as one of the first comprehensive attempts to define that process hypothesized by Sir John Eccles through which ". . . 'will' modifies the spatiotemporal activity of the neuronal network by exerting spatio-temporal 'fields of influence' that become effective through this unique detector function of the active cerebral cortex" (p. 124). Eccles went on to equate the act of will with some unknown agency acting in concert with the neurological activity of the brain. As he wrote in *Neurophysiological Basis of Mind:*

It is a psychological fact that we have ability to control or modify our actions by the exercise of "will," and in practical life all sane men assume that they have this ability. By stimulation of the motor-cortex (of the exposed brain of patients undergoing a brain operation) it is possible to evoke complex motor acts in a conscious human subject. The subject reports that the experience is quite different from that occurring when he "willed" a movement . . . there was the experience of having "willed" an action, which was missing in the other (Eccles, 1953).

The basic issue raised by such observations concerns volition: What is the nature and mode of operation of the act of will? For the first time, it is possible for science to address such issues objectively through the formal, systematic constructs of holographic and quantum mechnical models of the brain. We may ask, for example, is it possible that imagery is the phenomenological aspect of "spatio-temporal fields," or of "long-range quantum mechanical tunneling?" Modern physics has rendered a model of the brain as a highly sensitive, poised system wherein the discharge of any one neuron contributes directly and indirectly to the excitation or inhibition of millions of other neurons within the very brief time of 20 microseconds. The quantum mechanical view of brain function permits one to imagine how unobservable psychological factors could have profound effects therein.

When the body and mind were looked upon as solid versus ethereal, interaction seemed unlikely; that a subtle image could bear influence on a gross physical organ was an absurdity. However, as modern biophysics demonstrates that the body is a volatile, fluctuating, electromagnetic field (Cohen, 1975)—indeed, an infinitely interlocked series of fields within fields—a model of mind-body interaction emerges whereby the subtle properties of consciousness can be shown to have profound effects upon physical processes. These observations are of great importance in considerations of states of psychosomatic disorder and states of health as well as being a fundamental aspect of a science of consciousness.

Holographic models have given new impetus to considerations of the psychological concepts of imaging and imagery, including the internal imagery so characteristic of altered states. As Pribram has observed:

> Recent behavioral research has put a foundation under Imaging, and neurological research as well as insights derived from the information-processing sciences have helped make understandable the machinery which gives rise to this elusive ghost-making process. . . . Any model of perceptual processes must thus take into account both the importance of Imaging, a process that contributes a portion of man's subjective experience, and the fact that there are influences on behavior of which we are not aware (Pribram, 1971, p. 104).

Through images, sensations, and feelings (emotions), an individual manifests his basic orientation toward himself, others, and the world as a whole. In Chapter 6 of this book, we will see how it is possible that the individual's attention and sensitivity to his own internal images and sensations—generally, his psychosomatic self-awareness—is of vital importance in determining his state of health or illness. In Chapter 7, we will explore the possibility that there is an element of self-determination in death as well.

We have seen that processes at the quantum level are unobservable but seem to be organized in a manner analogous to the organization of mind. Support for the study of the nonphysical properties of mind comes from modern physics, the most advanced science of our era, and yet, ironically, this approach is shunned by most of contemporary psychology as "unscientific." Physics never hesitates to postulate an unobservable existence if that seems to be the only way to interpret the facts. Such unobservable existences abound in quantum physics—for example, electromagnetism, gravity, photons, virtual particles, and many others, as described in Chapter 2. Therefore, it would seem reasonable to expect that constructs such as mind, attention, awareness, and volition will serve equally well in the case of the interaction of brain and consciousness; i.e., their use will impart considerable explanatory power to theoretical problem-solving in this area. Niels Bohr considered his principle of complementarity to be a general philosophical principle that might be applicable to the relationship between mind and matter although he did not systematically work out this position.

Sir Arthur Eddington's early insight—that matter in liaison with mind would create a situation of matter which would be in direct contrast to the random behavior of matter postulated in physics (Eddington, 1939)—is still viable. Wilder Penfield's observation that consciousness and the physical brain are discrete but in interaction seems increasingly probable. This position, which has achieved a degree of acceptance in neurophysiology, has been succinctly stated by British neurologist Cyril Burt.

A comparison of the specific micro-neural situations in which consciousness does and does not arise suggests that the brain functions not as a generator of consciousness, but rather as a two-way transmitter and detector, i.e., although its activity is apparently a necessary condition, it cannot be a sufficient condition of conscious experience (Burt, 1968).

This statement echoes Aristotle's idea that mind is "attached to the body" and thereby hints at the enormous philosophical implications of contemporary research. In approaching this enigmatic area of psychosomatic interaction, it is necessary to adhere to the observable, empirical data of neurophysiology and also to acknowledge its limitations in addressing the phenomenology of consciousness. Too often the concept of consciousness has been relegated to a passive connotation of that which is experienced or to a minimally active role of sorting impinging stimuli. Now it has become necessary to postulate consciousness as an active, organizing principle that coordinates the divergent functions of the physical brain in a focused and purposive manner and operates at the quantum level where mind and matter are in inextricable interaction.

According to molecular biologist Gunther S. Stent in "Limits to the Scientific Understanding of Man," it is becoming incumbent upon researchers to approach the concept of a unitive principle of the "self." To this end, the phenomenology of mind noted in meditative traditions is highly instructive. In the next chapter we will see that these data are necessary complements to the otherwise obscure observations of the electrical activity of the brain. All individuals have a sense of a unitive principle of being, and everyone formulates his personal philosophy and way of life on the basis of that perception. What a magnificent event it is to discover that both science and deeply personal knowledge can share a common ground.

Biofeedback and Meditation

chapter 5

WE HAVE seen that the theoretical and experimental evidence points to an inextricable interaction between consciousness and the biological functioning of the body and brain. Much of the research we have reviewed so far would be merely academic were it not for the widespread use of biofeedback training and an equally great interest in the therapeutic aspects of meditation. The development of biofeedback is a clear example of the convergence of Eastern and Western sciences, of knowledge gleaned from ancient meditative systems and data gathered with the most sophisticated biomedical technology of the twentieth century. And in the interaction of the ancient and modern, the Eastern and Western disciplines, has come not only a regeneration of philosophical considerations, but also a series of major, pragmatic innovations in psychological and medical treatment. These innovations are discussed in this chapter and the next. Our major focus, however, remains on pointing the way toward a science of consciousness. By tracing the development of biofeedback and noting its similarities to ancient meditative systems it is possible to make further explicit links between neurophysiology and the phenomena of human consciousness.

Biofeedback training is based upon two fundamental principles. One is the biological feedback principle, which states that any neurophysiological function that can be monitored, then amplified by electronic instrumentation and fed back to an individual through any one of his five senses, can be brought under voluntary control by that individual. The second principle has been succinctly formulated by psychophysiologist Elmer E. Green:

> Every change in the physiological state is accompanied by an appropriate change in the mental-emotional state, conscious or unconscious, and conversely, every change in the mental-emotional state, conscious or unconscious, is accompanied by an appropriate change in the physiological state (Green, Green and Walters, 1969).

Taken together, these two principles require that both neurophysiological and phenomenological data be considered in the investigation of discrete state of consciousness. An overview of neurophysiological research reveals that very few investigators have taken these factors into consideration—mainly because they have not, until now, been recognized as significant variables. Present scientific paradigms tend to preclude the investigation of the psychological factors of consciousness in neurophysiological research because they are not readily measurable with existing procedures and instrumentation. This arbitrary limitation may be detrimental to progress in the field of conventional neurophysiology. Certainly one of the most persistent difficulties in research on the neurophysiology of states of consciousness—the cross-disciplinary field termed psychophysiology—has been the tendency of researchers to rely solely upon statistical correlations among multiple physiological indices such as the correlations between the electroencephalograph, heart rate, and muscle activity. After an extensive review of the major research in neurophysiology, Laverne C. Johnson has concluded:

> The frequent dissociation among physiological variables makes it difficult to conceptualize a simple psychophysiological model that would allow us to generalize as to the meaning and as to the probable response pattern of individual variables as the subject goes from one state to another, or for that matter, even when he remains within the same state. The multivariate approach will probably prove helpful and perhaps necessary in our efforts, but it is not sufficient (Johnson, 1970).

Simultaneous consideration of distinct states of consciousness and the neurophysiology of those states is essential in demonstrating the interaction between biological matter and such mind processes as attention, volition, and personal philosophy, and in translating these latter intangibles into detectable and quantifiable indices of the individual's neurophysiological functioning. Indeed, there is increasing evidence that rather than using physiological indices to define a state of consciousness, a more productive approach would be for the researcher to first determine the state and then interpret the physiological measures. In several of the examples in this chapter the experimental data are meaningless until the philosophy, or mind set, of the individual under study is taken into account.

It should be pointed out again, referring to the discussion of objectivity in Chapter 2, that this is a sword that cuts both ways, affecting both the individuals being studied and those doing the studying. In other words, the influence of one's personal paradigms creates an inescapable bias in his perceptual system that cannot be overlooked in any research setting. For example, during a symposium attended by seventy physicians at the Everett A. Gladman Memorial Hospital, Oakland, California, in 1971, the adept meditator Jack Schwarz gave a demonstration of voluntary control of bleeding and pain. Schwarz thrust a large-diameter, unsterilized knitting needle entirely through his left bicep, piercing the brachial artery. The needle in place, Schwarz requested the attending physician to take his pulse while he attempted to accelerate his heart rate. After two trials, the physician informed Schwarz that the pulse had not altered from its original level of seventy-two beats per minute, and that aspect of the demonstration appeared to have failed. A short time later, the meditator removed the needle and did control the bleeding from the puncture. (This demonstration of voluntary control was later confirmed in a more rigorous manner by my laboratory experiments.) Something else of importance took place in the auditorium that day, although it was not until several weeks later that I realized it. I received a letter from a cardiologist, Charles R. Ayers, telling me that a broad-gauge needle inserted through the brachial artery would have effectively blocked the peripheral pulse in that arm, making it undetectable. He also noted that a common error in palpating for a weak or thready pulse is that the observer may instead detect his own pulse beating in his fingertips. In retrospect, it seems likely that the physician had taken his own pulse, which would have remained steady at its normal level. Whether or not this was the case, what is important to note about the events of that day is that not one of the seventy physicians raised this question at the time. Their training had created a mental set, or personal paradigm, that predisposed them to view the voluntary control of arterial bleeding as impossible. Since the main task was regarded as impossible, none of the accompanying details such as peripheral pulse blockage was even noticed. This is an example of a pervasive phenomenon in scientific experimentation as well as in daily life: Expectations govern observations that in turn reinforce the initial expectations. Recognizing that the influences of personal paradigms are impossible to eliminate, it is incumbent upon researchers looking into the neurophysiology of consciousness to be alert especially to both experimenter effects and subjects' mind-set effects on experimental conditions as well as outcomes.

Voluntary control of autonomic functions (i.e., involuntary neurological and physiological processes) has probably been practiced by adept students of Zen and Yogic disciplines since the earliest years of these ancient ways of knowledge. Modern innovations in psychophysiological monitoring instrumentation have made it possible to verify the existence of these paradoxical states of autonomic control and to explore the nature of the accompanying states of consciousness. At the present time, however, the psychological processes by which an individual obtains voluntary regulation of a formerly autonomic function remain virtually unknown. Whatever these processes are, it is likely that they involve the most fundamental issues of mind-matter interaction and that their elucidation will draw upon evidence from scholarly fields ranging from quantum physics to Buddhist philosophy. Three major obstacles have hindered intensive investigation of this phenomenon: **(1)** In the laboratory, states of consciousness that characterize the interface of voluntary-autonomic control are exceedingly difficult to measure and assess because they can rarely be manifested upon request, and spontaneous occurrences are of very brief duration; **(2)** those few individuals who are capable of sustaining voluntary control are unable or unwilling to articulate that process in language that is comprehensible to Western psychology; and most importantly, **(3)** the prevailing paradigm of contemporary science mitigates against admitting consideration of internal phenomena. Despite these obstacles, basic research and clinical applications of biofeedback have demonstrated the pragmatic applications of meditative practices. While such applications are not necessarily the goal of meditation, they have been an impressive demonstration of empirical verification of systems of meditation that are thousands of years old.

Self-Regulation and the Paradigms of Meditation

The earliest research on the voluntary control of autonomic nervous system functions was conducted in India with practitioners of various forms of Yoga. French cardiologist Thérèse Brosse traveled afield in 1934 to study the yogis' claims of heart-rate control. The physiological measurements she later reported (1946) represented the first attempt of Western science to bridge the gap between East and West. World war interrupted this historic development, and it was not until years later that two French neurologists, Das and Gastaut (1955), went to India to research practitioners of Kriya Yoga. Using an electroencephalogram (EEG) to measure brain-waves, they found that the yogis exhibited strong beta activity of high amplitude during meditation: Beta waves of up to 40 Hz (cycles per second) with an amplitude of 30–50 microvolts were accompanied by a gradual acceleration of the heart rhythm. Additionally, they noted that various stimuli such as loud sounds applied during meditation did not produce the expected spiking in the EEG record. This high-activation meditation state was not verified in subsequent investigations, whose results suggested, on the contrary, that the meditation state could be characterized as a low-arousal condition, as indicated by the predominance of alpha waves (7–13 Hz) in the EEG records. At first puzzling, the reason for this discrepancy has emerged in the last few years as Westerners have come to realize that the different meditative disciplines—of which scores are known in the East—practice different forms of meditation, and that these various forms of meditation are associated with different EEG patterns. In view of this belated recognition, the findings of Das and Gastaut need to be reevaluated by taking into consideration the philosophy that informs the meditative technique of Kriya Yoga. Rather than attempting to develop a state of passive serenity, the cliché meditation goal, the disciples of Kriya Yoga focused their attention on internal visions and were actively involved in summoning kundalini energy. As their meditation progressed, this energy was purported to have uncoiled from its resting place at the base of the spine and rose up the spinal column until it reached the brain, where it ignited a state of ecstasy (Das and Gastaut, 1955). When this paradigm of Kriya Yoga is considered, the EEG not only becomes more intelligible but seems to affirm that the desired state of ecstasy—in this case, high activation—had been achieved. In retrospect, this prototypic study demonstrates that the philosophy and subjective experiences of meditators have to be taken into account in order to interpret the neurological and psychophysiological indices in a comprehensive manner.

In 1957 two American neurologists, B. K. Bagchi and M. A. Wenger, conducted an ambitious study of forty-five Indian yogis at sites ranging from university laboratories to a Himalayan mountain cave. Of considerable interest was their finding that one yogi exhibited no "alpha blocking" in response to an external stimulus of low intensity, such as a tapping sound within three to five feet of the yogi. Alpha blocking is the change in the EEG record from high-amplitude, low-frequency alpha to low-amplitude, high-frequency beta that occurs in response to an external stimulus. It is thought to be an invariate autonomic function of the central nervous system. Similarly the stimuli failed to elicit any change in the level of electrical resistance measured on the palm (galvanic skin response—GSR), which would normally have decreased involuntarily following the introduction of external stimuli. Although this information was objectively recorded in only one subject, it was supported by the verbal reports of two other subjects. These findings suggested that the invariate functions of the autonomic nervous system could be altered by an individual's adherence to a particular philosophy and the type of meditation used to implement this philosophy in daily activity. Although this pioneering research effort produced no definitive results it did indicate general procedures and directions for scientific research into yogic disciplines. Following these leads, Bagchi and Wenger planned other studies that focused primarily upon cardiovascular control with a secondary interest in the accompanying EEG states. These experiments are notable in part for their findings and in part because they reveal the great difficulties scientists encounter in attempting to document autonomic control and to assess the process by which that control is achieved.

In 1961 and 1963, research teams headed by Wenger, Bagchi, and B. K. Anand conducted a series of experiments with four yogis who claimed the ability to control their cardiovascular functions. Three yogis said they were able to stop their hearts, while one claimed he could slow his heart. The investigators found that three of the yogis could slow their heart rate not by controlling involuntary functions, but by performing the Valsalva maneuver. This involves tensing the striate muscles of the neck and abdomen in order to squeeze the vagus nerve and thereby to decrease the flow of blood from the veins into the chest. However, one subject was able to demonstrate a significant degree of control over his heart rate and blood pressure without recourse to the Valsalva maneuver or any other discernible means. This subject was able to stimulate and interrupt vagus nerve output to the sinoatrial node, establishing a "nodal rhythm." Electrocardiographic and plethysmographic records (the latter monitoring the pulse in a finger) indicated that the heart remained in continuous action although the rhythm was altered. Concurrently, there was a marked absence of the alpha rhythm in the EEG record.

This degree of cardiac control has more recently been affirmed by Elmer E. Green in his work with Swami Rama, a forty-five-year-old Indian yogi (Green, Ferguson, Green, and Walter, 1970). Swami Rama induced an atrial fibrillation of 300 beats per minute for 17 seconds; it was not clear, however, whether or not these results could be attributed to the "solar plexus lock" that the Swami said he used. Despite equivocal results with regard to stopping the heart, the Swami was able to demonstrate a significant degree of cardiovascular control by increasing and decreasing his heart rate on command.

To date, there are very few other studies that clearly indicate cardiac control by means of autonomic manipulation. Among these are: (1) a case study of a Hindu yogi, Sri Ramananda, in which the Valsalva maneuver was controlled during the experiment (Satyanarayanamurthi and Sastry, 1958); (2) a case report of a Danish aircraft mechanic studied at Lindsay Municipal Hospital in Lindsay, California (McClure, 1959); (3) clinical research indicating regulation and correction of tachycardia (Engel, 1967); and (4) instances of a modest degree of cardiac acceleration and deceleration in response to subjective thoughts (Schwartz, 1971). As preliminary and inconclusive as these studies are, they do demonstrate that some measure of voluntary control of cardiovascular functions is possible although the dramatic degree of control claimed by yogis remains equivocal.

Building upon the research of Bagchi and Wenger, several other researchers initiated more definitive experiments in the early 1960s. Notable among these were the studies of Anand, G. S. Chhina, and B. Singh (1961), who monitored the brain-wave activity of four Baj yogis during *samadhi*. *Samadhi*, or total bliss and fulfillment, is considered to be the end result of a form of meditation described as the "pin-pointing of consciousness" on different points in the vertex of the skull. The yogis were monitored before and during meditation. Two were exposed to distracting external stimuli that were photic (strong light), auditory (loud banging noise), thermal (being touched with hot glass tubing), and vibrational (being touched with a tuning fork). While meditating, neither of the yogis produced any alpha blocking in response to these external distractions; on the contrary, they continued to exhibit prominent alpha activity with increased amplitude modulation. Furthermore, when these same stimuli were presented to the yogis when they were not meditating, the EEG showed that they did not produce the usual habituation response, in which each subsequent stimulus elicits less and less response in the EEG, and which is considered to be an invariate norm of the autonomic nervous system. In other words, each stimulus was responded to with equal intensity each time it was introduced; the yogis did not habituate or adapt to the repeated stimulus. These results were highly interesting in that the EEG record indicated that the yogic goal of perceiving each event in the world with equal intensity and appreciation was being achieved.

Here again is a reminder of the necessity of considering the subjective purpose and underlying philosophy of an individual's behavior—in short, his intent or volition—in any attempt to understand his psychophysiological functioning. This is an extremely important finding that has had significant impact upon recent research in the related field of psychosomatic medicine. It seems that these early studies revealed time and again that there is a clear and demonstrable interaction between an individual's intention and his entire neurophysiological system. In this manner, the elusive concept of volition began to take on significant new meaning in the emerging science of consciousness. Since these data began accumulating in the mid-1950s, both psychologists and physicians have gradually come to recognize the critical role of personal philosophical and psychological factors in determining an individual's state of health or illness. It is now widely recognized in clinical practice that the negative interplay of mind and body factors results in disease while their positive interaction results in health and well-being. Startling feats of autonomic control nearly rivaling those of adept yogis are demonstrated by average individuals every day. What had been myth and rumor has become an integral aspect of modern medicine.

Another facet of the research by Anand, Chhina, and Singh suggested that alpha brain-wave activity might be the mediating factor of voluntary-autonomic control. They studied two yogis who could keep a hand immersed in icy cold water for forty-five to fifty-five minutes. Persistent alpha activity was recorded both before and during this practice. Normally, the noxious stimulus of severe cold would be associated with alpha blocking in the EEG. The absence of such blocking was additional evidence of a marked degree of self-regulation of autonomic activity. Further, as a consequence of findings, interest began to focus upon the significance of marked alpha activity. An earlier study by the Japanese psychiatrist, A. Kasamatsu (Kasamatsu et al., 1957) gained renewed interest. In this study electroencephalograms were recorded from four individuals; one expert practitioner of Zen, one practitioner of Yoga, and two control subjects whose baseline EEGs were similar to those of the practitioners selected. Kasamatsu and his colleagues reported that seventeen minutes after the Zen and Yoga practitioners began their meditations, alpha waves predominated in their EEG records; the EEGs of the control subjects remained unchanged. They also reported that while meditating, the practitioners' alpha waves were hardly affected by the sounds of hand claps or bells, but no objective record was obtained to substantiate this observation. By contrast, both control subjects exhibited alpha blocking in response to external stimuli of the same intensity. Thus, this small study seemed to lend support to the idea that brain alpha activity could be the link between a meditator's philosophical predisposition and his ability to self-regulate autonomic responses.

Building from these studies, Kasamatsu and T. Hirai (1966) undertook an intensive investigation of forty-eight disciples of Rinzai and Soto Zen. To date, this work stands as the most definitive study of the EEG correlates of meditation-induced altered states of consciousness. Kasamatsu and Hirai delineated several major aspects of meditation and autonomic control: (1) Alpha waves predominated in the EEG records of these Zen practitioners; (2) drowsiness was ruled out as being responsible for deep relaxation since the EEG record was monitored for periods of sleep onset; (3) alpha persisted with eyes open; (4) there were no EEG similarities between the hypnotic trance state and Zen meditation; (5) during and after Zen meditation, the meditators did not exhibit habituation to a click stimulus presented twenty times in succession; (6) rhythmical trains of theta waves (4-7 Hz) were observed in the records of those who had practiced meditation for the longest periods of time; (7) the more years of Zen training, the more change in state of consciousness was recorded in the EEG; and (8) evaluation by the Master of a student's competence in meditation was directly correlated with the amount of alpha or theta present in the EEG record. It is interesting to compare the *lack of response* to stimuli of Kriya Yoga students in the Das and Gastaut reports to the nonhabituating response to stimuli of the Zen practitioners in the study of Kasamatsu and Hirai. This is another pointer to the in-

teraction between philosophical systems and psychophysiological indices in that Kriya yogis attempt to shut out the
external stimulation of the world while the Zen doctrine
advocates being open to and appreciative of every aspect
of the phenomenal world. These philosophies, quite dissimilar, had the predicted effect upon the neurophysiological functioning of their adherents. As noted earlier, this
evidence of interaction of personal philosophy and physiology is of utmost importance to research concerning the
neurophysiology of consciousness. Additionally, the observation of the theta rhythm in advanced Zen meditators
provided another invaluable clue linking research in meditation, creativity, altered states, biofeedback, and autonomic control. It seems that both alpha and theta states
could be considered as mediating between brain functions
and certain altered states of consciousness. This possibility
will be more fully explored in the section below on theta
research.

Most of the studies reviewed above are commonly cited
in the biofeedback research literature, yet they are only a
few representatives of a large body of research concerning
the psychophysiology of meditation and altered states of
consciousness. In 1970 Yoshiharu Akishige of the Zen Institute of Komazawa University in Tokyo, Japan, who
compiled much of this research, could cite over 300 ar-
ticles ranging from Rorschach tests of Zen priests (Koga
and Akishige, 1970) to studies of respiratory rates and patterns during Zen meditation (Matsumoto, 1970). The plain
fact is that this substantial body of research literature concerning meditation states is largely unknown to Western
scientists. There are signs that this situation is changing,
fortunately. There are many points in common between
ancient meditative disciplines and modern biofeedback,

and Western science can only profit from discovering these rich sources of information—of interest to the biosciences as well as psychology.

The Alpha Rhythm

Paralleling the meditation studies of the 1960s was the pioneering biofeedback research of Joe Kamiya, who was then at the University of Chicago. Volunteer subjects were ordinary people with no special knowledge or experience of any mind-training disciplines. They were simply to guess whether or not they were producing alpha-wave activity. At each guess the experimenter, who was monitoring their EEG tracings, would tell the subject if the guess was correct or incorrect. Quite rapidly, the people in the experiment increased the accuracy of their guesses until they were able to say, more often than chance would have it, whether or not they were in an alpha state. In other words, they had apparently learned to recognize the subjective feelings accompanying alpha.

Next, Kamiya wanted to see if the subjects could learn to control the occurrence of alpha rhythms. To this end, subjects were instructed to induce alpha when a single tone sounded and to suppress alpha when a double tone sounded. This phase of the experiment was also successful. Kamiya then set up a procedure in which the EEG would emit a constant tone in the presence of sustained alpha activity. The same subjects were divided into two groups. One group was told to keep the tone from sounding altogether (i.e., produce no alpha), while the other group was required to keep the tone on for as long as possible. After a series of twelve training sessions, with the aid of the constant feedback tone, most of the people were able to turn their alpha activity on or off at will. For the first time in Western psychology, Kamiya (1962) had demonstrated that individuals are capable of voluntarily enhancing or suppressing alpha activity in the brain when allowed to monitor their EEG activity. When these individuals were questioned about their subjective experiences, they described the alpha state as a kind of relaxed vigilance that was serene, pleasant, and devoid of imagery. Moreover, they noted that in order to turn off the alpha rhythm, it was only necessary to exert any form of mental effort, such as solving a problem or invoking mental images. Of course, a good deal more has been learned about the alpha state since this seminal work of Kamiya's opened the biofeedback research field. Before surveying this material, however, it is useful to have a brief overview of the field as a whole.

Immediately following Kamiya's reports a major portion of biofeedback research focused upon optimizing the methodology for training the recognition of one's control of brain wave activity. More recent research has proceeded according to two discrete orientations: (1) clinical biofeedback, in which biofeedback is applied to problems in psychosomatic medicine and very little concern is given to formulating the psychodynamic processes by means of which voluntary control is achieved; and (2) explorations of these intrapsychic processes *per se* in order to discover the dynamics of interaction of the psychological and neurophysiological aspects of human consciousness.

Clinical biofeedback has made extensive use of electromyographic (muscle) feedback in disorders ranging from tension headaches (Haynes et al., 1975) to stroke paralysis (Basmajian et al., 1975), cardiac feedback (Weiss and Engel, 1975), and temperature control (Roberts et al., 1975). Electroencephalographic feedback has focused upon the subjective states accompanying various brain-wave states and upon such work as Barry Sterman's (1972) research indicating that some epileptic patients have learned to control or inhibit their seizures by enhancing the sensory motor rhythm (Gastaut, 1975; Kaplan, 1975). Other examples of the applications approach of biofeedback are: (1) decreased systolic blood pressure of essential hypertension (Benson et al., 1974; Miller, 1975); (2) control of pain (Gannon and Sternbach, 1971; Pelletier and Peper, 1977); (3) heart rate and blood pressure control (Shapiro et al., 1970; Brener and Kleinman, 1970; Kristl and Engel, 1975; (4) correcting tachycardia (Engel, 1966, 1967); (5) eliminating or reducing migraine headaches and inducing more restful sleep (Sargent et al., 1971); and many other examples which are too numerous to detail at this point. For an overview of each year of biofeedback research and clinical application, there is an annual publication entitled *Biofeedback and Self-Control*.

In contrast to this increasingly impressive array of clinical applications, very few research projects have attempted to examine how the control occurs. If the full range of applications of biofeedback is to be explored, then it will become increasingly necessary to clearly define the nature of the psychophysiological and phenomenological processes by which voluntary control is established.

One of the most innovative research projects concerned with the neurophysiological substrates of consciousness is that of Thomas Mulholland and Erik Peper who researched the link between visual perception and the alpha rhythm. Visual processing occurs in the parietal-occipital cortex, i.e., the lower back half of the cerebral cortex. Since alpha is conventionally monitored from that point, it is likely that the cortical processing of visual stimuli would have an effect upon alpha production. The reports of Kamiya's subjects, mentioned above, suggested that this was so, and previous experimentation had indicated that alpha was decreased when subjects reported visual imagery with eyes closed or responded to auditory stimulation (Mulholland, 1969). Mulholland and Peper determined that alpha attenuation, or blocking, was not due to simple visual attention but to specific oculomotor processes such as fixation, lens accommodation, and pursuit tracking (Mulholland and Peper, 1971). This finding is highly significant since it demonstrated that visual stimulation *per se* was not sufficient to cause continuous desynchronization, or mixed patterns, of alpha monitored from the parietal-occipital position. In short, it demonstrated that alpha can be maintained with eyes open; simple eyes-open attention and non-focused visual tracking of a target did not cause alpha blocking or desynchronization (Peper, 1970, 1971, 1972; Mulholland and Peper, 1971). The authors concluded from these results that the equation of visual stimuli or subjective imagery with alpha blocking is much too simple.

Alpha production and the phenomenology of that state has emerged as an area of subtle complexity. Alpha dominance cannot be characterized by any particular set of internal phenomena. This most recent conclusion is in accord with the findings of the earlier meditation research that noted a diversity of subjective, visual, and somatic phenomena associated with alpha dominance. More importantly, the recent work on alpha has revealed an interface shared by meditation, biofeedback, and autonomic autoregulation. This research has demonstrated that: (1) meditators exhibit high alpha production during their meditation practice; **(2)** individuals participating in experiments can also manifest high alpha production under conditions that diminish sensory input, e.g., a soundproof, darkened room; and **(3)** although a certain degree of autonomic control has been associated with enhanced alpha production, the precise relationship between alpha control and autonomic control of physiological processes remains enigmatic. To date, very few experiments have followed up these highly suggestive correspondences. How does prolonged alpha dominance affect other physiological functions? Is alpha activity the threshold to voluntary control of internal states? Few studies have employed the monitoring of multiple channels of neurophysiological indices combined with reports from the subjects of their psychological states to begin to resolve these critical questions.

"Paradoxical alpha," or "stimulus-enhanced alpha," has also been the subject of recent experimentation in alpha production enhancement and its relationship to internal states. Most often the production of an EEG frequency such as alpha is measured in "percent time," which refers to the amount of time during which an individual produces a specific frequency during a pre-selected interval. The research reports cited above have described alpha blocking in response to sensory stimulation or noted that such blocking does not occur when stimulation is debarred from registration as in deep meditation. A number of other studies report increased alpha production under certain stimulus conditions; this phenomenon has been termed paradoxical alpha, or stimulus-enhanced alpha (Kreitman and Shaw, 1965). As early as 1940, C. W. Darrow noted an increase in alpha amplitude and frequency during stimulus expectation and during mild fear. Darrow (1947), and later, M. Williams (1953), theorized that "stimuli which cause sudden mobilization of the reactive mechanisms'' might also facilitate alpha activity. Isolated instances of such alpha enhancement by stimuli were recorded by other investigators without further comment since such observations were tangential to their main purpose. In 1957, P. F. Werre noted that problem solving with eyes open led to increased alpha activity in approximately one-third of his subjects (Werre, 1957), and S. A. Lorens and Darrow (1962) found that although percent-time the subjects produced alpha significantly decreased during mental multiplication, examples contrary to this general trend did occur.

The reports of this anomalous alpha activity attracted little attention until a series of experiments by N. Kreitman and J. C. Shaw in the mid-1960s. In these experiments, eight volunteer subjects were given eyes-open and eyes-closed tests of auditory, visual, tactile, and mental arithmetic tasks while being monitored on an EEG. Kreitman and Shaw demonstrated that

> the enhancement of the alpha rhythm is to be viewed as quantitatively rather than qualitatively different from blocking. Enhancement has been found to occur more often with tactile than with visual stimuli and . . . although visual imagery, like primary visual activity, tends to be associated with a depression of the alpha band, this statement is true only as an average or trend, with exceptions that are numerous and of striking magnitude (Kreitman and Shaw, 1965).

In light of this and other research, it is clear that alpha enhancement is not always accompanied by a state of content-free, blank attention and deep relaxation, for alpha may also be enhanced by mild activation.

The research projects we have reviewed here amply demonstrate the complexity of alpha brain-waves and should serve to caution researchers and laymen alike against prematurely finalizing their classification of the contents and indices of this altered state of consciousness. The question of whether or not alpha production by means of biofeedback and alpha production during classical meditation are the same cannot be answered, but it is relevant to note that the intensive discipline of meditation doubtless involves far more subtle states of consciousness than any neurophysiological indices can measure. Meditators uniformly assert that all meditative practices postulate a system of interpreting intrapsychic phenomena as well as describing certain physical postures and exercises. By comparison, biofeedback offers the means of experiencing certain brain wave states but has not yet developed a comprehensive system of interpreting those states. It is also necessary to point out that neurophysiological indices of altered states of consciousness are not synonymous with the total experience of an individual in that state. Intensive and long-term discipline is necessary for the induction and sustained experience of the altered states evidenced in meditation and higher-order creative functions. Many subtle shifts involved in the mental processing of thoughts, images, and emotions do not appear to have any neurophysiological correlates. The absence of one-to-one correlations may simply be due to the hardware limitations of present-day neurophysiological instrumentation. Be that as it may, neurophysiological measures reflect only a limited portion of the total spectrum of human consciousness.

The Theta Rhythm

An equally intriguing area of research has been the study of theta brain-wave frequencies, which are even more elusive and evanescent than alpha and much less likely to be found to be dominant under normal waking circumstances. Theta rhythm (4–7 Hz) research has been more limited and more inconclusive, and results have been even more controversial than alpha rhythm experimentation. Only one observation concerning theta activity has considerable consensual validation: Theta dominance is associated with drowsiness and is recognized as the dominant electroencephalographic frequency of Stage-I sleep and sleep onset. Apart from this agreement, twenty years of sporadic research into the theta rhythm has succeeded only in producing a long list comprising highly disparate phenomena that apparently accompany this complex state.

Theta and delta (.5–4 Hz) EEG activity is more prominent in very young children than in adults. As children develop, these rhythms decline proportionately as alpha activity increases until the age of ten or eleven, when the normal adult EEG pattern of beta dominance becomes established. Pronounced theta activity in children has been regarded as a transitional state between the delta-dominant rhythms of infants and the beta-dominant rhythms of early adolescence. Beyond a certain chronological age prominent theta activity has been considered as indicative of maturation defects and related to cortical immaturity (Hill, 1952). A substantial body of research, especially studies of temporal lobe theta activity, has found theta dominance to be associated with a wide variety of neurological and psychopathological disorders. Examples are: (1) episodic rage (Jarvis, 1953); (2) psychopathic behavior (Kennard, 1953); and (3) high hostility scores on the Bender-Gestalt psychological test (Kennard et al., 1956). Prominent theta has been found in the EEG records of convicted murderers (Knott, 1956) and at the onset of convulsive disorders (Stevens, 1959). Offsetting this array of pathological disorders linked to theta are findings that associate theta prominence with: (1) extended periods of sensory deprivation (Saunders and Subek, 1967); (2) the recognition threshold of emotional words (Dixon, 1964); (3) vigilance to neutral stimulation (Daniels, 1967); (4) scanning for pleasurable activity (Walter, 1963); (5) hypnagogic and hypnopompic imagery, which are static mental images experienced usually when an individual is falling asleep or waking up (Green, 1973); (6) episodes of unusual creativity among artists, writers, and musicians (Rorvik, 1970); and (7) deep states of Zen meditation (Kasamatsu and Hirai, 1966). At present there is no widely accepted theory to account for this wide diversity of theta phenomena. An extensive overview and reinterpretation of the psychopathological states linked to theta is contained in my book *Consciousness: East and West* (Pelletier and Garfield, 1976). The emphasis in this discussion springs from the fact that adept meditators frequently report that they manipulate hypnagogic-like imagery to achieve and maintain autonomic control.

One of the most striking aspects of theta research is that it seems to be concerned with the enigmatic relationship between pathology and creativity, madness and genius. Writing in *New Mind, New Body* (1975), Barbara Brown suggests that the common denominator emerging from the research is the inability of those in a theta state to concentrate attention and to order the external environment in terms of significance. Brown maintains that prominent theta activity seems to be related to difficulties in problem solving, sorting and filing of incoming data, and retrieval of stored information. While this hypothesis does account for some of the results, particularly of the studies on the psychopathological correlates of theta, it is inadequate to account for the theta phenomena that have gained the most attention in recent research: the deliberate and often highly creative induction of this brain-wave state. Responding to these latter data, A. C. Mundy-Castle devised the following fourfold classification of theta rhythms.

THETA I— Theta rhythm which is suppressed by eye opening and/or mental activity, yet which is not an alpha variant. Like slow-alpha variant, it is rare in normal adults;

THETA II— Theta rhythm which is augmented during non-emotional activities, perceptual and/or imaginative, and which appears unrelated to affective changes;

THETA III— Theta rhythms which show variation during emotional activities, and are the classical theta most commonly discussed by theorists such as W. Grey Walter (1963);

THETA IV—Slow-alpha variants.

According to this tentative taxonomy (Mundy-Castle, 1957), Theta II is the type that has received the most attention from investigators concerned with both meditation and biofeedback.

Most of the recent research on the creative aspects of theta hypnagogic and hypnopompic activity has been conducted by Elmer and Alyce Green of the Menninger Foundation, Topeka, Kansas. Prior to the Greens' research, only one study had a bearing on this area—that of the Japanese investigators noted above, who recorded trains of theta activity occurring in meditators with twenty or more years of Zen practice (Kasamatsu and Hirai, 1966). The controlled occurrence of theta activity in the absence of hypnotic trance or drowsiness was a significant discovery because previous studies indicated that prolonged theta activity was incompatible with an alert, conscious state. It was also the first suggestion that controlled theta production was a positive creative function in contrast to the psychopathological properties of uncontrolled theta activity. The Greens' research at the Menninger Foundation was the first concerted effort to explore the controlled theta state as the neurophysiological analog of hypnagogic and hypnopompic imagery. Moreover, their ongoing research program is the most comprehensive attempt to define the psychophysiological parameters of altered states of consciousness. Although several earlier research projects had tried and failed to discover any definite empirical evidence linking physiological indices to subjective states (Barratt, 1956; Costello and McGregor, 1957; Drever, 1958; Mundy-Castle, 1957; Oswald, 1957; Slatter, 1960; Walter and Yeager, 1957), all were conducted prior to the advent of biofeedback, which has made it possible to sustain very transient physiological indices in order to research them more thoroughly. The Greens were among the first to develop biofeedback training techniques and it was their inspiration to combine the electronic hardware with elements of Johannes Schultz's Autogenic Training, as reported in their book *Beyond Biofeedback* (Green and Green, 1977).

The Greens began to work with seven male university students in 1969. In pilot experiments using electromyographic (EMG), or muscle, feedback to induce deep relaxation, they demonstrated that deep, muscular relaxation itself produced increasingly high percentages of alpha in the EEG. Feedback of the alpha rhythm was not used, although each subject was monitored for the occurrence of alpha. Another major finding was that alpha increased most markedly for those subjects who had a high percentage of alpha rhythm (above 20 percent) when their eyes were closed, and that alpha production was not easily manifested by those who normally produced less than 20 percent alpha with eyes closed. Additionally, the Greens noted that hypnagogic images were experienced by a number of the subjects in conjunction with periods of theta and low-frequency alpha rhythms. Encouraged by the correlation between theta rhythms and hypnagogic imagery, the Greens worked with three other individuals (a physicist, a psychiatrist, and a psychologist) who had trained in meditation for periods of 15 to 30 years (Green, Green, and Walters, 1970). Emphasis was upon prolonged theta activity since anecdotal and research evidence suggested a link between the hypnagogic images of the theta state and creativity. Unfortunately, it is extremely difficult for even trained individuals to sustain theta-wave activity without succumbing to drowsiness, and this seemed to impose a serious limitation on the delineation of the theta state. In order to discover whether individuals could learn to produce theta, the Greens trained ten other adults by means of biofeedback to sustain alpha and especially theta states. Each person entered into a biofeedback session once a month for seven sessions. The results showed that some subjects were able to increase the elapsed time of theta to the point where they could report the subjective contents of the theta state usually noted as vivid imagery of the hypnagogic type and spontaneous memory of childhood experiences. However, the difficulty of maintaining and monitoring the theta state has remained a vexing problem in this field of research.

More recently, the Greens have turned to intensive case studies of individuals adept at producing alpha and theta states as an efficient means of researching these altered states of consciousness. One of their first subjects, yogic master Swami Rama of Rishikesh, India, demonstrated the ability to sustain long periods of alpha, theta, and delta brain activity while yet remaining in a conscious state. According to Swami Rama, he was able to produce theta waves by "stilling the conscious mind and bringing forward the unconscious" (Green, 1971). One major difficulty in this research was that the Swami was not able to translate the metaphors of how he achieved and sustained that state into Western psychological terminology.

Extrapolating from the various subjective descriptions of controlled theta rhythm activity, the Greens have defined the properties of theta in much the same way as P. McKellar and L. Simpson, who characterized the state as having the qualities of vividness, independence from conscious control, originality, and changefulness. The Greens discovered that the theta state may be characterized by hypnagogic-like imagery in which unconscious processes are often revealed to the waking self in symbols, words, or gestalts. These properties are indicative of inwardly turned abstract attention and internal scanning—what the Greens term "reverie." Reverie is "differentiated from the state of attention normally associated with peripheral sensory processes, external scanning and concrete problem solving. There seems to be no simple differentiation between deep reverie and some dream-like states" (Green et al., 1970).

Other researchers have also noted the link between hypnagogic imagery and creativity in artistic as well as scientific endeavors. Stanley Krippner and his assistant (1970) cited the following instances wherein conscious manipulation of imagery led to creative insight and to discovery: **(1)** Bohr's model of the atom conceived in a reverie; **(2)** Loewi's breakthrough in chemical transmission of nerve impulses; **(3)** Howe's invention of the sewing machine; and **(4)** Descartes' reveries. In these and many other examples the individuals reported that hypnagogic-like imagery was the source of their inspiration. Naive subjects in related findings have also noted incidences of: archetypal imagery and spontaneous, vivid memories of early childhood experiences; dramatic changes in body image and profound integrative experiences; and instances of parapsychological phenomena such as precognitive perceptions. Thus, theta rhythm appears to be a link between conscious awareness and subconscious imagery and associations; as such, it could become an invaluable means of exploring the deep roots of mental phenomena. These studies indicate that controlled production of theta rhythm activity may be an important technique in the exploration of the phenomenology of consciousness. An even more intriguing area of inquiry is the role of theta activity in the voluntary control of autonomic functions. Given the present state of biofeedback research in this area, it is still not possible to link alpha and/or theta production definitively with autonomic control.

Nevertheless, in light of this research it is possible to posit a continuum of consciousness based upon neurological indices of attention focus. Beta (13 Hz to infinity) has been characterized as externally focused attention, alpha activity (7–13 Hz) as a threshold state of passive volition, or relative receptivity, while theta rhythms (4–7 Hz) seem to be indicative of a conscious, internal focus upon intra-psychic processes. The unique interface of conscious-unconscious processes occurring within the alpha/theta segment of the continuum seems to offer significant creative potential to the individual subject. In this interface state, an individual appears to be able to use his conscious mind to focus upon unconscious imagery in a paradoxical manner resembling controlled free association. The ability to focus on unconscious processes allows an individual to formulate more creative problem solutions—taking advantage of previously unavailable information from his subconscious mind. Despite these potentials, however, theta-rhythm research has remained limited for more than twenty years.

The model of a continuum of consciousness ranging from an extreme external focus of attention to an extreme inward focus of attention has been the subject matter of religions, philosophers, mystics, and scientists of all ages. At this point in our understanding, several critical issues concerning the relationship between the neurophysiology of the brain and the phenomenology of the mind remain unresolved, but at least we have begun to specify their dimensions. Several summations can be made from the research we have cited on self-regulation of autonomic functions. First, alpha and especially theta states of consciousness are difficult to manifest, maintain, and describe. Second, although most research has focused upon the alpha rhythm, the psychophysiological correlates of that state still remain equivocal. Third, theta state research is recent, minimal, and inconclusive; additionally, there is no known system by which an individual can be taught to maintain theta activity with sufficient duration for that brain wave and its psychophysiological correlates to be evaluated. Fourth, virtually no research has adequately differentiated the psychophysiological parameters of the alpha versus the theta states of consciousness; thus, the definition of these states remains a tautology at best, since the only evidence that these states are discrete relies upon their distinction according to EEG records. Fifth, there are a few, inconclusive indications that these states are subjectively distinguishable, although no intensive clinical study has empirically demonstrated that assumption. Last, no research has clearly demonstrated the function of alpha or theta production in mediating the voluntary control of autonomic functions. These are the issues outstanding in biofeedback research today. Their resolution in the coming years will dramatically forward the science of consciousness toward which we are striving.

Case Studies of Adept Meditators

In the summer of 1974 one of my research projects at the Langley Porter Neuropsychiatric Institute of the University of California School of Medicine in San Francisco attempted to monitor a variety of psychophysiological correlates of alpha and theta dominance and to discover if they played a role in mediating the voluntary control of bleeding and pain. One of my subjects for these studies was the Dutch meditator Jack Schwarz, a self-trained adept, with whom Elmer Green had conducted an informal study. In the Greens' laboratory at the Menninger Foundation, psychophysiological indices of stress, such as the GSR, muscle activity, and the EEG, were monitored while Schwarz pushed a broad-gauge knitting needle through his left bicep and then controlled the bleeding from that puncture. Alpha waves predominated during this action, and this and other data suggested no pain was experienced by the subject. Another unpublished study, by Erik Peper, described similar phenomena: One of Peper's subjects was able to control bleeding and pain while piercing his face, through both cheeks, with a sharpened bicycle spoke. Another, a thirty-one-year-old Korean Karate expert, placed a sharpened spoke through a fold of skin on his forearm and suspended a twenty-five-pound bucket of water from that spoke without evident pain and with no sign of blood (Pelletier and Peper, 1977a and 1977b). The psychophysiological data gathered by Green, Peper, and other investigators of unusual people was highly suggestive but inconclusive.

During my experiments of 1974, multiple neurophysiological indices of Schwarz's functioning were monitored, including two EEG measures, two skin conductance (GSR) measures, three electromyographic (EMG—or muscle activity) indices, electrocardiogram, thoracic and abdominal respiration rate and patterns. Schwarz's report of subjective events was the source of phenomenological data (Pelletier, 1974). During several sustained sessions over the course of one week the adept meditator engaged in alpha and theta feedback while all of the neurophysiological correlates were monitored simultaneously. It was clear from the intricate correlations that alpha and theta *do* constitute discrete states of consciousness.

In another phase of the experiment Schwartz pushed a large-diameter, unsterilized knitting needle through his left bicep and brachial artery while these same indices were monitored. The records show that he was capable of controlling pain at both the psychological and neurophysiological levels during this action. The records also demonstrate that he was able to control bleeding from the punctures. Alpha patterns were dominant in brain-wave activity measured from the left occipital, parietal, and temporal positions.

One additional finding, regarding respiration patterns, was of significance. Respiration patterns during alpha-dominant states consisted of thoracic activity equal to abdominal activity accompanied by a rhythmic pattern of inhalation equal to exhalation. Theta-dominant respiration patterns consisted of abdominal activity greater than thoracic activity accompanied by short, rapid inhalation and slow, prolonged exhalation. These respiration patterns may become extremely useful in clinical biofeedback practice: Patients may be instructed to use their own respiration patterns as feedback for maintaining alpha or theta dominance. In my own work the technique of respiration monitoring has been of greatest use in theta-state feedback, since theta is so volatile and fugitive a state that the intrusion of the audible feedback tone indicating the presence of theta actually distracts attention and disrupts it. Research with individual adept meditators, always intriguing, is most rewarding when it yields the means of translating their abilities into procedures that all individuals can learn to employ through training with biofeedback instrumentation.

Throughout this experiment the necessity of acknowledging the interaction between Schwarz's phenomenology and neurophysiology was repeatedly affirmed (Pelletier and Peper, 1977). The data only made sense when considered in an integrated manner. This and other recent studies on meditation and biofeedback support Laverne C. Johnson's observation that multivariate physiological analyses are necessary but insufficient in this field of research. These recent studies also complement the experience of the earlier meditation research projects indicating that neuro-physiological indices remain equivocal or uninterpretable in the absence of information on the paradigms of a practitioner's meditative discipline. Most of the early meditation research focused upon profound states of psychophysiological relaxation in deep meditation; that deep state is one that is seldom, if ever, carried over into daily activity. Nowadays, researchers interested in psychosomatic autoregulation and clinical applications of these processes focus on the extent to which the unstressed state achieved in deep relaxation remains present in normal activity.

By Jack Schwarz's own description, his meditative discipline is a form of Yoga known as Karma Yoga. It is the "path of action" (Schwarz, 1977), which consists of complete involvement in each daily activity while remaining in a positive state of open receptivity and awareness. Electroencephalographic and psychophysiological indices tend to confirm that description. Schwarz's alpha state could be characterized as paradoxical (as discussed earlier) in that high physiological activation was accompanied by an EEG record indicating a neurological state of deep relaxation. It is very important to note that this neurophysiological pattern of the Karma Yoga paradigm appears to be one that can be maintained indefinitely with no impairment of normal functions. Karma Yoga thus seems a form of meditation well suited to the prevailing high-activation life orientations of Western culture.

Another significant interaction between psychological and physiological indices was evidenced during the puncture demonstrations involving the voluntary control of bleeding and pain. All punctures were performed spontaneously at random intervals selected by the experimenters in keeping with Jack Schwarz's assertion that no special preparation was necessary. These spontaneous demonstrations of the control of bleeding and pain further support the validity of the concept of Karma Yoga wherein the meditator is in a perpetual state of "active passivity." Such a state has been recognized by Elmer E. Green who has noted that "a highest-level Guru does not need to practice or prepare himself for unusual demonstrations because, it is said, he remains continuously in a state of total mind-body control" (Green, 1973). On three separate occasions, Jack Schwarz demonstrated that degree of spontaneous autonomic control. Again, the significance of this demonstration resides in the fact that autonomic control may feasibly be established on an ongoing basis; this, in turn, opens up the possibility of individuals learning to control bleeding during surgery or following an accident, or to regulate high blood pressure or other deviant autonomic functions while maintaining normal daily activity.

Problems and Possibilities

Great discretion is required to transfer information and procedures from experimentation with adept subjects to that with average individuals. Experimental procedures and their outcomes must be rigorously evaluated before any attempt is made at research with subjects from the general population. In the face of current enthusiasm concerning biofeedback research and applications, a note of caution seems in order. Biofeedback is not a panacea, and uncritical substitution of biofeedback for medical care by specific pharmacological intervention or essential surgery is obviously unwarranted. Possible organic dysfunctions should be considered before the use of biofeedback is undertaken in the case of abdominal stress that might be appendicitis, or in a case of insulin shock induced by sudden stress reduction. Poorly supervised research or clinical experimentation with bleeding and pain control would certainly be hazardous and attempts at heart-rate control could be lethal. Uninformed brain-wave feedback could induce seizures in those prone to "petit mal" activity, while the deliberate induction of altered states of consciousness carries with it the responsibility of providing informed assistance to aid the individual so that he may integrate experiences in a meaningful, nondisruptive manner. There is no need to belabor the inherent dangers of biofeedback and altered states research; this area is as susceptible to abuse or misinterpretation as is any other research involving human beings. What does need to be recognized by researchers and laymen is that, current enthusiasm aside, biofeedback training *is* a powerful technique that should be applied with care by trained people.

At the leading edge of biofeedback and meditation research efforts is the development of a modality of research and treatment that is holistic in orientation. Biofeedback training and meditation practice are holistic in the sense that they evoke the individual's potential to self-regulate his mind, body, and external environment. Holistic medicine, research, or psychotherapy would seek to take into account the physical, emotional, mental, and transpersonal, or spiritual, aspects of the individual. That these functions are inseparably interacting in a holistic and integrated manner is one of the outstanding attributes of consciousness research. Furthermore, the interaction of subject and experimenter or patient and clinician needs to be carefully considered, particularly when working with sensitive and receptive states of consciousness. The expectancies of the experimenter may be critical in biofeedback and altered states research. Subjects or patients are in highly receptive states during alpha or theta training, and appear to be unusually sensitive to environmental influences. How this sensitivity biases or contaminates experimental or clinical outcome is an issue that has been partially illuminated by parapsychological research. Ideally, both of these disciplines take into account the interdependence of these realms of human functioning. Thus, all meditative disciplines recognize the necessity of adequately preparing initiates for each stage of intrapsychic exploration and autonomic autoregulation; and, increasingly, this need is coming to be recognized among those interested in biofeedback research and applications.

What cannot be quantified—and yet is clearly evidenced in biofeedback, meditation, and altered states research with both naive and adept individuals—is the phenomenon of volition. It seems that no matter how subtle the level of analysis or how sensitive the indices, researchers come to a limit beyond which they cannot probe. For this reason many researchers have concluded that the brain is a transducer or conductor of mind rather than the mind being an epiphenomenon of electrical or biochemical activity in the brain. Despite the philosophical complexity of such an issue, we are obliged to deal with the fact that the individual engaged in the simplest act of autonomic control phenomenologically experiences volition. This exertion of will appears to be the means by which he transcends the normal or habitual parameters of human functioning. While it is true that much of human behavior can be accounted for by unconscious choices, genetic endowment, and environmental conditioning, a simplistic view of all behavior that excludes purposive volition does not seem valid according to both empirical observation or phenomenological experience. Neurophysiological data may be regarded as incomplete indices of an exceedingly, perhaps infinitely fine-grained process, termed volition, that can be evoked to regulate macro-scale events of autonomic functioning. There are significant indications that such control may be used by individuals to regulate their own dysfunctional biological systems.

Ancient Eastern literature, poetry, mythology, alchemical texts, subjective accounts of mystics, saints, and modern astronauts—all have said that the experience of a higher self is a necessary prelude to the marked transformation of the individual personality. Research and clinical applications of biofeedback, meditation, and altered states have opened the way to this higher self and provided the means for an unprecedented exploration of human consciousness. Perhaps the ultimate enterprise of the twenty-first century will be the establishment of a Tranquility Base not on the moon, but within humankind.

Beyond
Psychosomatic Medicine

chapter 6

WESTERN psychology conceptualizes the effects of certain events or experiences upon individuals as engrams, or imprints, upon the person's mental functions. In a sense this is a physical model of consciousness that likens an experience to a small, isolated ball in the flux of mental activity, which may be removed or alleviated through effective analysis or therapy much as a tumor or growth may be surgically removed. There are numerous therapeutic systems for removing this disturbing imprint—from psychoanalysis to primal scream. Psychological metaphors such as this create a model of consciousness in which these problematic nodules can usurp psychological energy, as in repression or denial, or block unconscious contents, as in suppression (Pelletier and Garfield, 1975). No doubt there is some validity to this metaphor; certainly it is obvious in psychotherapy that blocks do occur in the midst of a person's mental processes and that these blocks are frequently manifest in physical symptoms such as ulcers, migraines, and other psychosomatic disorders. However, the drawback of conceptualizing negative experience as an isolated tumor is that it obscures the dynamic properties of mind.

Contrasting with this model is one presented in the Buddhist text of the *Abhidharma,* one of the three major divisions of early Buddhist canon (Guenther and Kawamura, 1975). According to Buddhist doctrine an influence in an individual's perceptions is like a drop of ink placed into clear water. Rather than remaining as a drop, it disperses and colors the entire solution. Analogous situations occur in consciousness when basic mental and emotional difficulties are not specific to individual circumstances but affect an individual's entire mode of perception. *Abhidharma* doctrine states that every action is composed of momentary events termed dharmas (Govinda, 1974). By diligent practice in perceiving each moment, an individual can see that his ignorance causes his sufferings and can begin to exercise choice and initiate change in his life patterns. Or as expressed by Shakyamuni Buddha, "That which has the nature to arise, also has the nature to cease." Clearly, this is a highly sophisticated concept of how will and volition play the central role in an individual becoming aware that his states of consciousness profoundly effect his psychological and physical well-being.

Throughout the history of medicine, physicians have puzzled about the seemingly inexplicable recovery of mortally ill patients and the sudden morbidity of patients who should have recuperated fully. Only recently have the hidden and subtle influences of psychological outlook upon healing been regarded seriously. Just as psychological factors seem to play a considerable part in the etiology and duration of illness, they also appear to exert a profound influence in healing, sometimes swinging the balance between life and death (Hutschnecker, 1972). Psychogenic factors may explain the so-called miraculous recoveries brought about through an individual's "will to live," by an "act of faith," or by ingesting a placebo dosage of vitamins or an organic compound. Jerome D. Frank addressed this question of the "miraculous cure" in an article, "The Faith that Heals" (1975), noting the "rapidly growing accumulation of scientific evidence that mental states can affect bodily processes, and thereby health and illness, to a significant degree."

The last decade, especially, has seen a renewed interest in phenomena that previously were looked upon as unexplainable and nonscientific—spontaneous remission, miracle cures, shamanistic rituals, faith healings, and placebo effects. All of these point to an as yet undetermined factor in the healing process. Perhaps the missing element is the consciousness of both the patient and doctor and the interaction between them. The psychodynamic aspects of the healing relationship have been extensively considered by anthropologists, psychologists, and physicians but have generally not been incorporated into the current medical model of disease, which remains predominantly based upon biochemical and physiological principles (Kiev, 1975). Research into the role of individual consciousness in healing has not been considered compatible with that biomedical paradigm, because the latter focuses primarily upon the alleviation or cure of manifest disorders, while the consciousness-based studies have concentrated on issues of etiology and the prevention of disorders and disease. Recent advances in research in psychosomatic aspects of disease and its alleviation by psychosocial interventions has demonstrated that these two approaches are compatible and mutually enriching. Writing in *Science,* physician George L. Engel has stated this position most succinctly:

> To provide a basis for understanding the determinants of disease and arriving at rational treatments and patterns of health care, a medical model must take into account the patient, the social context in which he lives, and the complementary system devised by society to deal with the disruptive effects of illness (1977).

Such an approach forms the foundation of an extended model of disease that emphasizes the consciousness of the individual patient and clinician. It is a comprehensive model in which both psychosocial and biomedical approaches have been reconciled by examining the role of stress in the etiology of psychosomatic disorders. Within this framework of inquiry consciousness becomes an implicit factor in the etiology of both disease and health.

While this enunciation of a psychosomatic paradigm of health and disease may seem the product of recent insights, it has rarely been so eloquently stated in our time as by Plato in 536 B.C.

> We must conceive of that compound of soul and body which we call the living creature. Whenever the soul within it is stronger than the body (and is in a very passionate state) it shakes up the body from within and fills it with maladies. And whenever the soul ardently pursues some study or investigation, it wastes the body; and when the soul engages in public or private teachings and battles of words carried on with controversy and contention, it makes the body enflamed and it shakes it to pieces and induces ca-

tarrhs and thereby it deceives the majority of so-called physicians and makes them ascribe the malady to the wrong cause. On the other hand, when a large and overbearing body is united to a small and weak intellect, the motions of the stronger part prevail and augment that part but make the soul obtuse and dull of wit and forgetful and thereby produce within it that greatest of diseases—ignorance. One salvation from both evils: neither exercise the soul without the body, nor the body without the soul (Plato, *Timaeus*, p. 88).

Plato's analysis and his prescription for the exploration of the function of consciousness in states of disease and health is precisely accurate. After reading this and other passages, our contemporary efforts seem rather like reinventing the wheel.

Numerous clinical researchers have attempted to discover decisive psychological factors concerning which patients would recover from illness and which patients would grow worse. Behavioral scientists are beginning to formulate how feelings, stress, anxiety, depression, and other such states influence the body to create or aggravate organic disorders (Selye, 1956). Researchers are also seeking ways to reverse this process of degenerative pathology and to maximize the conditions under which positive attitudes, beliefs, and life-style changes can alter and heal severe organic pathology and create lasting changes. Among the issues raised in this research are: What is the etiology of psychological and physical illness? What is the nature of the interaction between mind and body that so clearly manifests itself in the negative consequences of psychosomatic disease? (Cannon, 1967; Simeons, 1961) To what extent do psychological factors influence recovery from organic illness, and what are these hidden influences that modulate the course of healing? One of the most fruitful sources for clues is the literature concerned with the psychosocial factors leading to the onset of disorders and with the positive influences of these same variables leading toward spontaneous remission (Pelletier, 1977). In searching the medical journals for such information one finds innumerable "reasons" for spontaneous remission, ranging from testimonials of individuals' cures by faith healers to cases that were inexplicable to both patients and attending physicians (Pelletier and Peper, 1975). There are over 2,000 well-documented cases of such remissions from terminal prognoses, which point toward an extremely important facet of self-healing and personal growth.

Drawing upon the neurophysiological research cited in Chapter 3, it is possible to extend the communication model of mind-body interaction in order to approach the problem of the genesis of psychosomatic disorders. Theoretical and research considerations of mind and body as an interactive unit versus Cartesian dualism seems to weigh heavily on the side of an integrated interaction between psyche and soma. Cartesian dualism has had a long and potent history but now it appears to be an erroneous dichotomy whose usefulness is limited to purely academic debate. Nowhere is the evidence for mind-body interaction more graphically evident than in psychosomatic disorders such as migraine, hypertension, and perhaps even cancer (Simonton, 1975; Stein, Schiaui, and Camerino, 1976). An assumption at the root of psychosomatic medicine is that there is both a psychological and physiological component to all diseases and, a more recent addition to this, that individuals can and do exercise a marked degree of volition in the development, aggravation, and alleviation of these disorders. Personal psychological beliefs and belief systems have a pronounced effect upon whether a person maintains health or contracts a disorder that may end in biological death. Estimates concerning the role of psychological factors and psychophysiological stress in both psychosomatic and physical disorders range from a conservative 50 to 70 percent, according to *Harrison's Principles of Internal Medicine,* to a full 100 percent. A basic assumption in the latter estimate is that all psychological, psychosomatic, and physical disorders and illnesses are either caused or aggravated by psychophysiological stress, and that therefore all illness and disease is comprised of the interaction of psychological and physical factors.

Traditionally, the term "psychosomatic" has connoted disorders that were "imaginary" in the sense that symptoms or complaints persisted in the absence of clearly diagnosed organic pathology. This sense of psychosomatic denoted diseases such as peptic ulcer, migraine, mucous and ulcerative colitis, bronchial asthma, hay fever, Raynaud's disease, hypertension, hyperthyroidism, paroxysmal tachycardia, rheumatoid arthritis, impotency, urticaria, edema, and many others that are considered to be classical stress-induced syndromes (Wintrobe et al., 1974). However, even at best, this group comprises only a limited range of disorders when one considers that recent research has demonstrated a higher percentage of cases in broader diagnostic categories that are attributable to psychological and physiological stress factors. Here the term "psychosomatic" is used to denote states of illness, disease, or health that are characterized by a particular interaction of mental and physical factors (Brown, 1975). Psychosomatic is a neutral term connoting neither illness nor health but acknowledging the interplay of psychological and biological processes in both instances. From neurology, psychology, and biofeedback research there is substantial evidence that individuals can modify their bodily functions to a very large degree and that these alterations can be either positive or negative. In order to make this point more graphic, it is necessary to consider the evidence linking mental activity to alterations in the biological processes of the body.

Cortical Censorship of "Fight or Flight"

This section is by no means intended to be a reductionistic equation of neurological and psychological processes. For the purposes of this discussion we shall assume that activity of the neurological system is electrical while that of psychological processes is symbolic, and neither can be totally reduced or transformed into the other. With that distinction kept clearly in mind, we may proceed on the accepted convention of localizing conscious processes within the cerebral cortex and unconscious processes in the subcortical, or diencephalic, areas of the brain (Eccles, 1966). A substantial body of research and theoretical evidence supports the use of this convention despite the fact that researchers increasingly agree that such a one-to-one correlation is merely a convenient fiction.

Based upon extensive research at Harvard Medical School, Walter B. Cannon formulated one of the earliest modern theories concerning the neurophysiological substrates of consciousness. Cannon considered the two basic anatomical components of the brain, the diencephalon, or thalamus, and the cerebral cortex, or gray matter. In his day, the brain functions localized within and regulating the autonomic nervous system were assumed to function independently of conscious control. Cannon's classic study,

The Wisdom of the Body (1942), focused primarily upon the physical and biochemical reactions that occur spontaneously when any animal is confronted with stress or danger. Responding to a threatening stimulus, the animal's nervous sytem initiates a series of "emergency reactions," or "fight-flight" reactions, in which "respiration deepens, the arterial pressure rises; the blood is shifted away from the stomach and intestines to the heart and central nervous system and the muscles, and the spleen contracts and discharges its content of concentrated corpuscles, and adrenalin is excreted from the adrenal medulla" (Cannon, 1942, p. 136). More recent observations of these biological alterations have been conducted by Walter R. Hess, who termed them the "ergotropic response." The brain areas that participate in this response extend from the anterior midbrain toward the hypothalamus, and their activity is mediated by the sympathetic (a functional division of the autonomic) nervous system. The response is characterized by increased heart rate, blood pressure, and respiration, as well as pupil dilation and hyperexcitability. All of these activities are initiated as an undifferentiated aggregate leading to a generalized state of high arousal. According to Hess:

> In the diencephalon, we are dealing with a *collective* representation of a group of responses which includes responses of the autonomic system as they make their appearance in the form of synergically associated mechanism (Hess, 1957, p. 35).

From both Cannon's and Hess's accounts the most significant factor to note is that threatening or stressful stimuli initiate an intense, overall state of undifferentiated hyperarousal. The biochemical and physiological alterations involved in this response have been most clearly and precisely defined by Hans Selye in his two books, *The Stress of Life* (1956) and *Stress Without Distress* (1974). Selye termed the phenomenon the general adaptation syndrome, or the biological stress syndrome. He noted that an individual's stress reaction initiates such marked alterations as adrenal overaction, transient heart rate and blood pressure elevation, as well as a myriad of other relatively short-term reactions. When stress is prolonged or repeated, then more drastic and potentially pathological reactivity occurs, such as a shrinking of the thymus, spleen, and lymph nodes, and development of peptic ulcers in stomach and intestine. All of these neurophysiological and biochemical changes and their concomitant perceptual alterations are dramatic and long lasting; they are subjectively experienced as fear, rage, or extreme, undifferentiated anxiety.

Under most circumstances such autonomic reactions would be coordinated with voluntary efforts on the part of the animal to flee or engage in a struggle. In researching this complex process Cannon concentrated upon the unified interaction of the cortical and subcortical systems. This focus enabled him to elaborate a principle of the preservation of biological homeostasis within the brain and the physiological organism. Homeostasis is a term borrowed from physiology which describes the compensatory adjustments that the psychosomatic system makes to adapt to changes in the external environment. Actually, the process has come to connote a general balancing function within the organism. However, this explication of the homeostatic principle does not consider the possibility that conflicting reactions may emanate from the diencephalon and the cerebral cortex, which would result in physiological as well as psychological confusion and intraorganismic conflict.

By neglecting to deal with this aspect of the issue, Cannon inadvertently contributed to the preservation of a dualistic model of the brain wherein subcortical levels govern crude sensations and cortical levels govern highly differentiated conscious experiences. In such a model, the introduction of discrepant intracerebral information raises the question of which of the two systems will dominate the organism's reaction. Clearly, this neurophysiological model has had extensive impact upon a whole generation of psychological theorists concerned with the question of unconscious drives versus cognitive control. Additionally, within this framework the autonomous unconscious is alternatively viewed as essentially negative and requiring control, as in psychoanalytic theory, or as essentially positive and a potential source of liberation, as in bioenergetics.

As discussed in Chapter 3, this controversy, although much in evidence in contemporary psychology, is based upon outmoded concepts of neuroanatomy. The most recent neurophysiological research, particularly the studies illuminating the reticular activating system, afford a more subtle and satisfactory view of cortical-subcortical relations. From a purely neurological level of analysis, the functions of the reticular activating system provide a means of mediating conflicting information between the cortical and subcortical areas of the brain through a continual process of selecting which information will be attended to and dominate the individual's perceptions. However, this communication model of continual information exchange of a purely neurological nature is not sufficient to account for the onset or alleviation of psychosomatic disorders. Psychological factors involved in stress situations play an extremely important part in the dynamics of cortical to subcortical information processing.

Writing in 1961, neuropsychiatrist A. T. W. Simeons proposed a communication model of psychosomatic disease that has much to recommend it. Simeons based the model on thirty years of his own work enriched by evidence from neurology, paleontology, and anthropology. In brief, Simeons contended that the cortex of the brain has evolved to the point where it now asserts excessive control over subcortical, diencephalic processes, and that cortical formulations are guided by moral precepts which have arisen solely out of the cultural environment that man has created. These moral sanctions are purely cortical, i.e., consciously formulated; they have no biological basis. Thus, according to Simeons, in response to the increased stresses of contemporary society, man has imposed increasingly stringent cortical censorship over his more biologically based reactions to those stresses.

For example, people often attend cocktail parties or dinners that are an important part of their business although they may have little if anything to do with pleasure or relaxation. At such a gathering, Mr. Smith begins to talk to Mr. Jones, who is important because of social, economic, or business reasons. Mr. Smith does not actually like Mr. Jones but is impelled to be polite, social, and attentive for innumerable covert reasons. Throughout the conversation, Mr. Smith smiles and appears to be having a delightful exchange. However, Mr. Smith notices that, despite his efforts at concealment, his stomach is beginning to burn at each drink of his cocktail, his upper back and neck muscles have tightened to the point where his smile is forced, and his heartbeat has accelerated inexplicably. Actually, Mr. Smith may feel more like running away from Mr. Jones or engaging him in a fight than he can consciously acknowledge. Given normal social constraints compounded by other self-imposed limitations, the alternatives of "fight or flight" are not open to Mr. Smith, despite the fact that he is unconsciously prepared for one or the other of those reactions in response to an unpleasant and stressful situation. On a purely biological level, Mr. Smith is reacting totally normally. But, since his cortex has decreed that he can neither fight nor flee, he gradually learns to ignore these physical symptoms of stress and to maintain a composed personal presentation. This example is but one minor case of a process that is repeated again and again by every individual from the onset of socialization at two or three months of age throughout his entire life.

Clearly there are enormous benefits for the individual who adheres to cultural norms and exhibits an acceptable degree of socialization. However, when socially dictated behavior repeatedly takes precedence over more pressing biological mandates, the price of excessive restraint may be the onset of a psychosomatic disorder. Consider the number of times per day that most individuals ignore such vital body functions as sweating; tight muscles in the back, neck, or face; a slight heart-rate acceleration; pressure behind the eyes; or other more subtle indications of stress. Ignoring these physical and psychological precursors of more pronounced symptoms does not alleviate the condition and may aggravate matters even further. In the case just cited, Mr. Smith is more likely to feel angry about the betrayal of his stomach growling at an inopportune moment than he is to recognize the sensation as a signal for him to remove himself from a highly stressful situation. Most people gradually learn to dissociate from and desensitize themselves to physiological indices of stress. Sometimes this is a conscious decision, but more often it is due to the fact that they do not comprehend the meaning of these signals. There are many situations in which such desensitization is useful and even beneficial; but when an individual systematically and incessantly ignores this information, these stresses accumulate out of awareness until a more clearly recognizable symptom is manifest, such as an ulcer, migraine headache, or tachycardia. Recent research indicates that the specific disorder can frequently be predicted, given certain information about the individual's personality and important psychosocial factors in his immediate family and environment. A good analysis of such factors is undertaken in *Type A Behavior and Your Heart* (1974) by Meyer Friedman and Ray H. Rosenman, both cardiologists, of Mt. Zion Hospital in San Francisco.

Cortical censorship may also be understood as a process of misinterpreted communications between cortical and subcortical brain systems rather than an inherent, irremediable conflict between conscious and unconscious processes. Briefly, the basic observation of Simeons is as follows:

> Modern man's cortex, having censored the diencephalic reactions at the level of consciousness, is unable to interpret the bodily preparations for flight correctly. His cortex cannot understand that his primitive diencephalon still reacts in the old way to threats which the cortex no longer accepts as such. When these once normal and virtually important reactions to fear do not reach his conscious awareness, he interprets them as something abnormal and regards them as afflictions. He speaks of indigestion when apprehensiveness kills his appetite, and insomnia when fright keeps him awake at night. . . . The increased heartbeat becomes palpitation, the sudden elimination of waste matter he calls diarrhea, the clenching of his back muscles he calls lumbago, and so forth. It is man's civilization which prevents him from realizing that such bodily reactions may be merely the

normal results of diencephalic alarm and the mobilization of those marvelous flight mechanisms to which he owes his existence as a species (Simeons, 1961, p. 52).

How ironic it is that normal subcortical or diencephalic reactions are misinterpreted in the cortex as indications of disease which, in turn, increase the individual's anxiety. Perfectly normal stress reactions are labeled as disturbing or even pathological by the individual who views them as inconveniences to be overcome rather than vital signals that he is under stress. Essentially, an accumulating cycle of minute stress symptoms that is ignored rather than halted appears to be the means by which psychosomatic disease becomes established.

While the basic instincts of sex, hunger, sleep, and fear are governed by subcortical systems in the brain, the wide range of human emotions such as pity, shame, hope, guilt, and joy are considered to be cortical elaborations or interpretations of the more basic instincts. This observation is the basis of a theory of emotional states formulated by psychologist Stanley Schachter, who writes:

> Given a state of physiological arousal for which an individual has no immediate explanation, he will "label" this state and describe his feelings in terms of cognitions available to him. . . . One might anticipate that precisely the same state of physiological arousal could be labeled "joy" or "fury" or any of a great number of emotional labels, depending on the cognitive aspects of the situation (Schachter and Singer, 1962).

Numerous studies have confirmed Schachter's basic theory, among them one recently conducted by psychologists Donald Dutton and Arthur Aron at the University of

British Columbia (Dutton and Aron, 1974). Using an ingenious research design, they instructed an attractive female interviewer to approach male students as they were crossing a suspension bridge. The interviewer explained that she was conducting a psychology experiment and asked the subjects to write a brief, dramatic story based on a picture of a young woman covering her face with one hand and reaching out with the other hand. The same procedure was used with male subjects who were approached in a small park on the other side of the bridge after they had already crossed. Results showed that the young men who wrote their interpretation while on the bridge had more sexual imagery in their stories than did the men who were in the park. The researchers interpreted these findings as follows: The men standing in the middle of the suspension bridge were in a physiologically more aroused state than the men who were sitting in a sheltered park. The men on the bridge labeled or subjectively experienced their arousal as sexual because they were in the presence of an attractive woman. Men in the park, on the other hand, although in the company of the same woman, did not experience a significant level of arousal that they would have had to understand or label as sexual arousal. Labeling a physiological state of arousal according to readily observable environmental cues essentially induces subjective understanding. Once an individual can label why he is upset, he feels better, despite the fact that the cognitive labeling may be distorted or incorrect. Similar experiments have emphasized the subjects' cognitive labeling of ambiguous states of physiological arousal in a social situation.

Experiments such as these, while not concerned specifically with psychosomatic disease, utilize much the same evidence cited by Selye, Simeons, and other stress researchers. They demonstrate the behavioral correlates of "tonic activation," the generalized state of subcortical arousal that is cognitively labeled. An equally important process concerns "phasic activation," the other half of the two-way communication between cortical and subcortical processes. According to Simeon's communication model of psychosomatic illness, phasic activation of the subcortex by cortical processes is the neurological basis of stress diseases such as ulcers, arteriosclerosis, diabetes, obesity, and psychological disorders such as guilt and depression. Overall, Simeons' major point is that an individual's physiology is ill suited to cope with the extended stress and anxiety common to contemporary society. With rare exception, when the individual's body and subcortical brain react to social stress by preparing for fight or flight, he must consciously restrain himself. Immobility is interpreted by the subcortex as evidence of insufficient preparation for fight or flight and it initiates more vigorous biochemical reactions. Subjectively the individual experiences this biochemical alteration as mounting tension. The termination or interruption of this highly destructive cycle may be the key to alleviating psychosomatic disorders.

Notes on Stress

Most of the preceding research concerns the dynamic by which distorted exchanges of information between the cortex and subcortex and the conscious and unconscious can create nonspecific stress anxiety that can result in more severe psychosomatic disorders. Undifferentiated stress per se is not responsible for the development of severe symptoms. A certain degree of stress is unavoidable, necessary, even pleasurable. However, stress that is prolonged, un-abated, and nonspecific seems to be primarily responsible for these disorders (Pelletier, 1977). The capacity of modern man's physiology to respond appropriately to stress and then to unstress or relax after the stressful situation has passed has been seriously disrupted.

Unfortunately, most stress-inducing stimuli in a modern environment consist of noise or air pollution, subtle social or business pressures, familial problems, food, toxins such as caffeine or white sugar, environmental contaminants such as lead and excessive hydrocarbons which irritate the lungs, and other ambiguous or abstract stressors. The result is that modern man lives in an unabated state of high stress and anxiety for no specific reason and therefore with no specific means of alleviating those tensions. His biological system does not have the opportunity to react and then to terminate the reactivity and assume a state of compensatory relaxation (Benson, 1975; Pelletier, 1977). Habitual, chronic, unabated stress has replaced such immediate threats as loss of life, starvation, or territorial combat which characterized the stresses of primitive man and animals. Very few contemporary stressors are immediate or identifiable, and individuals are left with a physiological state of arousal for which they have no cognitive label. Contemporary man is in a perpetual state of nonspecific arousal much like the individuals standing in the middle of a suspension bridge. Perfectly normal stress-reducing responses have become pathological, while maladaptive behavior is sanctioned as normal and acceptable. Thus the system of stress and stress-related disorders becomes closed and self-reinforcing, perpetuating and amplifying itself toward destructive ends. Such prolonged autonomic response is damaging to a person's psychological state much as racing an automobile engine will lead eventually to overheating and breakdown. One solution would be to interrupt one part of this progressively degenerative cycle before it has accelerated beyond control. To restore an individual's capacity to identify, react to, and then relax from stressful conditions appears to be the critical point of resolution. Such an intervention based upon individual autoregulation is both necessary and possible.

Absence of stress does not, however, necessarily imply presence of relaxation, just as absence of a clearly diagnosed illness does not necessarily imply health. Unstressing or relaxation is an active state and the absence of stress does not imply a state of lethargy (Benson, 1975; Luthe, 1973). From a purely neurophysiological perspective, a period of parasympathetic rebound, or a "relaxation response," can be deliberately induced by stress-management techniques such as clinical biofeedback, autogenic training, and related methods. However, this neurophysiological principle is complicated by the fact that whether or not that compensatory period occurs is also determined by psychological factors. As both benefactors and victims of the Protestant ethic, most individuals in our culture incorrectly assume that relaxation is a shameful luxury having connotations of nonproductivity, laziness, lethargy, and other such tragic personal shortcomings. Despite these ruminations of guilt, it appears that unstressing is not a luxury at all but absolutely essential to the maintaining of mental and physical well-being. Another misconception is that the ability to relax is inherent and simply occurs when work or other stressful situations are absent. On the contrary, the reacquisition of a harmonious state of mind-body integration requires both effort and training to establish and sustain.

Another qualification of this increasingly complex definition of stress is that stress is not due to exclusively unpleasant or negative circumstances. In fact, subjectively pleasant events may contribute equally to an individual's experience of tension and stress. Researchers have found that stress is closely related to the sheer number of changes that may occur in a person's life. This question has been studied most extensively by Thomas H. Holmes of the Department of Psychiatry and Behavioral Sciences at the University of Washington (Holmes and Rahe, 1967). According to Holmes, the quality and quantity of a person's "social readjustments" are critical factors in creating tension and stress. He observed that a certain number of specific types of events often occurred in a subject's life just prior to the onset of disease or disorder. Among these stress-inducing occurrences were obvious and negative precursors of stress such as the loss of a job, divorce, a jail sentence, financial difficulties, or the death of a spouse or other close family member. However, also predictive of increased stress were such seemingly positive changes as pregnancy; marital reconciliation; job promotion; changes in eating, sleeping, or personal habits; and even vacations. The main characteristic of all these events is "change," which implies the necessity of social readjustment to a new set of life and personal circumstances. Based on these empirical findings, Holmes developed a psychological test profile called the Schedule of Recent Experience Scale (SRE) (Holmes and Rahe, 1970). The profile lists 42 life changes and gives an average numerical value to each experience according to how much adjustment would be required after that particular event. Average values of these events range from a low of 11 for "minor violations of the law" to a high of 100 for "death of spouse." This simple, self-administered, self-scoring scale has extremely high predictive value in pinpointing those individuals most likely to contract a disease or manifest a disorder. The evidence points to a high correlation between the number and intensity of life changes and onset of illness for both psychological and physical disorders. High life-change scores predict a high probability of illness while low life-change scores predict a low probability of illness onset.

The predictive power of the SRE has been borne out in a series of research studies. Richard Rahe and Thomas Holmes did a prospective study of 84 resident physicians, using their life changes for the previous 18 months as the quantitative measure for predicting the onset of illness in the near future. Each physician was given the SRE profile and then assigned to one of three groups: a high-risk group of those who scored 300 or more "life-change units," a medium-risk group of those who score 200–299 life-change units, or a low-risk group who scored 150–199 life-change units. Eight months later, the research demonstrated that illness was reported by 49 percent of the high-risk group, 25 percent of the medium-risk group, and only 9 percent of the low-risk group. A very high degree of predictability relates life-readjustment needs to illness onset in these findings.

In a similar study, Richard Rahe did a two-year follow-up on medical students and noted the same incidence of illness as seen among physicians (Rahe, 1973), over half (52 percent) reporting some illness during the two-year period following the administration of the SRE profile. Of these medical students, 85 percent of those who had high-risk scores reported illness, while 48 percent of those who had medium-risk scores and only 33 percent of those who had low-risk scores reported illness. Additionally, Rahe noted that the high-risk group who reported major illness also reported more minor illnesses, such as stomach aches, minor cuts and bruises, and colds, than the low-risk group. Part of the degenerative cycle noted by Hans Selye and A. T. W. Simeons is that when any specific disorder becomes manifest, it in and of itself becomes another source of stress, laying the ground for further, usually more severe complications. A progressively degenerative spiral, wherein symptoms aggravate stress which creates further symptoms, is a major element in all illness and disease. Generally, those individuals who had the fewest number and smallest magnitude of life changes were less susceptible to both major and minor illnesses.

To account for these results and similar findings made by themselves and others (Holmes and Holmes, 1970; Meyer and Haggerty, 1962; Rahe, 1968), Holmes and Masuda (1973) postulated that excessive life readjustments have the effect of lowering physical resistance and enhancing the probability of illness or disease. In short, an individual's attempts to deal with stress, if unsuccessful, may contribute to an increase in the stress level. These observations are in accord with and affirm the earlier models of Cannon, Selye, and Rahe himself, all of which cite the negative effects of prolonged, unabated stress. Psychological stress due to the need to adapt to life changes can also lead to further stress. If this adaptation is ineffective and repetitive, then it too can be cumulative and lead to more severe psychosomatic illness. The types of illness may vary from psychological disorders, such as depression or anxiety, to classical psychosomatic disorders, such as hypertension and migraine, and may extend to disorders considered to be purely physical, such as infectious diseases and cancer. While stress and psychosomatic disorders have been clearly linked, interestingly, some of the most striking correlations between stress and illness come from research with diseases such as tuberculosis and pneumonia (Meyer and Haggerty, 1962), and traumatic injuries such as sudden death (Engel, 1978) not conventionally classified as psychosomatic. Most of the influences on health—the psychological, physiological, familial, and environmental factors that require adaptative changes—operate outside of an individual's normal awareness at a subliminal level. Even though adequate adjustment to the new circumstances may occur at a conscious level, the subliminal perception research cited earlier makes it abundantly clear that subliminally perceived stimuli do have a very marked effect upon a person's psychological outlook and physical well-being. Although an individual may adapt to noise and air pollution or ignore interpersonal difficulties, these still have the effect of elevating that person's overall level of neurophysiological activity. When those influences are recognized and worked with through an effective stress-management method, then a state of optimum health can ensue.

The Relaxation Response

Our theoretical neurophysiological model of mind-body interaction is supported by extensive evidence linking stress to illness when this interaction tends in a negative direction. The same model forms the basis of a positive alternative for the alleviation and prevention of these life-threatening disorders. The interruption of the degenerative spiral of a disorder is an effective means of accomplishing this unstressing. However, while the curative frequently prescribed for emerging psychosomatic disorders is relaxation, often no specific instructions on how that state is to be achieved are supplied. In fact, the suggestion or directive "you must relax" is a classic double-bind message since the content of relaxation is undetermined by its necessity. "You must relax" is not only a logical contradiction; it is a biological impasse that can only succeed in creating further stress. A physician may thus prescribe one of a wide variety of major or minor tranquilizing drugs to induce relaxation. Or the patient may embark on a self-medication program involving alcohol or marijuana as relaxants. Neither practice is viable or effective; nor are they the only alternatives available.

If stress is due to numerous factors operating outside of or below an individual's normal threshold of awareness, then it is incumbent upon researchers and therapists to discover a means for that individual to become aware of and rectify those influences. Herbert Benson of the Harvard Medical School proposes a solution through activation of what he terms "the relaxation response" (Benson, Beary, and Carol, 1974). Essentially, Benson's notion is based upon Walter R. Hess's trophotropic response. Hess discovered that parallel to the "fight-flight," or ergotrophic, system in the brain is the "relaxation," or trophotropic, area. That part of the brain is located in the anterior hypothalamus and extends into the supra- and preoptic areas, septum, and inferior lateral thalamus. Stimulation to this area is mediated by the parasympathetic (a functional division of the autonomic) nervous system and results in "hypo- or adynamia of the skeletal musculature, decreased blood pressure, decreased respiratory rate, and pupil constriction" (Benson et al., 1974). The trophotropic response is considered to be a protective mechanism meant to guard the body against having too much stress induced via the ergotrophic system and also to promote restorative processes. These dynamic effects are opposed to ergotrophic reactions, which are oriented toward increased oxidative metabolism and utilization of energy. Given that there are these two systems available, the question then arises of how to change from a stressful ergotrophic response to a more relaxed trophotropic response, or how to change from stressed Type A behavior to unstressed Type B behavior.

Benson and his colleagues have provided an invaluable insight and contribution to the solution of this problem based upon evidence drawn from ancient meditative disciplines such as Zen, from more modern systems such as Transcendental Meditation, and from contemporary meditation and biofeedback research. They enumerate the preconditions for eliciting the trophotropic or relaxation response in four basic elements:

> **(1)** Mental Device.—There should be a constant stimulus—e.g., a sound, word, or phrase repeated silently or audibly, or fixed gazing at an object. The purpose of these procedures is to shift from logical, externally-oriented thought. **(2)** Passive Attitude.—If distracting thoughts do occur during the repetition or gazing, they should be disregarded and one's attention should be redirected to the technique. One should not worry about how well he is performing the technique. **(3)** Decreased Muscle Tonus.—The subject should be in a comfortable posture so that minimal muscular work is required. **(4)** Quiet Environment.—A quiet environment with decreased environmental stimuli should be chosen. Most techniques instruct the practitioner to close his eyes. A place of worship is often suitable, as is a quiet room. (Benson et al., 1974).

These conditions prescribe a clear, simple, straightforward set of guidelines for stress reduction. They are also the essential factors in all meditative systems. A note of caution is necessary: Meditation that has the stated goal of stress reduction is no longer meditation, which properly has no goals. Perhaps stress reduction, or relaxation response induction, is a good initial impetus, but it too can become another "you must relax" situation unless one remembers the second condition, that of a passive attitude, of not trying or striving to attain anything. Among the applications of focused attention and the maintenance of optimum states of health are projects in the field of athletics. Psychologist Richard M. Svinn of Colorado State University has trained Olympic athletes in a method he terms "visuo-motor behavior rehearsal" (Svinn, 1976). His training proceeds in three steps, the first being relaxation through Jacobson's progressive relaxation. Second, the athletes practice visualization and imagery, which involves tactile, auditory, muscular, and emotional as well as visual imagery. Lastly the athletes use their skills to practice a specific routine. Techniques similar to this have been noted by the skier Jean-Claude Killy and elaborated in Michael Murphy's *Golf in the Kingdom* (1972). For example, during several sessions Svinn recorded electromyographic (muscle) activity from an Alpine skier as he rehearsed a downhill run. According to the record, "By the time he finished this psychological rehearsal of the downhill race his EMG recordings almost mirrored the course itself. There was even a final burst of muscle activity after he had passed the finish line, a mystery to me until I remembered how hard it is to come to a skidding stop after racing downhill at more than 40 miles an hour" (Svinn, 1976). Svinn cites the impressive records of the athletes he has trained as objective evidence of the value of this method and points out that athletes of the Soviet Union, Austria, and Great Britain employ similar techniques. Most significant for our purposes is the demonstration of psychosomatic factors in eliciting states of optimum performance.

Practitioners of meditation embark on a multidimensional discipline for attaining a state of clarity of awareness. To free the mind and body from confusion and fragmentation can be of beneficial effect to an individual's health. A central point throughout this book has been that the brain is a highly sensitized organ that functions at quantum levels of activity involving infinitesimal amounts of energy. Given the evidence that has been presented here and elsewhere, it is highly probable that such subtle factors as thoughts and images, acting in accord with neurophysiological amplification and feedback systems, are precisely the critical elements in psychosomatic interaction. For this reason alone, it is imperative to explore various meditative disciplines to discover the process by which psychosomatic influences might be optimized to alleviate disorders and to create states of health.

Meditation is most effective when the meditator voluntarily desists from actions and thoughts that would lead to involvement in strong affect or other distractions to his attention. Essential to the practice is stable attention and the establishment of a patient attitude toward attention that wanders and vacillates. Two researchers at Stanford University, Deane H. Shapiro, Jr. and Steven M. Zifferblatt, have analyzed Zen meditation from a behavioral perspective and have conceptualized five steps in the movement toward a deep meditative state.

> First, it is a type of relaxation training. The individual sits in a physically centered posture and breathes in a calm, effortless way. Second, the person learns to focus attention

on one thing—his breath—and to do so in a relaxed, yet deliberate fashion. Third, the person learns to be self-conscious (i.e., to self-observe) without a reactive effect and without habituating to the task. Fourth, the individual is able to desensitize himself to whatever is on his mind: thoughts, fears, worries. And fifth, the meditator is able to eventually remove all covert thoughts and images, thereby allowing him to "let go" of cognitive labels, "reopen" the senses, and be more receptive to internal and external stimuli; or, in the words of the Zen master, the individual learns "to be able to see the flower the five hundredth time as he saw it the first time" (Shapiro and Zifferblatt, 1976).

An outcome of this process is that the individual is capable of being immediately operational in present time, because he is free of past influences, future anticipations, or present-time distractions.

The end point of meditative discipline has been described by M. Csikzentmihalyi, who studied a wide range of rewarding experiences and found them to be characterized by a state of "flow." Key elements in this concept of flow have been summarized by Daniel Goleman as:

(a) the merging of action and awareness in sustained, nondistractible concentration on the task at hand, (b) the focusing of attention on a limited stimulus field, excluding intruding stimuli from awareness in a pure involvement devoid of concern with outcome, (c) self-forgetfulness with heightened awareness of functions and body states related to the involving activity, (d) skills adequate to meet the environmental demand, (e) clarity regarding situational cues and appropriate response (Goleman, 1975).

When this state is achieved and maintained, it can be brought to bear upon all life circumstances and all intrapsychic phenomena. According to Buddhist doctrine an essential characteristic of man is the pain and suffering arising from ignorance (*avidya*), emotive instability (*kleshas*), and a lack of satisfaction (*dukkha*). Of great interest to psychosomatic medicine is the fact that once these conditions are realized through meditation, then a means of ending the suffering becomes the primary focus of an individual's consciousness.

Life, Death, and Rebirth

chapter 7

*T*HROUGHOUT the history of humanity as a rational species, the experience of death has remained a focal point of any adequate theory of the universe. At the center of all philosophical and religious systems, Eastern and Western as well as primitive and modern, lies the eternal mystery of individual death. In an excellent compilation of humanity's attempts to comprehend the meaning of life and death, Choron (1964) traces the history of this quest from Greek civilization through contemporary times. One consistent theme throughout virtually all religious traditions is the need to gain a comprehension and control over the idea of death and its effects upon the physical and spiritual aspects of the individual living being. Complex death systems, replete with detailed rituals and rites of passage, are an essential aspect of all cultures. These cultural

208

mechanisms, as well as individual preoccupations and fears surrounding the subject of death, must be given close scrutiny by any discipline that purports to address itself to the intricacies of human consciousness.

Biological death of the body is certainly the most evident and feared concept of death, but equally important and potentially more disconcerting is the psychological confrontation with death. After reviewing the extensive literature concerning individuals who have been close to death or clinically declared dead and then revived, it is evident that the greatest degree of despair and anxiety occurs prior to the moment of physical death. Death appears to have no antecedent experience and its unique finality is a potential source of terror. Meditation systems exhort their practitioners to see themselves literally dying and being reborn with each word and deed. This concept is intellectually quite acceptable, but to achieve it as a life orientation requires great sincerity and sustained efforts. Most recently, this prescription was offered by Don Juan during Carlos Castaneda's initiation as a warrior:

> When your body is properly tuned to the world and you turn your eyes to your left, you can witness an extraordinary event, the shadow-like presence of death. When death stands to your left you must create your world by a series of decisions. There are no large or small decisions, only decisions that must be made now (*Journey to Ixtlan*).

Death is always potentially imminent and unexpected; the perception of that fact free from anxiety or fear permits an individual to act with spontaneity from one life event to the next. Since it appears that the psychological confrontation with death is the critical point of resolution, the emphasis in this chapter is primarily upon that issue: how an individual may learn to confront his own death. That starting point will take us through an exploration of those aspects of consciousness that allow an individual to rehearse periods of "nonbeing" during meditation.

Social historians have cited the enormous rapidity of change and the consequent discontinuity in contemporary social systems as contributing to the increasing difficulty for cultures to maintain stable organizing principles, especially regarding death. Central to establishing or maintaining a sense of continuity is a belief termed "symbolic immortality" by Yale psychiatrist Robert Jay Lifton, who has researched the survivors of cataclysmic events such as Hiroshima. In *Living and Dying,* Lifton notes that symbolic immortality is the pervasive feeling in people that something of their essence will live on after death in the form of work, children, art—intangibly, in their influence upon others, or simply as part of the great flow of nature. However, the unprecedented degree of change in modern society and the very real possibility of nuclear war which could make the planet uninhabitable have vitiated the basis of that belief. Hence, death has become more unpalatable for modern society than it ever was for previous cultures and less integrated with life.

Western civilization has offered two general approaches to overcoming one's fear of death. The first rests on belief in immortality or future existence. Although acknowledged as the most effective means of diminishing fear of death, it is unacceptable to many because it depends on untestable assumptions. This solution to man's fear of death is most clearly articulated by traditional Christian dogma with its doctrines of salvation and an eternal afterlife. But, since death is unknowable, the untestable assumptions of this approach are in direct conflict with the predominant paradigm of the modern scientifically fixated culture. A second approach is the existential notion of actively coming to terms with the finality of death. In this system an individual need make no assumptions about a hypothetical afterlife; one focuses entirely upon the process of living. Such a philosophy contends that only when one has consciously accepted the inevitability of his annihilation can he fully realize the supreme importance of the here and now and its myriad possibilities. However, the existentialists fail to provide any concrete advice about accepting one's inevitable nonbeing that might lead to a reduction of the attendant fear of death.

Our cultural norms not only dictate a reduction in the most human interactions, which by nature are far more emotional than rational, but also inhibit the individual from gaining awareness of his attitude toward the most irrational fact of all—the end of life. From the vantage point of much oriental as well as occidental philosophy, our culture appears to be based upon hyper-rationality. Moreover, it is evident that a high premium is placed upon self-control, and a narrow sense of personal identity is fostered under the guiding principle of individualism.

One means of bridging the gaps between death, psychological states, and the neurophysiological dimensions of consciousness is a concept offered by Arthur Deikman, a psychiatrist at the University of California School of Medicine in San Francisco. Deikman has conceptualized two modes of human organization, active and receptive, which have both psychological and biological dimensions (Deikman, 1971). According to his theory the active mode is characterized by: **(1)** a manipulative orientation toward one's environment; **(2)** physiological emphasis upon the striate muscle system and the sympathetic nervous system;

(3) psychological emphasis upon focal attention, electroencephalographic predominance of beta-wave emissions, object-based logic, heightened boundary perception, dominance of formal over sensory characteristics, and preference for shapes and meanings rather than colors and textures; (4) phenomenological emphasis upon a state of striving directed toward achieving personal goals, e.g., nutrition, defense rewards, pleasure; (5) future orientation. In contrast to this, the receptive mode of psychobiological orientation is characterized by: (1) an orientation toward the maximal intake of one's environment; (2) physiological emphasis upon the sensory-perceptual system and the parasympathetic nervous system; (3) psychological emphasis upon diffuse deployment of attention, paralogical thought processes, decreased boundary perception, dominance of sensory over formal characteristics, and electroencephalographic predominance of alpha waves; (4) a maximal functioning during infancy, with subsequent dominance by the active mode as a result of the progressive development of striving activity; (5) "here and now" orientation. In the context of this system, Western man's orientation toward death reveals his clear preference for the active mode of functioning. Or, in terms of the neurophysiological dimensions of consciousness, Western man tends to be dominated by the rational left hemisphere at the expense of those capacities residing dormant within the right hemisphere.

In most people these characteristics occur in a certain mix, or blend, and their emergence is shaped by the demands of a particular situation. During maturation the active mode is frequently favored as it enhances the development of biological survival skills. Out of this may arise a powerful inclination toward regarding the active mode as the one most suitable for all of adult life. When a person's primary goal is to maximize his ability to manipulate the environment, the active mode of manipulation rather than the receptive mode of acceptance is the more functionally appropriate. Excessive reliance upon the active mode of functioning, coupled with a highly seductive cultural mystique that equates the cultivation of this orientation with self-esteem and material gain, are sufficient conditions for the inordinately high level of thanatophobia—the fear of death.

Consequences of the predominance of this orientation are extensive. Any perceived impairment on the individual's part of his capacity to manipulate his environment is anxiously experienced as a loss of self-control and a threat to his personal integrity. In our culture, one's own death represents the ultimate failure of the active mode. Death must be denied, for it cannot be contemplated without experiencing overwhelming anxiety. Phenomenologically, the individual's experience of being in the world is characterized in Martin Buber's terms by the I–it rather than the authentic I–thou relationship. There is a sense of the individual being separate and isolated from his environment, which is perceived as threatening since so much of it is beyond control. Writing in *The Natural Mind,* Andrew Weil has noted:

> The ultimate distinction that the intellect makes is the one between "self" and "not-self"; the sense of "I" as distinct from everything else in the universe is the very root of ego-consciousness. Further, in the ego's own terms, all that is not-self is potentially threatening because it has the capacity to undermine the whole conceptual scheme built up so carefully by the intellect. Consequently, persons who have not yet learned to let go of ego consciousness must

necessarily experience the profound sense of isolation that some philosophers consider the normal human condition. Along with this existential loneliness comes the inevitable conviction that one is surrounded by a hostile universe. Everything out there that is not-self seems bent on destroying the fragile, isolated bubble of self (Weil, 1972).

With this orientation, clearly the most ominous threat from the uncontrollable external environment is death itself. Despite the cultural pervasiveness of this perception, it is a highly limited and unnecessarily constrained view of the vast realms of human consciousness.

In close parallel to Deikman's concept of the active and receptive modes of consciousness, Kastenbaum and Aisenberg (1972) have derived a scheme contrasting two different forms of response to death. One is an overcoming response to death, which is seen as highly probable when there exists: (1) a conceptualization of death as an external contingency; (2) a view of the context of the anticipated death as possessing overtones of failure, defeat, or humiliation; (3) a highly developed need in the individual for achievement and independence; (4) a technological (or magical) prospect, i.e., a social or cosmic system for supporting one's objectives; and (5) cultural or group values that require an assertion of power against the devastating or malicious forces of the environment. By contrast to this, an individual is more likely to develop a participatory relationship toward death when: (1) death is conceptualized as possessing an internal locus; (2) the context of the anticipated death carries overtones of honor, reunion, or fulfillment; (3) the individual has a highly developed sensitivity for cooperative behavior, sharing, and affiliation; (4) techno-magical props against death are not conspicuous; moreover, there are positively valued social channels available through which the dying person can express himself and distribute meaningful symbols or tokens; and (5) the culture feels itself to be in a natural and intimate relationship with its environment. It should be obvious that our culture is characterized by the overcoming response to death.

This has not always been so in the West. For twentieth-century man, and particularly for us of postindustrial American society, the current position of death-denial is radically different from past views. Noted French social historian Phillippe Ciriès has documented this shift in *Western Attitudes Toward Death,* which traces the changing attitudes toward death from the early Middle Ages to contemporary society through an examination of customs, literature, and art. His conclusion is that Western attitudes have changed from a resignation to death as an inevitability to an outright denial and rejection of death. It is as if La Rochefoucauld's classic remark that "one can no more look steadily at death than at the sun" has been taken to a ludicrous extreme in an attempt to avoid the profound consternations that arise with the thought of personal extinction. There is no doubt that the dissipation of traditional value systems and religions has compelled modern man to regard the universe as devoid of purpose and meaning, and condemned him to a life that is often little more than an insatiable acquisition of material goods. From this perspective, modern man views death as an intrusion upon the scientific community's quest for immortality. One thanatologist, Herman Feifel, has observed:

> In the presence of death, western culture, by and large, has tended to run, hide and seek refuge in group norms and actuarial statistics. The individual face of death has become

blurred by embarrassed incuriosity and institutionalization. The shadows have begun to dwarf the substance. Concern about death has been relegated to the tabooed territory heretofore occupied by diseases like tuberculosis and cancer and the topic of sex. We have been compelled, in unhealthy measure, to internalize our thoughts and feelings, fears, and even hopes concerning death . . . profound contradictions exist in our thinking about the problem of death. Our tradition assumes that man is both terminated by death and capable of continuing in some other sense beyond death. Death is viewed on the one hand as a "wall," the ultimate personal disaster . . . on the other, death is regarded as a "doorway," a point in time on the way to eternity (Feifel, 1959).

Unconscious fears and conflict cannot be resolved until they are acknowledged and expressed, and a Westerner in this situation is doubly bound by the cultural sanctions against exploring the taboo realm of death as well as his internal predicament of acknowledging death as a personal experience. By contrast, Eastern cultures have long held an attitude toward death as an integral aspect of the eternal cycle of life, death, and rebirth. While this orientation is not absent from Western philosophy, being evidenced in mythology and alchemy, it is definitely a minority position.

No expression of the difference between Eastern and Western attitudes could be more clear-cut than a comparison of the image of a flagellated and bleeding Christ on the cross with that of the utterly serene Buddha reclining peacefully on his deathcouch. In the former, death is at best a painful deliverance, while in the latter it calls to mind the Zen anecdote in which a nobleman asked Master Hakuin, "What happens to the enlightened man at death?" "Why ask me?" "Because you're a Zen master!" "Yes, but not a dead one!" While training in a meditation discipline it is possible to experience deathlike, or thanatomimetic, states wherein an individual confronts and experiences his deepest fears regarding extinction. In some meditations the experiences intensify to such a degree that the practitioner may go beyond a self-conscious state and may no longer know that he is not actually dying. In this manner the fear of death can be experienced intensely prior to actual biological death.

Despite the fact that thanatophobia has received extensive consideration in both theology and philosophy, it was not until Herman Feifel's classic work entitled *The Meaning of Death* (1959) that researchers in psychology seriously considered death and dying as significant factors in the comprehension of human behavior. A few years later Kastenbaum (1965) outlined the following fertile areas for psychothanatomological research: **(1)** the developmental sequence through which an individual forms his idea of death; **(2)** the specific attitude toward death as a manifestation of the principles governing an individual's attitudes in general; **(3)** studies of sensory deprivation, psychosomatic illness, and other phenomena that may contain features comparable to those of the dying process; **(4)** the thanatomimetic phenomena that are the primary focus of this chapter. This fourth category includes a wide range of observations that share the common feature of being experiences of death in organisms that are still alive. According to Kastenbaum, "Material is to be found in zoology, medicine, and other fields, but within the psychologic ground there are also hints that partial and/or temporary 'deaths' constitute phenomena deserving close scrutiny . . . one might refer to Freud's analysis of Dostoyevsky's death-counterfeiting seizures." The fifth category is the relationship between psychosocial variables and longevity. In this area Kastenbaum raises the possibility that psychological and psychosocial variables may have a bearing upon the manner and timing of an individual's death. Actually this issue has an ancient lineage; meditation literature is replete with reports of spiritual masters who willed their moment of death. One step removed from such accounts are the reports by anthropologists noting instances of "voodoo death," wherein individuals die from no apparent organic causation.

Drawing upon the evidence in *Mind as Healer, Mind as Slayer* (Pelletier, 1977), it is feasible to hypothesize that severe conditions of stress induced by extreme fear could result in instantaneous death. Such a hypothesis, extensively treated by Walter B. Cannon (1942) and C. P. Richter (1957), has been explored anew by Barbara W. Lex of Western Michigan University. Lex defined the neurophysiological mechanisms that might account for the phenomenon of voodoo death. In concluding her overview of this area of research, she writes:

> Suggestion in this context is accomplished by the practitioner's manipulation of the autonomic nervous system through the victim's cognitive apprehension of the meaning of witchcraft. The extreme fright experienced by the individual who has been thus singled out can be as fatal as a dose of poison (Lex, 1974).

Her observations are analogous to the neurophysiological and immunological response impairments noted in the discussion of the genesis of psychosomatic disorders detailed in Chapter 3. Such hypotheses suggest intriguing areas for research into the role of volition in an individual's recovery from illness or surgery versus a movement toward death. If subtle thought processes profoundly affect states of health and illness, then these factors may also be effective agents in the phenomenon of an individual's active participation in his own death.

Altered-State Rehearsals of Death

Ultimately, an individual's personal belief system and attitude govern his orientation toward death. Within this subjective complex are considerations such as social processes, demographic and life-status variables, and personality dynamics, which may very well have direct correlations with an individual's longevity and/or confrontation with his personal death. In 1967 D. Lester undertook a comprehensive review of the three major approaches that have been used to assess an individual's fear of death. One method is the direct use of questionnaires, interviews, and rating scales. Another involves projective techniques, such as the thematic apperception tests and sentence completion tests (Rhudick and Dibner, 1961). Third are physiological methods, such as the galvanic skin response (GSR) to words presented in a word-association exercise or to a tachistoscopic recognition procedure (Alexander and Adlerstein, 1958, 1960). For example, Meissner took GSR measures on forty Roman Catholic seminarians, recording their responses to death-symbolic terms selected from the psychoanalytic literature—such as journey, bird, candle burning out, across the bridge, and two control words. Death-symbolic words elicited more affective response as indicated by a larger GSR deflection (Meissner, 1958). Interpreting these results, Lester notes, ". . . Religious belief does not affect the intensity of the fear of death, but rather channels the fear onto the specific problems that each religion proposes.'' In concluding this review Lester states:

> It can be seen that much of the evidence conflicts. Part of this may be due to the wide variety of subjects used: normal adults, college students, elderly psychiatric patients, etc. The better designed studies . . . show that within a single group, demographic variables have little effect on death attitudes. Age will obviously affect attitudes until mental development is complete. Thereafter, it would seem that personality factors and life experiences are the important determinants of the fear of death (Lester, 1967).

Emphasis upon personality factors and life experiences suggests that altered states of consciousness may be a means of allowing an individual to experience an ego-dissolution of thanatomimetic proportions prior to the actual confrontation with death itself.

Another provocative observation may constitute a link between the lack of altered-state experiences in some individuals and their thanatophobia. Recent research supports the concept of a drive to alter consciousness arising from the brain's innate neurophysiological appetite for novel stimuli (Maddi, 1968). This drive is countered by social sanctions against experiences that are regressive or pathological from the consensus perspective of ego consciousness (Pelletier and Garfield, 1976). Sanctions are imposed very early in life: Children are encouraged to repress memories of altered-state experiences, such as those induced by spinning around or hyperventilating, just as they learn from their elders to repress speaking about death. An important link between the cultural denigration of altered-state experience and a positive, or receptive, mode of orientation toward the possibility of death is offered by Kastenbaum and Aisenberg, who posit an intentional thana-tomimetic to all altered-state experiences. According to their theory, "Any state that bears a resemblance to death can be used symbolically as a death-equivalent or substitute" (Kastenbaum and Aisenberg, 1972). All of this leads to the hypothesis that individual functioning more characteristically receptive to death, a condition achieved in part through various altered-state "rehearsals," would diminish the culturally induced fear of death perpetuated by an excessive dominance of the active mode. In fact, the fear of helplessness during the anticipatory period as an individual approaches death is the most anxiety-laden aspect of the experience. Within this framework, the inordinate fear of death in Western cultures may well have been created by the lack of ego-loss experiences and the absence of rituals or rites of passage to help comprehend the psychological impact of imminent death.

Some years ago Walter B. Cannon wrote a striking description of the devastating impact that the lack of social support may have upon an individual's experience of death:

> In the first movement, the community contracts; all people who stand in kinship relation with him withdraw their sustaining support. This means that all his fellows—everyone he knows—completely change their attitudes toward him and place him in a new category. He is now viewed as one who is more nearly in the realm of the sacred and taboo than in the world of the ordinary where the community finds itself. The organization of his social life has collapsed, and, no longer a member of a group, he is alone and isolated. The doomed man is in a situation from which the only escape is by death. During the death-illness which ensues, the group acts with all the outreachings and complexities of its organization and with countless stimuli to

suggest death positively to the victim, who is in a highly suggestible state. In addition to the social pressures upon him, the victim himself, as a rule, not only makes no effort to live and to stay a part of his group but actually, through multiple suggestions which he receives, cooperates in the withdrawal from it. He becomes what the attitude of his fellow tribesmen wills him to be. Thus he assists in committing a kind of suicide (Cannon, 1942).

This elaborate description of the final stages of impending death is a fair account of the process a terminal patient endures during confinement to his home or in a hospital setting in Western culture of the twentieth century. Yet, surprisingly, this passage actually begins, "There are two definite movements of the social group by which black magic becomes effective on the victims of sorcery." In this excerpt, Cannon was describing the devastating effects of social isolation in the voodoo ritual of a primitive culture. Ironically enough, the isolation a patient undergoes remarkably resembles the deliberate attempt of a primitive tribe to kill one of its members. There is little need to ponder the fear of death when other members of the society unconsciously, or consciously, hasten the process. Acceptance of death must be avoided—not for the sake of the dying person, but for society and for those people close to the dying person. According to Phillippe Ciriès, the shift toward death-denial accelerated between 1930 and 1950 due to the displacement of the site of death away from the home and family to the hospital, where doctors waged heroic warfare against death. All of the unbearably strong emotions caused by the dying process disrupted the modern fantasy purporting that life is, or at least should seem to be, always happy. Death in an institution is not the occasion of ritual ceremony, and in the majority of cases, the person has already lost consciousness some time before and has long since been removed from family. Cannon's description of voodoo rites stands as an indictment against the way of death in modern, postindustrial societies of the West, though the issue was probably not foremost in his mind as he observed the workings of a primitive culture.

Compounding the fear of isolation and helplessness as an individual anticipates death is the unimaginable event of the end of life. Certainly it is quite evident that death is the most contradictory and illogical of human experiences. It is impossible to employ a purely logical approach to this phenomenon. Writing in 1969, Guthrie noted four basic paradoxes at the root of the fear of death. The first paradox is that although death is an inevitable and universal event about which nothing can be done, it is at the same time an event that we cannot relegate to the status of a common, everyday occurrence. Second is the paradox that while we know intellectually that we are going to die, experientially we have great difficulty in believing it. The third paradox is that death is both a biological and a spiritual phenomenon. Last and most important is that although death is the terminus of life, it is not simply isolated at life's end since its reality permeates the whole of our existence. That these paradoxes have been dealt with in Western cultures largely by denial is due in part to the inability of contemporary religion and philosophy to address the subject of death satisfactorily. The failure of these systems is, in turn, at least partially due to the lack of those thanotomimetic experiential systems that constitute the core of all culturally viable death rituals. This experiential base places the fact of individual annihilation in the context of a system of knowledge as is found in the Egyptian and the Tibetan books of the dead. In direct contrast, the belief systems of Western cultures have only vaguely defined these rites of transition.

Given the hyper-rational nature of our culture, the ideal man of contemporary mythology is possessed of fully conscious, willful, rational control of himself. With such a premium placed upon control, any state or condition in which there is a loss of control constitutes a threat and induces extreme anxiety. The great societal ambivalence concerning the entire area of altered states of consciousness, such as those induced by meditation, psychedelic drugs, or spontaneous mystical experiences, stems from the culturally relevant fear of the diminution of rationality and self-control. Unlike the death-accepting cultures of the East, Western civilization rarely presents acceptable altered-state experiences. Thus, when a Westerner confronts the reality of his own death, and faces the ultimate loss of control and rationality, he has no inner resources to sustain him. He feels both dependent and inadequate; "in a sense the ego is no longer master of its own fate nor the captain of the self" (Grotjahn, 1960).

Extremely important to note is that the fear of ego dissolution is a culturally relative phenomenon (Pelletier and Garfield, 1976). The ego dissolution that is anathema for a Westerner is precisely that state of consciousness so clearly advocated by Eastern religions. In fact, Freud's description of the operation of Thanatos, or death instinct, approximates the phenomenological accounts of the Eastern notion of the highest states of consciousness, such as satori and nirvana. A good description of Thanatos is the following:

> Finally, there is a fear of those internal instincts within one's self that always push us to retreat from the outer world of reality to a primal world of fantasy and bliss.

Throughout life, our ego fights against this internal pull to an eternal primordial existence. Freud called it thanatos—instinct to death. Whatever the theoretical grounds, it does appear that the dying person begins to return to a state of being at one with the world where there is a helplessness and timeless existence, where I (the ego) and you (outer world) no longer are differentiated. At this point, one is rapidly approaching the state of surrender to the process of renunciation of life and return to union with the earth out of which we have sprung (Pattison, 1967).

Depending upon an individual's attitudes, belief systems, and orientation toward death, this experience can either be feared or accepted. The point is, there is a choice: Agonizing fear for the individual and family is not an integral part of death and dying.

Accounts of Near-Death

The most striking evidence for this last observation are the reports of individuals who have undergone near-death experiences. Their stories coincide in certain important respects and serve to focus our attention upon death itself rather than the anticipatory, dehumanizing treatment generally administered to the terminally ill.

Recently at the University of Iowa College of Medicine, Russell Noyes, Jr., a psychiatrist, and Roy Kletti, a clinical psychologist, analyzed 114 near-death experiences of 104 persons whose median age at the time of the event was 24 years. All were normal adults who were suddenly confronted by the possibility of imminent death. The study's findings were similar to those of previous studies in the area of depersonalization in that, in 64 percent of the events, people reported experiencing a sense of detachment; 50 percent reported feeling no emotion, while 23 percent experienced a joyful feeling. Although one out of three found the experience hard to describe, many reported vivid memories and had excellent recall. The most frequently reported experience, by 75 percent of these people, was an altered state of consciousness in which external events slowed down, like a film running in slow-motion. Also, 68 percent experienced a speeding up of their internal thought processes and were astounded by the number of mental images that went through their minds in a few seconds or less. A twenty-four-year-old mountain climber who nearly fell 2,000 feet recalled, "My thoughts speeded up, time slowed down. . . . [I got] an understanding of death as something beautiful." A twenty-one-year-old woman reported that as her car was spinning toward a bridge abutment she "entered a calm, dreamlike state accompanied by a feeling of being at peace with everything. It was all very much like sitting in a movie theatre and watching it happen on the screen." A physician who had narrowly escaped drowning recalled, "Once I realized I could not rescue myself, an indescribable feeling of calmness and serenity came over me that I have often wished desperately to experience again." Overall, pleasurable reactions to imminent death occurred when the person resigned himself to dying while anger was more common when the person persisted in rescue efforts throughout the period of danger. Researchers Noyes and Kletti concluded,

> One may today take comfort from the fact that suddenly confronted by death, he might find within himself the resources for coping with that frightful prospect. In such an

urgent moment, strength might be found to effect a rescue, but failing in that, to face life's end with serenity, even acceptance (Noyes and Kletti, 1976).

This observation comes from another source: "The letting go, the giving in, the abandonment of striving to maintain object relationships and acceptance of passivity is intrinsically a joyous or pleasurable state" (Hunter, 1967). These are not the words of an oriental or occidental mystic but those of an American psychiatrist attempting to interpret the near-death experiences of a middle-aged patient. From such observations Noyes has proposed three phases that people near death commonly undergo. First there is resistance followed by a recognition of danger, fear, struggle, and acceptance of death. Then there is the experience of life review, a rapidly changing flicker of images and scenes from the person's entire past. Finally there comes an experience of transcendence, a state of mystical consciousness or ecstasy, and spiritual rebirth phenomena. Reactions such as these, which are frequently reported, lend support to the concept that fear of death may be much more a fear of the antecedent conditions—particularly pain—than of the event itself.

Working from a somewhat different perspective, a psychiatrist at the University of California School of Medicine in San Francisco has undertaken intensive studies of individuals who survived jumping from the Golden Gate or the San Francisco–Oakland Bay bridges. According to David H. Rosen, there was a great surprise in his results: The survivors uniformly described their experiences as tranquil and peaceful. "All of them experienced transcendence and spiritual rebirth phenomena" (Rosen, 1975). Seven survivors of these leaps did not experience the phases of resistance and life review noted by Noyes, but this may be due to the fact that the person who has planned his own death has most likely worked through the resistance and may in fact be blocking on the life review aspects. However, the suicide survivors did consistently experience the transcendent phase of near-death. Rosen summarized the interviews as follows:

> Most recorded a feeling of submission or surrender, as if they were guided or controlled by God or a higher power. The survivors reported emotions of extreme calm and peace, or ecstasy. They have gone through a unique experience of surviving planned and almost certain death. . . . Most of the survivors, during and after their jumps, experienced mystical states of consciousness characterized by the loss of the conventional sense of time, space and self. And they experienced a sense of oneness or unity with other human beings in the entire universe (Rosen, 1975).

All six survivors of leaps from the Golden Gate Bridge favored the construction of a suicide barrier, as did one survivor of a jump from the San Francisco–Oakland Bay Bridge. According to Rosen, the experience of ego-death and subsequent spiritual rebirth is perhaps the underlying factor in the survivors' advocacy of a suicide barrier. This accords with the observation of Stanislav Grof, who has written, "After the ego-death the individual sees human existence in a much broader spiritual framework—no matter what the personal problems are, suicide does not appear to be a solution any more" (Grof, 1973). Grof's statement raises the possibility that profound mystical experiences sometimes provoke a distancing response in the very individuals who sought ways to attain them. An individual may create sanctions against the experience for himself as well as counsel others to take intermediate steps to reach the altered state that he experienced immediately. Or he may feel, in the extreme, that no one should have such an experience. This seems to be true of the survivors in Rosen's study, as it may well be for someone who had had an intense drug- or meditation-induced altered-state experience and cautions others not to follow in his path.

Phenomenologically, individuals' accounts of the point of death, from which they escaped, are astoundingly similar to the eloquent descriptions of adept meditators regarding their altered states of experience (Roshi, 1978). It is intriguing to reflect on the possible psychothanatological concomitants of those altered-state experiences that might move an individual toward an acceptance of ego-loss states. If the fear of ego extinction, or ceasing to be, can be regarded as the fundamental fear of death, then the ego-loss experiences described as precursors of altered states of consciousness gain added significance as thanatomimetic experiences. The clinical work of Stanislav Grof (1972) offers extraordinary accounts of such ego-dissolution experiences occurring under the influence of LSD. The LSD sessions provided his subjects with an experiential base for acquiring partial insights into the nature of death, and a degree of satisfaction of that innate drive to experience a variety of modes of consciousness. The implication of Grof's work is that individuals with extensive altered state experiences, of whatever kinds, may have obtained a means to explore their own nonbeing without actually surrendering their being permanently.

These links between thanatomimetic, altered-state experiences and human confrontation with the ultimate specter of death suggest a means of alleviating the inordinate anxiety provoked by death in Western culture. Another way of distinguishing between Deikman's active and receptive modes of consciousness is Andrew Weil's concept of "straight thinking" versus "stoned thinking." Straight thinking is characterized by reason and strictly logical connections, while stoned thinking is characterized by intuition and holistic perceptions. According to Weil,

> At the least, we can conclude that altered states of consciousness have great potential for strongly positive psychic development. They appear to be the way to more effective and fuller use of the nervous system, to development of creative and intellectual faculties, and to attainment of certain kinds of thought that have been deemed exalted by all who have experienced them . . . so there is much logic in our being born with a drive to experiment with other ways of perception. True, it exposes the organism to certain risks, but ultimately it can confer psychic superiority. To try to thwart its expression might be psychologically crippling for individuals and evolutionarily suicidal for the species (Weil, 1972).

Perhaps a society's ability to allow individuals to experience altered states and integrate them into the ongoing culture is the key to Western civilization's reacceptance of death.

As modern rites of passage emerge, it is so very, very important that they be humanistic in the broadest sense—addressing themselves to the body, mind, and spirit of each individual. One hopes that we will be spared a regiment of death specialists as yet another fragmented aspect of an already overly compartmentalized health-care system. Unimaginative technicians administering psychoactive agents or meditation as hollow palliatives whose effects they themselves do not understand would impart abhorrence, not enlightenment, to the process. Researchers and clinicians would do well to reflect upon the rich humanistic heritage of insight into death and its rituals that exists even in our modern culture. Such a sensitive and insightful source, among many others, is *I Heard the Owl Call My Name* by Margaret Craven. Above all else, death will not yield to intellectualizing. It is an irreducible human experience.

Symbolic Death

Mythology, the traditional vehicle of collective values, contains the most elemental responses of the psyche to the eternally repeated needs and longings of the human experience. Fundamental forces in man's development, the benevolent and malevolent urges that have attended his spiritual adventures and the aspirations that have prompted him, all are to be found in myth. Throughout mythology, death and the fear of death appear as elements of the psyche of all times and geographic locations. Most commonly, death does not stand as a final act of annihilation, but rather is represented as part of a cycle of death and rebirth or as the condition necessary to create transcendence of life in an experience of resurrection. This theme of symbolic death followed by rebirth is prominent in the imagery of mythology, religion, and alchemy. It is a primordial affirmation of the cycle of degeneration and regeneration that pervades all of nature and life itself.

Perhaps the most important myth pertaining to thanatology is the hero myth, with its emphasis upon the eternal cycle of life, death, and rebirth. From the extensive work by Joseph Campbell, the journey of the hero can be summarized as follows:

The mythological hero, setting forth from his common day hut or castle, is lured, carried away, or else voluntarily proceeds, to the threshold of adventure. There he encounters a shadow presence that guards the passage. The hero may defeat or conciliate this power and go alive into the kingdom of the dark (brother battle, dragon battle, offering, charm), or be slain by the opponent and descend into death (dismemberment, crucifixion). Beyond the threshold then, the hero journeys through a world of unfamiliar yet strangely intimate forces, some of which severely threaten him (tests), some of which give magical aid (helpers). When he arrives at the nadir of the mythological round, he undergoes a supreme ordeal and gains his reward. The triumph may be represented as the hero's sexual union with the goddess-mother of the world (sacred marriage), his recognition by the father-creator (father atonement), his own divination (apotheosis), or again if the powers have remained unfriendly to him, his theft of the boon he came to gain (bride-theft, fire theft); intrinsically it is an expansion of consciousness and therewith of being (illumination, transfiguration, freedom). The final work is that of the return. If the powers have blessed the hero, he now sets forth under their protection (emissary); if not, he flees and is pursued (transformation, flight, obstacle flight). At the return threshold the transcendental powers must remain behind, the hero re-emerges from the kingdom of dread (return, resurrection). The boon that he brings restores the world (elixir) (Campbell, 1949).

Such is the journey of any individual who embarks on an inner quest to know life and its meaning as fully as possible. In that quest the individual will actually experience his own death, not in metaphor but in fact. If life is to be known then so must death. During an inner journey facilitated by meditation it is possible to experience a state in which the individual ego no longer exists. Ego awareness must literally die, for any awareness other than the pure experience requires a split in consciousness between the observer and the observed, a quality that diminishes the experience by far more than half. These are not metaphorical abstractions but experiences more real than those of any ordinary daily activity.

Throughout Evan-Wentz's *Tibetan Book of the Dead,* a translation of an eighth-century text of Mahayana Buddhism, there are numerous passages elucidating a synthesis of symbolic and biological experiences of death and rebirth. The text sets forth instructions for a dying man concerning the experiences he will encounter after his soul leaves his body. It tells him how to behave in the "bardos," the realm intermediate to this life and the next. His reactions to the situations met in this plane will determine whether his soul is to be reborn again on earth or in one of the heaven or hell worlds. In this way he becomes an active participant, a judge as it were, in his own death. From the psychological point of view this is a most sophisticated and well-developed concept. At one stage of the journey through the bardos he will meet the "wrathful deities," who will appear as terrifying demons of lust, anger, and hatred. Instructions given to him in this event are: "O Nobly born, whatever fearful or terrifying visions thou mayest see, recognize them to be thine own thought forms" (Evan-Wentz, 1960). If the individual is able to overcome this fear and achieve this degree of insight, he will be subsequently released from their power, their forms will disappear, and he is free to pass on to the next trial. This signifies that as soon as man becomes conscious of the fact that the demons that appear to be external are simply reflections of unrecognized and threatening unconscious forces operating within his own psyche, he is freed from their influence. Such is the task of the hero's journey in preparation for death.

Hindu mythology aptly symbolizes similar intrapsychic

cycles of death and rebirth as a timeless series of events without the suggestion of any end in view. This is the subject of the dance of Shiva. According to Hindu myth, the god Shiva is the destroyer, the god of death who marks the passage into new life rather than into nonexistence. In this manner Shiva represents a fundamental energy of the universe that destroys form and creates it in an unending cycle. The eternal movement of Shiva's dance represents "the release of souls from the snare of illusion"; "the place of the dance, the center of the universe, is within the heart" (Coomaraswami, 1957). In Hindu mythology the universe comes into being with the birth of Brahma in the center of a thousand-petal lotus. In this way, according to the Rig Veda, the universe is born and develops from a core or central point, which is seen as a navel from which creation can promulgate. Creation occurs in a cosmic unit of time, which is the "kalpa," or day, of Brahma the creator. When Brahma reaches the hundredth year of his life all the universe, including Brahma himself, is resolved into a great cataclysm. After a hundred years of chaos another Brahma is born. Thus the myth provides an affirmation of timeless regeneration.

For Western cultures alchemical doctrines provide a counterpart to the regeneration process in the transmutation of base metals into silver and gold by the agency of the philosopher's stone. Through these metals the medieval alchemist projected symbols of man in the various stages of his spiritual development. Gold, the most precious of the metals, was to the alchemist the symbol of regenerate man and called a "noble metal." A maturing process was essential to effect the transmutation of the base metals. The first step of this process was to reduce the metals to their "prima materia." From an intrapsychic perspective, the reduction of the metals to their primary substance parallels the immersion of consciousness in the unconscious (Edinger, 1972). Thus the alchemical process is one of purification by putrefaction, the metals must die before they can be resurrected and truly live; through death alone can they be purified. Death becomes oxidation and rebirth becomes reduction. Alchemists sought to destroy the body or outward form of the metals in the hope that they might discover the living essence they believed to be immanent within. The relationship of alchemical metallurgy to the mystical doctrine of self-renunciation lies in the fact that the soul must die to itself before it can emerge into life everlasting. Hence the alchemists dissolved the imperfect creations of the soul, reduced the latter to its materia, and then crystallized it anew into a nobler form. Death and rebirth, the emerging of consciousness from unconsciousness, are universal stages.

Religion, insofar as it is something more than a profession of faith, enables an individual to reconcile aspects of his inner and outer life that he has thus far failed to accomplish by his own efforts. According to biblical scholars, the modern ritual of sprinkling a few drops over the head of an infant in baptism is a mere shadow of the original rites. St. John, in writing of baptism, stated, "It represents death and burial, life and resurrection. . . . When we plunge our heads into the water as a sepulchre, the old man is immersed, very holy, when we come out of the water, the new man appears at the same time" (John XXV). During the early baptismal rituals John Chrysostom immersed adults in the waters of a river to the point where they would believe that they were about to drown. This brush with actual, physical death induced a thanatomimetic altered state sufficiently intense to instill in the baptized a new appreciation for life. Inevitably there must have been individuals who drowned in this ritual and, as time went on, it became less thanatomimetic and more a symbolic matter.

It is possible to view all mysticism and religion as a search for the unity and completeness of being. Essentially this is also the search of the psychotic individual. Perhaps this relation between mystical and schizophrenic states can account for many psychotic individuals' obsessions with religion and death. This course of schizophrenic experience can be viewed as analogous to the mythical voyage, in that whoever undertakes this perilous journey into the darkness by descending, whether intentionally or unintentionally, soon finds himself in a landscape of symbolic figures. Gregory Bateson, in the introduction to *Perceval's Narrative,* an autobiographical account of a schizophrenic, notes the following:

> It would appear that once precipitated into psychosis the patient has a course to run. He is, as it were, embarked upon a voyage of discovery which is only completed by his return to the normal world, to which he comes back with insights different from those of the inhabitants who have never embarked on such a voyage. Once begun, a schizophrenic episode would appear to have as definite a course as an initiation ceremony—a death and a rebirth—into which the novice may have been precipitated by his family life or by adventitious circumstances, but which in its course is largely steered by endogenous processes (Bateson, 1961).

As has been demonstrated in *Consciousness: East and West* (Pelletier and Garfield, 1976), the psychic productions of a psychotic experience are closely analogous to the ancient myths of renewal and rebirth. The motifs are similar—destruction and re-creation, chaos and order, darkness and light. Jungian psychiatrist John W. Perry has also found that the primary features of the contents, or image sequences, of a psychotic episode can be seen as steps in a process and "the progress of reconstituting the self seems to have an astonishing regularity of occurrence of motifs from patient to patient" (Perry, 1974). Whether the hero's journey is precipitated by a psychotic episode, induced by a psychoactive agent, or elicited by meditative practice, there is always the potential for a loss of ego awareness permitting emergence into the greater realms of consciousness and a profound understanding of death itself.

Perhaps the arcane realms of mythology and alchemy, the turmoil of psychosis, and the tranquility of meditation may seem to be disjunctive elements when considering the phenomena of death. However, these few and extremely brief examples are intended to move the consideration of death away from the dreaded image of hospices that are little more than way stations for those patients who are certain to die sooner than others relegated to convalescent homes. More than any other area, the phenomenology of death requires that we consider the subtle realms of mind, emotion, and spirit in conjunction with objective assessments of physical phenomena.

Ordinarily, science provides meaningful conceptualizations and reliable information about phenomena, but *knowledge* is quite another matter. Psychology and other sciences can provide information about the relationships among thanatological phenomena, and it is certainly possible that thanatomimetic situations can be systematically simulated to gain phenomenological clues into experiences that verge on nonbeing. One may reasonably expect scientific inquiry to yield new information in thanatology,

Life, Death, and Rebirth   237

but here one may expect a different kind of information, i.e., experiential or "inside" information, from what science generally provides.

In considering death, the phenomenology of consciousness is essential to comprehensiveness. Reams of data would be hard pressed to provide as insightful and serious a view of death as Bertrand Russell has given:

> An individual's human existence should be like a river—small at first, narrowly contained within its banks, and rushing passionately past boulders and over waterfalls. Gradually, the river grows wider, the banks recede, the waters flow more quietly, and in the end, without any visible break, they become merged in the sea and painlessly lose their individual being (Russell, 1956).

Consciousness requires the study of internal phenomena, including all the products of the mind expressed in poetry and the arts. Any inquiry considering less is limiting to the observer rather than to the realms of human consciousness.

On the Evolution of Consciousness

chapter 8

Evolutionary Considerations

*I*NCREASES in brain size that occurred from the earliest manlike primates of the Australopithecus genera to Homo sapiens are traditionally attributed to changes in the environment and mode of life as the anthropoid apes moved away from arboreal habitation. By descending to the ground, the apes ostensibly freed their hands for the performance of progressively more refined skills, such as developing found pebble "tools" into the true axes of the Paleolithic era. However, if a biologist had observed life before the origin of the hominids, he could not have predicted that the human species would eventually evolve (Dobzhansky, 1962). Although there is a tendency among those not familiar with its complexities to consider evolu-

239

tion as deterministic—i.e., proceeding along specific lines of progressive development—the fossil records reveal no central trend leading directly from a protozoan to man. Rather there are numerous series of intricate branchings of evolutionary trends, showing repeated changes in both rate and direction of development, with man as the end point of one branch. Our "end point" is but one small design in the infinitely patterned tapestry of evolution.

Those who subscribe to classical Darwinian evolutionary theory frequently overlook this fact, just as they usually ignore the theory's gaps. Central to Darwinian theory is the selection and increased specialization of adaptations, such as the lengthening of the horse leg and the trunk of the elephant. However, in order for selection to operate there must be variation from which selection can take place, and this has been a difficult issue. Usually this is resolved by reference to DeVrie's theory that cosmic radiation would alter chromosomes and selection would operate to eliminate undesirable changes. Although this has considerable application, it still cannot account for other instances of biological evolution such as the development of hollow bones and elevated body temperatures in birds prior to achieving flight. Birds with hollow bones were not better suited to survive prior to flight than other land animals and this phenomenon cannot be accounted for by selection and increased specialization (Young, 1976). Not only is classical evolutionary theory lacking in a complete explanation of biological evolution, but nowhere do Darwinists address nonmaterial phenomena such as man's aspirations and his ability to reflect upon himself. On the contrary, Darwin's theory may be taken to imply that man is merely an inordinately clever animal that arose in the course of a randomly generated biological process. This concept has certainly contributed to a lessening of man's stature. Jesuit paleontologist Teilhard de Chardin strove throughout his long and distinguished career to correct this error. An impassioned spokesman for including phenomena of consciousness in any evolutionary theory, he directly challenged the materialistic assumptions of Darwinism with his declaration "Evolution is an ascent toward consciousness" (Chardin, 1965). One of the most important problems facing the emerging science of consciousness is to begin articulating phenomenological and evolutionary data. A critical aspect is the need to consider whether properties of human, or humanlike, consciousness were present at earlier stages of evolution and are manifested today in dimensions outside the limits of classical observation. Perhaps these properties are evidenced in humans as well as in species such as the dolphins (Lilly, 1974). When evolutionary theory addresses both mental and biological evolution, then it is possible to hypothesize a humanitarian view that consciousness is represented to some degree on a planetary level in all organisms.

If consciousness cannot be adequately attributed to an epiphenomenon of neurophysiological and biochemical processes unique to the human brain, then one may reasonably search for indications of properties of consciousness that have occurred throughout the course of the evolution of life on earth and, indeed, are occurring now. Although little headway has been made in this area as yet, Sir John Eccles feels the time may be at hand for a breakthrough theory of psychophysiology, one that will do for this problem what relativity theory did for physics at the turn of the century (Eccles, 1970). According to Eccles, the most important aspect of relativity theory as it applies to the evolution of consciousness is that the observer is not passive in the act of physical observation. An observer always participates in a frame of reference common to that of the observed and also is subject to the interference inherently generated in any system under observation. Eccles urges psychophysiologists to recognize that all observations of the external world are derivative of the perceptual world of the observer, just as the making of scientific hypotheses or philosophical systems are high-order activities of consciousness. Having probed the material universe to its limits, the quantum physicist is left with a highly ambiguous stimulus field analogous to a Rorschach pattern. His situation is not unlike that of an individual practicing the meditative discipline of sitting with eyes open upon a blank wall to project the contents of consciousness upon that screen. Upon such ambiguous stimuli the physicist projects the phenomena of his own consciousness rather than deduces a definitive description of an outer, material reality. An integrated concept of matter and consciousness is clearly indicated in quantum physics. For individuals to be able to speculate about the nature of evolution requires recognition of aspects of the self that go into such a process. Self-reflexive awareness is the unique property of consciousness that permits mind to introspect upon itself unhampered by limitations of physical instrumentation. When researchers approach the threshold between observable neurophysiological activity and the phenomenology of consciousness, then there is the need of a revised form of inquiry most clearly evidenced in the ancient meditative traditions. Before addressing this point let us look at the work of psychiatrist Gordon G. Globus and philosopher Arthur M. Young, each of whom has proposed an integrative theory of evolution.

Gordon G. Globus of the Department of Psychiatry at the University of California at Irvine contends that

> . . . all matter which embodies events is conscious—or perhaps better, protoconscious—as a function of the com-

plexity and parameters of the events embodied by the particular matter. Although it may seem absurd to propose that all organizations are conscious, this apparent absurdity may reflect human chauvinism about consciousness (Globus, 1973).

This proposal is not a naive, pantheistic attribution of a human type of consciousness to inanimate matter or other animate organisms. Each level of organization in matter represents an aspect of potential consciousness directly proportional to its position in the evolutionary chain—from inorganic matter to sentience. Drawing evidence from philosophy, physics, and medicine, Globus adduces evidence of conscious activity as far down in the scale of animal evolution as the metazoa. At these levels of biological organization he finds indications of a "selective attention" that foreshadows higher properties of consciousness; indeed, this property seems inherent, in some degree, at even the simplest levels of organization. Thus, in this view, differences between the human brain, other living tissue, and inorganic matter are quantitative rather than qualitative, although the magnitude of differential function may be many billion times. If one adopts this perspective consciousness is no longer bifurcated from the rest of nature; rather it is relativized according to specific levels of organization that encompass all of material reality.

Although there is nothing in the scientific method that precludes the identification of these prototypic properties of consciousness, such considerations have long been excluded as a common convention. However, as the physical and life sciences probe deeper, both cross the limits of observation and approach the realm of uncertainty. Writing in *Across the Frontiers* (1974), Werner Heisenberg observed:

In biology we are beginning to understand that the control of biological processes in the organism is often linked with particular properties of certain complex substances at the level of atomic physics. Here, too, we are obliged to leave the realm of immediately perceptible living processes in order to recognize the connections at work. It seems, therefore, that developments in many fields of science and technology are running in the same direction: away from the immediate sensory present into an, at first, uncanny emptiness and distance, whence the great connections of the world become discernible (p. 68).

Despite the significance of insights such as this, they are not sufficient to reconcile scientific inquiry with the phenomenology of consciousness. What is required is a comprehensive system that relates specific aspects of the natural sciences with specific properties of consciousness and is based on the recognition that a "prototypic" consciousness permeates man's animate and inanimate environment.

Although such a task might seem virtually impossible, it has been accomplished by Arthur M. Young in two works entitled *The Geometry of Meaning* and *The Reflexive Universe* (1976). Young's integrated model proceeds from philosophical principles to the elaboration of a scientific theory encompassing the empirical data of the natural sciences. A central thesis presented in *The Reflexive Universe* is that each successive level of organization in matter—ranging from the fundamental particles in physics to biological organisms—expresses a particular aspect or property of consciousness. From this point, Young draws evidence from contemporary quantum physics, biochemistry, psychology, as well as ancient mythology, to build a theory of mind-matter integration with implications for all models of inquiry. Young's theory proposes that atomic and molecular organization are protoconscious and provide the basis for more complex expressions of awareness. Such properties gradually accumulate and develop, foreshadowing the characteristics of human consciousness, just as the intrauterine embryo anticipates the adult of the species. The differences between human awareness, other living organisms, and inorganic matter represent discrete steps in the evolution of consciousness. Thus, for example, processes within an animal's body exemplify a level of consciousness more complex than the plants upon which it feeds, which are, in turn, more complex than the earth out of which the plants grow, and so on, in the progressive stages of the organization of mind. Rather than isolating human consciousness from the material universe, this paradigm postulates a continuum of consciousness linking material, biological, and psychological entities.

Basic to Young's theory is the Einstein-Eddington equation for the volume of the universe as a hypersphere or torus of $2\pi^2r^3$. This is the volume of the torus, which is a three-dimensional, doughnut-shaped form with an infinitely small hole. Mathematicians developed the field of topology, the science of surfaces, to describe the properties of such forms, which are so much more complex than geometry. For both geometry and topology, a key mathematical operation is "mapping" in order to distinguish one area of a surface from another. For an ordinary surface or plane such as a map of the globe, no more than four colors are required to create such distinctions. However, seven different colors are required to map the surface of a torus such that any one part of the surface is differentiated from all others. According to calculations by Young, these seven distinctions constitute a fundamental, mathematical property in differentiating one part of the universe from another. Perhaps this scientific rendering correlates with ancient creation myths of the Hindu, Zoroastrian, Christian, and other traditions that divide the process of creation into seven discrete stages. In any case, Young proposes a seven-stage process by which consciousness evolves from its first prototypic manifestations in the photon through nuclear particles, atoms, molecules, plants, animals, and finally to man.

At the first stage, the photon, uncertainty prevails. While science has long regarded indeterminacy with dismay, believing that it hampers inquiry, Young points out that the formula 2π provides for the possibility of a connection between uncertainty and purpose. This is an extremely important point but a difficult one to grasp since it is dependent upon the recognition that one of the 2π elements in the equation for the volume of the 2π torus represents the space-time curvature postulated in Einstein's Relativity Theory. According to Arthur M. Young,

> As Eddington pointed out, the curvature of space-time can be replaced by the phase dimension whose measure is 2π, and this 2π is the uncertainty inherent in quantum theory. In other words, Eddington recognized that the curvature of relativity is the same thing as the uncertainty of quantum theory! (Young, 1976, p. 265)

Later in his theory, Young builds upon this observation and notes,

> . . . the extra 2π makes control possible. It is the entry of consciousness into the universe . . . by Eddington's profound recognition that the curvature of relativity is equivalent to the uncertainty of quantum theory. We add that both are the capacity of consciousness to act upon the universe, or to control determinism (Young, 1976, p. 267).

246 Toward a Science of Consciousness

Thus, uncertainty is not merely a limitation upon science, it is also the condition that allows the positive introduction of purpose and choice at the most fundamental level of matter. Nearly two centuries ago Leibnitz also observed that light behaved as though it was purposive, in the sense that it selected the shortest possible path in its movement from one point to another, and he believed this evidenced "an ubiquitous higher reason ruling all of nature." From this starting point of total uncertainty, Young's theory traces how the element of choice is maintained in the nuclear, atomic, and molecular levels of organization. At the higher stages of evolution, including plants, animals, and man, this quality of uncertainty or choice becomes increasingly voluntary and conscious. These brief examples will serve to suggest the scope of Young's work. However, it should be reiterated that the theory is comprehensive and addresses itself to accepted data of each of the disciplines noted above, indicating how these can be viewed as instances of the prototypic properties of consciousness in the process of evolution.

As discussed earlier, scientific discovery is not simply a process of logical deduction but is much akin to a revelation or sudden insight into an order underlying an observed series of events. Insight and creativity are certainly not the exclusive provinces of modern science, for humans of all ages and perspectives have expressed understandings about the functions of consciousness. And yet, the insights required to create a theoretical schematic of the structure of the universe do not guarantee an understanding of the purpose of such an order. Scientific data tend to give a single, static glimpse of one experiment at one time and its results. That description of the whole range of possible observations and outcomes is analogous to a single still photograph attempting to represent the complexity of a full motion picture. Any comprehensive theory of the nature of reality needs to consider both the fixed images obtained by experimentation as well as the dynamic properties of our ongoing experiences as individuals who are evolving. When this perspective is adopted, the universe assumes a more organic and less mechanistic quality. An early attempt to describe the universe of science as a dynamic, purposive process led J. H. Jeans to conclude in 1937 that "the universe begins to look more like a great thought than a great machine." No accounting of the empirical data of science or the metaphors of mythology would add up to a complete description of reality without addressing itself to the proposition that the universe itself is in the process of evolution. Arthur M. Young has accomplished the formidable task of articulating a paradigm of a dynamic, reflexive universe wherein science and mysticism, data and values, structure and purpose equally coexist.

The Evolution of Science

Theoretical paradigms such as Arthur M. Young's, in integrating the disparate aspects of research in physics, biology, and psychology, point toward the emergence of a profound revision in the contemporary concept of science. The word itself derives from the Latin *scire* (to know), yet the initial power of this human undertaking has gradually been perverted into scientism, which is a reductionist philosophy complete with dogmatic views of objectivity, cause-and-effect relationships, and a materialist imperative. In order to revise this limited and sterile derivative of science and return to its root motive, we need to redefine what constitutes acceptable scientific data as those findings gathered by trained observers and verifiable by others. Thus, when defined procedures are repeated by other trained researchers and the same results are obtained, then the findings become acceptable as scientific data. Any observation needs to fulfill the major criteria that the phenomena be real, hence that they are verifiable, and that they allow for predictions.

A pertinent example here is the recent analysis of the *Yoga Sutras* of Patanjali. Two researchers, Mishrital Jain and Kamal M. Jain of the Maryland Psychiatric Institute, have demonstrated how Patanjali's classic conforms to all the essential criteria of the scientific method in defining the precise methods by which a trained practitioner might experience very precise phenomenological states (Jain and Jain, 1973). The pertinence of the reference to Yoga as science is to recall the fact that consciousness has been found to be a central phenomenon in both the natural and psychosocial sciences and yet one that is not explainable or reducible to materialistic models. This position is stated most succinctly by Roger Sperry:

> The conscious mind in this scheme, far from being put aside as a byproduct, epiphenomenon, or inner aspect, is located front and center, directly in the midst of the causal interplay of cerebral mechanisms. Mind and consciousness are put in the driver's seat, as it were: They give the orders, and they push and haul around the physiology and the physical and chemical processes as much as or more than the latter processes direct them. This scheme is one that puts mind back over matter, in a sense, not under or outside or beside it. It is a scheme that idealizes ideas and ideals over physical and chemical interactions, nerve impulse traffic, and DNA. It is a brain model in which conscious mental psychic forces are recognized to be the crowning achieve-

ment of some five hundred million years or more of evolution (p. 78).

Consideration of this perspective is essential in constructing a science of consciousness in the West, even though precise methodology for the verification of these hypotheses may not yet be available.

Evidence and data need to modify—not be dismissed by—philosophical assumptions of scientific inquiry. Numerous facts and observations are verifiable, but do not fit within the framework of science as it is now practiced and interpreted. Indeed, this situation has reached such proportions that it has been given the name "prematurity" by researcher Guenther Stent, a biochemist from the University of California at Berkeley. He defines a discovery as premature "if its implications cannot be connected by a series of simple logical steps to canonical, or generally accepted knowledge" (Stent, 1972). Instances of the dismissal of "premature" but accurate data abound in the history of science, as illustrated by the French Academy's dismissal of meteors as impossible in 1772 (since stones could not fall from the sky), or the controversies that have characterized the interpretation of fossil records and the earliest computations of Copernicus. Innovative theories need to be formulated to incorporate the rapidly accumulating and often "premature" data regarding a comprehensive science of consciousness.

Quantum physics occupies a unique position in the contemporary evolution of the scientific enterprise. Subatomic particles, having no meaning in and of themselves, can only be understood as products of an interaction between experimental conditions and the subsequent measurements. Hence, the Cartesian dualism that splits the observer from observed is simply no longer applicable. According to physicist Fritjof Capra:

> Quantum mechanics thus reveals a basic oneness of the universe. It shows that we cannot decompose the world into independently existing smallest units. As we penetrate into matter, nature does not show us any isolated basic building blocks, but rather appears as a complicated web of relations between the various parts of the whole, and these relations always include the observer in an essential way (Capra, 1974).

If such an observation holds true in experimentation with the inanimate subject matter of physics, then it certainly should be verified for the life sciences, whose subject matter is, by definition, reactive to environmental influences. Separating the observer from the act of observation, or an aspect of consciousness from its physical counterpart, is at best a convention and at worst an impediment. Relativity theory anticipated and created the groundwork for this extended paradigm by rendering a major revision in concepts of space and time. Einstein's theory demonstrated that space is not three-dimensional nor time a separate entity. Rather both are interconnected to form the four-dimensional continuum of "space-time," wherein space is inseparable from time and time exists only in reference to space. Analogously, our concepts of body and mind are being profoundly revised by contemporary scientist-philosophers. Emerging developments are yielding a concept of "mind-body" in which their interconnectedness is a given factor in hypothetical formulations and experimental research design.

Physicists are actively engaged in the search for an umbrella theory that would cover both quantum mechanics and relativity theory. Although such a unified theory is still not an accomplished fact, there is one formulation in this area—termed "bootstrap theory"—that appears to be promising (Chew, 1968). It is a relativistic theory that addresses itself to certain aspects of quantum activity, and also has significant implications for research into consciousness.

> The basis of the bootstrap model is the idea that nature cannot be reduced to fundamental entities, like fundamental building blocks of matter, but has to be understood entirely through self-consistency. All of physics has to follow uniquely from the requirement that its components be consistent with one another and with themselves (Capra, 1974).

Central to the bootstrap theory is the premise that everything in the universe is connected to everything else. Hence, the theory dispenses with the concept of fundamental entities, be they laws, equations, or principles. Only the requirement of self-consistency must be satisfied. Consequently, the properties of various parts can be understood not through the discovery of fundamental laws but through an understanding of the interrelated properties of all the other parts. Actually this concept is also consistent with a further observation by Arthur M. Young regarding the topology of the torus. An inherent problem in physics, cosmology, and the great religions of the world is the reconciliation of individual separateness and universal unity. Perhaps a property of the topology of the torus can provide an intriguing model of resolution through a concept Young terms "connectivity." Young gives the example that when a circle is drawn around a point on a plane surface, that point is isolated from the rest of the plane. However, when that same operation is performed mathematically with certain points on the surface of a torus, those points remain connected to the whole (Young, 1976). With reference to the topology of the torus, it is possible to conceptualize entities as being simultaneously separate and connected. Among the other implications of bootstrap theory are Western counterparts to the metaphors of Eastern philosophies that emphasize the unity and interconnectedness of all phenomena. Historian Joseph Needham has noted in his study of Chinese civilization that its science never included a concept of fundamental laws. Their term closest to that idea is *Li,* which translates as "dynamic pattern" (Needham, 1956). This concept is given poetic expression in a Buddhist scripture of the 10th century:

> In the heaven of Indra, there is said to be a network of pearls, so arranged that if you look at one you see all the others reflected in it. In the same way each object in the world is not merely itself but involves every other object and in fact is everything else. In every particle of dust, there are present Buddhas without number (Eliot, 1959).

Foremost in Eastern philosophy and a basic insight of diligent meditative practice is the knowledge of the interconnectedness of all objects and events. Bootstrap theory yields a model for demonstrating this reality in mathematical terms.

Western psychology, by and large, has not caught up with the pace of evolution set by modern physics. Much of the literature of the last decade is a morass of meaningless diagrams and idiosyncratic jargon regarding mind and its manifestations in various altered states of consciousness. Each researcher seems intent upon adding yet another construct to the psychological vocabulary rather than adhering to the basic tenet of parsimony. With a few notable exceptions such as Charles Tart's *States of Consciousness* (1975) and Julian Jaynes' *The Origin of Consciousness in the Breakdown of the Bicameral Mind* (1976), the literature amounts to an orgy of "psychologizing." When psychological concepts are unhinged from the necessity of acknowledging neurophysiology, biology, evolutionary theory, and the natural sciences, then such wanderings in the labyrinth are inevitable. In contradistinction to such indulgences are the highly refined phenomenological accounts that have been developed in a disciplined manner and made intelligible in publications such as *Mind in Buddhist Psychology,* translated from the Tibetan by Herbert V. Guenther and Leslie S. Kawamura (1975), and *The Psychological Attitude of Early Buddhist Philosophy* by Lama Anagarika Govinda (1974). Govinda provides a systematic translation of the Buddhist *Abhidhamma,* which is essentially a periodic table of consciousness. While Western science was busy extending Mendeleyev's periodic table of the elements, the internally oriented sciences of Asia continued their tradition of mapping discrete states and properties of consciousness. Actually, the intent of such works was to instruct an individual in the transformation and transcendence of various psychological states that would lead to an experience of perception devoid of intellectual constructs and rationalizations. On the whole, Western psychology has failed to come to grips with the data already on hand—in both the physical and phenomenological sciences—that lead toward the development of a science of consciousness.

Mind and matter appear to be organized according to principles that translate into the particular language of the discipline practiced by the scientist involved in the act of observing. By juxtaposing data from physical science experiments with those concerning consciousness itself, both sets of information are constrained by having to account for the data from each, and yet both are greatly enriched. A case in point is the group of recent studies of electromagnetic radiation emanating from the human body as in the work of orthopedic surgeon Robert O. Becker (1976, 1977), or that of physicist David Cohen, whose extensive research at the Massachusetts Institute of Technology is done with a detector named SQUID (an acronym for superconducting quantum interference device), developed by James Zimmerman (1972). This instrument, in conjunction with a shielded room, reduces the interference of the earth's electromagnetic field in order to measure magnetic fields from the human body, which are as weak as 1×10^{-9} gauss, or about one-billionth of the earth's magnetic field (Cohen, 1975). To date the researchers can detect distinct fields from the brain, which appear to be the strongest at 3×10^{-8} gauss, as well as heart, lungs, and muscle complexes. Potential applications of the findings include detecting defects in cardiac activity or the presence of environmental pollutants in the lungs. In addition to possible advances in medical diagnosis, perhaps these detectable electromagnetic fields will have some spillover impact on a science of consciousness. Psychology has endlessly considered the issue of the effect of one person upon another; although there has been some degree of clarity in these discussions, there has been no resolution. Now psychologists may experiment with the detection of electromagnetic fields, which will enable them actually to observe the effects of one individual upon another and perhaps add some understanding to the positive effects of concepts such as "empathy," or to both the positive and negative influences of such notions as "placebo."

Research in fundamental science and its applications for understanding the process of consciousness promises to be a highly productive orientation. Certainly there are limits to a correlation between detectable electromagnetic fields and the phenomenology of mind, but until those limits are probed, it is mindless to abandon the effort. Until a science of consciousness is formulated that can acknowledge this necessity, the proliferation of increasingly obscure jargon, diagrams, idiosyncratic labels, and redefinitions will persist. Any discipline becomes mired in its own specialization when it loses contact with significant data from other sources. For a science of consciousness to emerge as truly comprehensive, data from many disciplines need to be considered and integrated.

At present there is a great void separating a psychology of consciousness from the basic natural and biological sciences. The historical basis of this unfortunate split can be traced to the fact that much of the psychological material pertaining to consciousness rests on the theories of Freud, Piaget, and Skinner, who for the most part ignored neurophysiology. The contemporary trend to the reunification of mind and body in a holistic science of consciousness promises to revitalize psychology's ties to the natural and life sciences. An example is the research of Mel J. Konner, a Harvard biological anthropologist, who has engaged in cross-cultural studies of emotional responses. His research is based on the fact that in the first year of life, the brain nearly doubles its volume and attains 80 percent of its adult size. According to Konner, this spectacular rate of growth is accompanied by specific changes in the brain and nervous system that give rise in a fixed sequence to specific emotional and social behaviors (Greenberg, 1977). Thus, despite vast differences in climate, rearing practices, and culture, the development of behaviors such as smiling, withdrawal, and aggression follows an identical time schedule in children all over the world. Biologically it appears that substantial growth of myelin must take place in the central nervous system before the neuromuscular behavior termed smiling can even occur. Further, Konner correlates the emergence of the "fear of separation" with the child's ability to achieve independent locomotion, observing that only when a child can actually leave its mother does the possibility of separation and an attendant fear emerge psychologically. Konner does not argue for a causal sequence but for an integrated, holistic model of the development of human consciousness in tandem with a fundamental base in neurophysiology. His work, and that of others, circumvents purely psychological theorizing, which may be inaccurate or abstract simply because it ignores or violates basic principles readily observed in the biological and natural sciences. An inquiry into the nature of human consciousness need not be limited by the biological sciences, but it cannot ignore them either. When a science of consciousness is based upon supportive information from multiple disciplines, it can finally proceed in a productive mode.

A Science of Consciousness

Scientific method is based upon measurement, and advances in neurophysiology and physics are making it possible to measure certain subtle aspects of the phenomena of the mind. Although consciousness itself cannot be measured directly, researchers can measure numerous psychophysiological correlates (Green and Green, 1971; Pelletier, 1975;

Woolfolk, 1975). Thus the study of consciousness can be conducted under many of the conventions and methodologies of contemporary science, although limitations also need to be acknowledged. As researchers begin to define a continuum of consciousness, perhaps the inquiry will indicate a spectrum of consciousness composed of various qualities analogous to the electromagnetic spectrum of various vibratory bands. Drawing such analogies from the physical sciences may certainly be of major significance in formulating an inner science. One such example can be cited, again from the work of Gordon G. Globus:

> According to the complementary principle, light is not just a wave, not just a particle, and surely not a "wavicle" (both). What light is depends on the experimental arrangement used to determine what light is and light has no reality independent of that experimental arrangement. The relation of the present application of Bohr's complementarity principle to the problem of mind and matter would seem to be deeper than a simple analogy to its application in quantum physics. Rather, both applications illustrate the use of a general philosophical principle (Globus, 1973).

This one principle resolves the noncompatibility of mind and matter by relativizing their noncompatible properties as a function of mutually exclusive experimental procedures. By analogy, whether a researcher derives a physical or a psychological theory of consciousness is dependent upon the chosen experimental conditions and cannot be construed to be a property of consciousness per se in either case. Each observation is equally true, each is one aspect of a unitive principle of consciousness.

Throughout the centuries, mystics and accomplished meditation practitioners have uttered pronouncements about the highest state of consciousness as one of transcendent unity. They report that consciousness in its pure form is immobile, extemporal, and exquisitely serene. Enlightenment is freedom from the bondage of the incessant activity of the mind—a state in which it is devoid of all thoughts, desires, volitions. According to Zen Buddhism, mind is contentless and insubstantial in its absolute state of satori (Kennett, Roshi, 1978). This state has been variously termed—inner light by Quakers, mystical self by Vedas, supramental consciousness by Sri Aurobindo, and "stopping the world" in the sorcery of Don Juan. Among the most profound insights of history is that the mystical experience has been essential to the deepest understanding of both nature and man. What is required now is a balance between the scientific inquiry concerning neurophysiology and the mapping of the phenomenology of consciousness through disciplined introspection.

Individuals reside within an evolving universe in the sense of the arcane dictum "Know thyself." An individual's consciousness can reflect upon and know itself and the universe of which it is a part. Deep space probes, Eastern meditation and philosophy, incessant warfare, ecological upheaval, human-potential growth centers, information fragmentation, and the decline of orthodox religion have conspired to turn man's attention toward considering his place in the universe with urgency and humility. In that spirit, insights from all disciplines are converging to create an emergent science of consciousness in the latter part of the twentieth century.

Bibliography

AARONSON, B., and OSMOND, H., EDS. 1970. *Psychedelics: The Uses and Implications of Hallucinogenic Drugs*. New York: Doubleday.

ABRAMS, R., FINK, M., DORNBUSH, R. L., ET AL. 1972. Unilateral and bilateral electroconvulsive therapy. *Arch. Gen. Psychiatry*. 27: 88–91.

ADEY, W. R. 1975. Introduction: Effects of electromagnetic radiation on the nervous system. *Ann. N. Y. Acad. Sci.* 247 (February 28, 1975): 15–20.

ALDINE, ATHERTON. 1970. *Yearbook—Biofeedback and self control*. An Aldine annual on the regulation of bodily processes and consciousness. DNLM WI B1664K. Chicago.

ALEMA, G., ROSADINI, G., and ROSSI, G. F. 1961. Psychic reactions associated with intracarotid Amytal injection and relation to brain damage. *Excerpta Medica*. 37: 154–55.

ALEXANDER, I. E., and ADLERSTEIN, A. M. 1958. Affective responses to the concept of death in a population of children and early adolescents. *J. Genet. Psychol.* 93: 167–77.

————. 1960. Studies in the psychology of death. In *Perspectives in Personality Research,* ed. H. P. David and J. C. Brenglemann, pp. 65–92. New York: Springer.

ALFVEN, H. 1966. *Worlds-Antiworlds.* San Francisco: W. H. Freeman.

ANAND, B. K., CHHINA, G. S., and SINGH, B. 1961. Some aspects of electroencephalographic studies in yogis. *Electroenceph. Clin. Neurophysiol.* 13: 453–56. Reprinted in Tart (1969).

ARBIB, M. 1972. *The Metaphorical Brain.* New York: Wiley-Interscience.

ARENDT, H. 1958. *The Human Condition.* Chicago: Univ. of Chic. Press.

ARIÈS, PHILIPPE. 1974. *Western Attitudes Toward Death.* Baltimore: John Hopkins Press.

————. 1976. *Sur La Mort.* Paris: Le Seuil.

ASANUMA, H., and OSAMU, O. 1962. Effects of transcallosal volleys on pyramidal tract cell activity of cat. *J. Neurophysiol.* 25: 198–208.

ASERINSKY, E., and KLEITMAN, N. 1955. Two types of ocular motility occurring during sleep. *J. Appl. Physiol.* 8: 1.

ASHVAGHOSHA. Ca. first century A.D. *The Awakening of Faith.* Translated by D. T. Suzuki. Chicago: Open Court, 1900.

ASSAGIOLI, R. 1965. *Psychosynthesis.* New York: Hobbs, Dorman & Co.

AUGER, P. 1963. Structure and complexity in the universe. In *The Evolution of Science,* ed. G. S. Metraux and F. Crouzet. New York: Mentor Books.

AUROBINDO, S. 1957. *The Synthesis of Yoga.* Pondicherry, India: Aurobindo Ashram Press.

————. 1958. *On Yoga II.* Pondicherry, India: Aurobindo Ashram Press.

————. 1972. *The Future Evolution of Man.* Compiled with a

summary and notes by P. B. Saint-Hilaire. Pondicherry, India: Aurobindo Ashram Press.

Austin, M. D. 1971. Dream recall and the bias of intellectual ability. *Nature*. 231: 59.

Avorn, J. 1973. The varieties of postpsychedelic experience: An interview with Robert Masters and Jean Houston. *Intellectual Digest,* March, 1973, pp. 16–18.

Bagchi, B. K., and Wenger, M. A. 1957. Electrophysiological correlates of some yogi exercises. *EEG and Clinical Neurophysiology.* 7: 132.

Bakan, P. 1969. Hypnotizability, laterality of eye-movements and functional brain asymmetry. *Percept. Mot. Skills.* 28: 927–32.

————, and Putnam, William. 1974. Right-left discrimination in brain lateralization. *Arch. Neurol.* 30 (April, 1974): 334–35.

Barber, T. X., ed. 1970, 1971. *Biofeedback and Self Control.* Chicago: Aldine, Atherton.

Barnett, Lincoln Kinnear. 1948. *The Universe and Dr. Einstein.* New York: W. Sloane Associates.

Barnothy, M., ed. 1971. *Biological Effects of Magnetic Fields.* Vol. 2. New York: Plenum Press.

Barratt, P. E. 1956. Use of the EEG in the study of imagery. *Brit. J. Psychol.* 47: 101–14.

Barron, F. 1969. *Creative Person and Creative Process.* New York: Holt, Rinehart & Winston.

Bateson, G. 1972. *Steps to an Ecology of Mind.* New York: Ballantine Books.

Baudouin, C. 1922. *Suggestion and Autosuggestion.* Translated by E. and G. Paul. New York: Dodd Mead & Co.

Beal, J. B. 1973. Electrostatic fields, electromagnetic field, and ions: mind/body/environment interrelationships. In *Proceeding of Symposium and Workshop on "The Effects of Low-frequency Magnetic and Electric Fields on Biological*

Communication Processes," Sixth Annual Meeting of the
Neuroelectric Society. Vol. 6. Snowmass-at-Aspen,
Colorado.

BEALE, G. 1971. Social effects of research in human genetics.
In *The Social Impact of Modern Biology*, ed. W. Fuller.
London: Routledge & Kegan Paul.

BECKER, R. O. 1972. Augmentation of regenerative healing in
man: A possible alternative to prosthetic implantation. *Clin.
Orthop.* 83 (Mar.–Apr.): 255–62.

————. 1974. The basic biological data transmission influenced
by electrical forces. *Ann. N. Y. Acad. Sci.* 238: 236–41.

————, and Spadaro, J. A. 1972. Electrical stimulation of partial limb regeneration in mammals. *Bull. N. Y. Acad. Med.*
48 (May): 627–41.

————, ET AL. 1963. Geomagnetic parameters and psychiatric
hospital admissions. *Nature.* 200: 626.

BELLMAN, R. 1970. Acceptance speech for the first Norbert
Weiner prize for applied mathematics. Laramie, Wyoming.
Quoted from *Consciousness and Reality,* ed. C. Musès and
A. Young, p. 289. New York: Outerbridge and Lazard.

BENSON, H., BEARY, J. F., and CAROL, M. P. 1974. The relaxation response. *Psychiatry.* 37: 37–46.

BERLUCCHI, G., HERON, W., HYMAN, R., et al. 1971. Simple
reaction times of ipsilateral and contralateral hand to
lateralized visual stimuli. *Brain.* 94: 419–30.

BERNAL, J. D. 1965. Molecular structure, biochemical function,
and evolution. In *Theoretical and Mathematical Biology,*
ed. T. H. Waterman and H. J. Morowitz, chapter 5. New
York: Blaisdell Publishing Co.

BEVAN, WILLIAM. 1964. Subliminal stimulation: a pervasive
problem for psychology. *Psychological Bull.* 61 (2): 81–99.

BEVER, T. G., and CHIARELLO, R. J. 1974. Cerebral dominance
in musicians and nonmusicians. *Science.* 185: 537–39.

BIDDER, T. G., STRAIN, J. J., and BRUNSCHWIG, L. 1970. Bilateral and unilateral ECT: follow-up study and critique.
Am. J. Psychiatry. 127: 737–45.

BLOCH, H. 1972. *Civilization and Science*. New York: Ciba Foundation/Elsevier.

BOGEN, J. E. 1969. The other side of the brain: I. Dysgraphia and dyscopia following cerebral commissurotomy. *Bull. Los Angeles Neurol. Soc.* 34: 73–105.

———. 1969. The other side of the brain: II. An appositional mind. Ibid. 34: 135–62.

———. 1969. The other side of the brain: III. The corpus callosum and creativity. *Ibid.* 34: 191–220.

———, DeZure, R., Ten Houten, W. D., et al. 1972. The other side of the brain: IV. The A/P ratio. Ibid. 37: 49–61.

BOGEN, J. E. 1973. The other side of the brain. In *The Nature of Human Consciousness,* ed. R. Ornstein. San Francisco: W. H. Freeman.

BOHM, D. 1971. Fragmentation in science and society. In *The Social Impact of Modern Biology,* ed. W. Fuller. London: Routledge & Kegan Paul.

———, and HILEY, B. 1975. On the intuitive understanding of nonlocality as implied by quantum theory. *Foundations of Physics.* 5: 93–109.

BOHR, N. 1934. *Atomic Physics and the Description of Nature.* Cambridge, Eng.: Cambridge Univ. Press.

———. 1958. *Atomic Physics and Human Knowledge.* New York: John Wiley & Sons.

BOISEN, A. T. 1936. *The Exploration of the Inner World: A Study of Mental Disorder and Religious Experience*. Reprint. Philadelphia: Univ. of Pennsylvania Press, 1971.

BONDI, H. 1964. *Relativity and Common Sense*. New York: Doubleday. Quoted by M. La Brecque in "The Quantum Cat." *The Sciences* (October, 1971), p. 8.

BOULDING, K. E. 1961. *The Image: Knowledge in Life and Society*. Ann Arbor, Mich.: Univ. of Michigan Press.

———. 1964. *The Meaning of the Twentieth Century*. New York: Harper Colophon.

BOYD, DOUG. 1974. *Rolling Thunder*. New York: Random House.

BRADSHAW, J. L., ET AL. 1972. Ear asymmetry and delayed auditory feedback, effects of task requirements and competitive stimulation. *J. Exp. Psychol.* 94: 269–75.

BREMERMANN, H. J. 1965. Quantum noise and information. In *Proc. Fifth Berkeley Symposium on Mathematical Statistics and Probability.* Berkeley, Cal.: Univ. of California Press.

BRENER, J., and KLEINMAN, R. A. 1970. Learned control of decreases in systolic blood pressure. *Nature.* 226: 1063.

BRINTON, C. ET AL. 1955. *A History of Civilization.* Vol. 2. Englewood Cliffs, N.J.: Prentice Hall, Inc.

BROOKS, L. R. 1970. An extension of the conflict between visualization and reading. *Q. J. Exp. Psychol.* 22: 91–96.

BROSSE, T. 1946. A psychophysiological study. *Main Currents in Modern Thought.* 4: 77–84.

BROWN, B. B. 1970. Awareness of EEG-subjective activity relationships detected within a closed feedback system. *Psychophysiology.* 7: 451–64.

———. 1975. *New Mind, New Body.* New York: Harper & Row.

BUCHSBAUM, M., and FEDIO, P. 1969. Visual information and evoked responses from the left and right hemispheres. *Electroencephalogr. Clin. Neurophysiol.* 26: 266–72.

———. 1970. Hemispheric differences in evoked potentials to verbal and non-verbal stimuli in the left and right visual fields. *Physiol. Behav.* 5: 207–10.

BUCKE, R. M. 1960. *Cosmic Consciousness.* 20th edition. New York: Dutton.

BUCKLEY, W., ed. 1968. *Modern Systems Research for the Behavioral Scientist.* Chicago: Aldine, Atherton.

BURT, CYRIL. 1967. Psychology and parapsychology. In *Science and E.S.P.,* ed. J. R. Smythies. New York: Humanities Press.

———. 1968. Brain and consciousness. *British Journal of Psychology.* 59 (1): 55–69.

CAMPBELL, D. T. 1959. Methodological suggestions from a comparative psychology of knowledge processes. *Inquiry.* 2: 152–84.

————. 1966. Evolutionary epistemology. In *The Philosophy of Karl R. Popper*. The Library of Living Philosophers, edited by P. A. Schlipp. La Salle, Illinois: Open Court Publishing Co.

CAMPBELL, JOSEPH. 1949. *Hero with a Thousand Faces*. New York: World Publishing Co. Reprint. Meridian Book Edition, 1956.

————. 1968. *The Masks of God: Creative Mythology*. New York: Viking Press.

CANNON, WALTER B. 1942. *The Wisdom of the Body*. New York: W. W. Norton.

CAPEK, M. 1961. *The Philosophical Impact of Contemporary Physics*. Princeton, N. J.: D. Van Nostrand.

CAPRA, F. 1974. Modern physics & eastern philosophy. *New Dimensions*. 3 (2).

————. 1975. *The Tao of Physics*. Berkeley: Shambhala.

CASTANEDA, C. 1968. *The Teachings of Don Juan*. New York: Ballantine Books.

————. 1971. *A Separate Reality*. New York: Simon & Schuster.

————. 1972. *Journey to Ixtlan*. New York: Simon & Schuster.

————. 1974. *Tales of Power*. New York: Simon & Schuster.

CELLARIUS, R. A., and PLATT, J. 1972. Councils of urgent studies. *Science,* 177: 670–75.

CHAI, C. V., and WANG, S. C. 1962. Localization of central cardiovascular control mechanisms in the lower brain stem of the cat. *Am. J. Physiol.* 202: 25–42.

CHAITANYA, K. 1972. *The Physics and Chemistry of Freedom*. Bombay, India: Somaiya Publications.

CHARDIN, P. TEILHARD DE. 1961. *The Phenomenon of Man*. Translated by B. Wall. Introduction by J. Huxley. New York: Harper Torchbooks.

————. 1965. *Hymn of the Universe*. New York: Harper & Row.

CHAUDHURI, H. 1965. *Integral Yoga*. London: George Allen & Unwin.

CHEW, G. F. 1968. "Bootstrap": a scientific idea? *Science.* 161: 762–65.

———. 1970. Hadron Bootstrap: triumph or frustration? *Physics Today.* 23: 23–28.

———. 1974. *Impasse for the Elementary Particle Concept.* The Great Ideas Today. Chicago: Encyclopaedia Britannica.

———, GELL-MANN, M., and ROSENFELD, A. H. 1964. Strongly interacting particles. *Scientific American.* 210: 74–83.

CHORON, J. 1964. *Modern Man and Mortality.* New York: Macmillan.

———. Ca. fourth century B.C. *Inner Chapters.* Translated by Gia-Fu Feng and Jane English. New York: Vintage Books, 1974.

Ciba Foundation. 1972. *Civilization and Science.* New York: Elsevier.

CLARK, K. B. 1971. Psychotechnology and the pathos of power. *Amer. Psychologist.* 26 (12): 1047–57.

COHEN, B. D., BERENT, S., and SILVERMAN, A. J. 1973. Field-dependence and lateralization of function in the human brain. *Arch. Gen. Psychiatry.* 28: 165–67.

COHEN, DAVID. 1975. Magnetic fields of the human body. *Physics Today.* (August, 1975): 34–43.

COHEN, R. A. 1969. Conceptual styles, culture conflict and non-verbal tests of intelligence. *Am. Anthropol.* 71: 828–56.

COLLINS, MICHAEL. 1974. *Carrying the Fire: An Astronaut's Journeys.* New York: Farrar, Straus & Giroux.

COLQUHOUN, W. P. 1971. *Biological Rhythms and Human Performance.* New York: Academic Press.

COMMONER, B. 1971. *The Closing Circle.* New York: Knopf.

CONANT, J. B. 1951. *Science and Common Sense.* New Haven, Conn.: Yale Univ. Press.

COOMARASWAMI, A. K. 1943. *Hinduism and Buddhism.* New York: Philosophical Library.

————. 1969. *The Dance of Shiva*. New York: The Noonday Press.

COSTELLO, E. G., and McGREGOR, P. 1957. The relationship between some aspects of visual imagery and the alpha rhythm. *J. Mental Science*. 103: 786–95.

COULTER, HARRIS L. 1975. *Divided Legacy: A History of the Schism in Medical Thought* (Vols. I–III). Washington, D.C.: Wehawken Book Co.

CRAVEN, MARGARET. 1973. *I Heard the Owl Call My Name*. New York: Doubleday.

CRITCHLEY, M. 1953. *The Parietal Lobes*. London: Edward Arnold & Co.

————. 1967. Creative writing by aphasiacs. In *Neurological Problems*, ed. J. Chorobski, pp. 275–86. London: Pergamon Press.

CRONIN, D., BODLEY, P., POTTS, L., et al. 1970. Unilateral and bilateral ECT: a study of memory disturbance and relief from depression. *J. Neurol. Neurosurg. Psychiatry*. 3: 705–13.

CROSLAND, M. P., ED. 1971. *The Science of Matter*. History of Science Readings. Baltimore, Md.: Penguin Books.

CSIKSZENTMIHALYI, MIHALY. In Press. Play and intrinsic rewards. *J. Humanistic Psychol*.

CUMMINS, G. 1952. *The Road to Immortality and Beyond Human Personality*. London: Psychic Press.

DANIELS, R. S. 1967. Alpha and theta EEG in vigilance. *Perceptual and Motor Skills*. 25: 697–703.

DARROW, C. W. 1947. Psychological and psychophysiological significance of the EEG. *Psychological Review*. 54: 157–68.

DAS, N. N., and GAUSTAUT, H. 1955. Variations de l'activité electrique du cerveau, du coeur et des muscles squelletizers au cours de la meditation et l'extase Yogique. *Electroenceph. Clin. Neurophysiol*. Supplement No. 6, pp. 211–19.

DAVID-NEEL, A. 1936. *Tibetan Journey*. London: John Lane.

DAVIDSON, R. J., SCHWARTZ, G. E., PUGASH, E., and BROM-
FIELD, E. 1975. Sex differences in patterns of EEG asym-
metry. *Proceedings of the Society for Psychophysiological
Research,* Toronto, Ontario, Oct. 16–19, 1975.

DEGEEST, H., LEVY, M. N., ZIESKE, H., et al. 1965. Depression of ventricular contractility by stimulation of the vagus
nerves. *Circ. Res.* 17: 222–35.

DEIKMAN, A. J. 1963. Experimental meditation. *J. Nervous and
Mental Diseases.* 136: 329.

———. 1971. Bimodal consciousness. *Arch. Gen. Psychiatry.*
25: 481–89.

———. 1973. The meaning of everything. In *The Nature of
Human Consciousness,* ed. R. Ornstein. San Francisco:
W. H. Freeman.

DELGADO, J. 1969. *Physical Control of the Mind: Toward a
Psychocivilized Society.* New York: Harper & Row.

D'ELIA, G. 1970. Comparison of electroconvulsive therapy with
unilateral and bilateral stimulation. *Acta Psychiatr. Scand.*
215: 30–43.

DEMENT, W. C. 1960. The effect of dream deprivation. *Science.*
131: 1705–07.

DENHYER, K., and BARRETT, B. 1971. Selective loss of visual
information in STM by means of visual and verbal in-
terpolated tasks. *Psychol. Sci.* 25: 100–102.

DERENZI, E., and SPINNLER, H. 1966. Visual recognition in patients with unilateral cerebral disease. *J. Nerv. Ment. Dis.*
142: 515–25.

DE ROPP, R. S. 1957. *Drugs and the Mind.* New York: Grove
Press.

———. 1972. *The New Prometheans.* New York: Delacorte
Press.

DEUTSCH, M. 1959. Evidence and inference in nuclear research.
In *Evidence and Inference,* ed. D. Lerner. Glencoe, Ill.:
The Free Press.

DIJSTERHUIS, E. J. 1961. *The Mechanization of the World Picture.* Oxford, England: The Clarendon Press.

DIXON, N. F. 1964. Incidence of theta rhythm prior to awareness of a visual stimulus. *Nature*. 203: 167–70.

————. 1971. *Subliminal Perception: The Nature of a Controversy.* New York: McGraw-Hill.

DOBZHANSKY, T. 1962. *Mankind Evolving: The Evolution of the Human Species.* New Haven, Conn.: Yale Univ. Press.

————. 1971. Determinism and indeterminism in biological evolution. In *Man and Nature,* ed. R. Muson. New York: Delta Books.

DOLE, S. H., with ASIMOV, I. 1954. *Planets for Man.* New York: Random House.

DOMHOFF, G. W. 1969–70. But why did they sit on the king's right in the first place? *Psychoanal. Rev.* 56: 586–96.

DREVER, J. 1958. Further observations on the relation between EEG and visual imagery. *Am. J. Psychol.* 71: 270–77.

DUBOS, R. 1965. *Man Adapting.* New Haven, Conn.: Yale Univ. Press.

————. 1967. Man adapting. In *Environment for Man,* ed. W. Ewald, Jr. Bloomington, Indiana: Indiana Univ. Press.

————. 1968. *So Human an Animal.* New York: Scribner's.

————. 1973. Humanizing the earth. *Science.* 179: 769.

————, and WARD, B. 1972. *Only One Earth.* Harmondsworth, Middlesex, England: Penguin Books.

DUNN, E. S., JR. 1971. *Economic and Social Development: A Process of Social Learning.* Baltimore: Johns Hopkins Press.

DUNNE, J. W. 1939. *An Experiment with Time.* London: Faber & Faber.

ECCLES, JOHN C. 1953. *The Neurophysiological Basis of Mind: The Principles of Neurophysiology.* Oxford, England: The Clarendon Press.

————. 1966. Conscious experience and memory. In *Brain & Conscious Experience,* ed. J. C. Eccles, pp. 314–44. New York: Springer Verlag.

————. 1970. *Facing Reality.* New York: Springer Verlag.

———. 1973. *The Understanding of the Brain*. New York: McGraw-Hill.

EDDINGTON, A. S. 1928. *The Nature of the Physical World*. Cambridge, England: Cambridge Univ. Press.

———. 1935. *New Pathways in Science*, Cambridge, England: Cambridge Univ. Press.

———. 1939. *The Philosophy of Physical Science*. Cambridge, England: Cambridge Univ. Press.

———. 1946. *Fundamental Theory*. Cambridge, England: Cambridge Univ. Press.

EDELSTEIN, K. L. 1957. Recent trends in ancient science. In *The Roots of Scientific Thought*, ed. P. Wiener and A. Noland. New York: Basic Books.

EDINGER, E. F. 1972. *Ego and Archetype*. Baltimore: Penguin Books.

EFRON, R. 1963a. Effect of handedness on the perception of simultaneity and temporal order. *Brain*. 86: 261–84.

———. 1963b. The effect of stimulus intensity on the perception of simultaneity in right and left-handed subjects. *Brain*. 86: 285–94.

EHRLICH, P. R. 1970. *Population, Resources, Environment: Issues in Human Ecology*. San Francisco: W. H. Freeman.

EIDELBERG, E. 1969. Callosal and non-callosal connections between the sensory motor cortices in cat and monkey. *Electroencephalogr. Clin. Neurophysiol.* 26: 557–64.

EINSTEIN, A. 1930. Religion and science. *New York Times*, November 9.

———. 1934. *Essays in Science*. New York: Philosophical Library.

———. 1950. *Out of My Later Years*. New York: Philosophical Library.

———, et al. 1923. *The Principle of Relativity*. New York: Dover.

ELIADE, M. 1969. *Myths and Symbols*. New York: Search Book Translation/Edition.

ELIOT, C. 1959. *Japanese Buddhism*. London: Routledge & Kegan Paul. Reprint. 1969. New York: Barnes & Noble.

ELLUL, J. 1967. *The Technological Society*. New York: Knopf.

ELSASSER, W. 1966. *Atom and Organism*. Princeton, N.J.: Princeton Univ. Press.

EMMET, D. 1969. Religion and the social anthropology of religion: III Myth. *Theoria to Theory*. 3 (April, 1969): 42–55.

ENGEL, B. T., and CHISM, R. A. 1967. Operant conditioning of heart rate speeding. *Psychophysiology*. 3: 418–26.

ENGEL, B. T., and HANSEN, S. P. 1966. Operant conditioning of heart rate slowing. *Psychophysiology*. 3: 176–87.

ERIKSON, E. 1958. *Young Man Luther*. New York: Norton.

EVANS-WENTZ, W. Y., trans. *The Tibetan Book of the Dead*. New York: Oxford Univ. Press, 1960.

FARADAY, A. 1972. *Dream Power*. New York: Berkeley.

FARRINGTON, D. 1953. *Greek Science*. London: Penguin Books.

FEIFEL, HERMAN. 1959. *The Meaning of Death*. New York: McGraw-Hill.

FENZ, W. D., and PLAPP, J. M. 1970. Voluntary control of heart rate in a practitioner of yoga: negative findings. *Perceptual and Motor Skills*. 30: 493–94.

FERENCZI, S. 1926. An attempted explanation of some hysterical stigmata. In *Further Contributions to the Theory and Technique of Psychoanalysis*. London: Hogarth Press.

FEYNMAN, R. P., LEIGHTON, R. B., and SANDS, M. 1966. *The Feynman Lectures on Physics*. Reading, Mass.: Addison-Wesley.

FILBEY, R. A., and GAZZANIGA, M. S. 1969. Splitting the normal brain with reaction time. *Psychol. Sci.* 17: 335.

FINGARETTE, H. 1963. *The Self in Transformation*. New York: Basic Books.

FINLEY, WILLIAM W. 1971. The effect of feedback on the control of cardiac rate. *J. Psychol.* 77 (1): 43–54.

FISCHER, C. 1957. Study of the preliminary stages of the construction of dreams and images. *J. Am. Psychoanal. Assoc.* 5: 5–60.

————, and PAUL, I. H. 1959. The effect of subliminal visual stimulation on images and dreams: a validation study. *J. Am. Psychoanal. Assoc.* 7: 35–83.

FISCHER, E. D., and MANN, L. B. 1952. Shift of writing function to minor hemisphere at the age of 72 years: report of case with advanced left cerebral atrophy. *Bull. Los Angeles Neurol. Soc.* 17: 196–97.

FISHER, CHARLES. 1954. Dreams and perception: the role of preconscious and primary modes of perception in dream formation. *J. Am. Psychoanal. Assoc.* 2: 389–445.

————. 1956. Dreams, images, and perception: a study of unconscious-preconscious relationships. *J. Am. Psychoanal. Assoc.* 4: 5–48.

————. 1957. A study of the preliminary stages of the construction of dreams and images. *J. Am. Psychoanal. Assoc.* 5: 5–60.

FLEMINGER, J. J., DEL HORNE, D. J., NAIR, N. P. V., ET AL. 1970. Differential effect of unilateral and bilateral ECT. *Am. J. Psychiatry.* 127: 430–36.

FORBES, R. J. 1968. *The Conquest of Nature.* New York: Praeger.

FORD, K. W. 1965. *The World of Elementary Particles.* New York: Blaisdell.

FOULKES, D. 1964. Theories of dream formation and recent studies of sleep consciousness. *Psychol. Bull.* 62: 236.

FOX, S. W. 1971. Chemical origins of cells, part 2. *Chemical and Engineering News,* December 6, 1971.

FRANK, J. D. 1972. The bewildering world of psychotherapy. *J. Social Issues.* 28 (4): 27–44.

FRENCH, J. D. 1957. The reticular formation. *Scientific American.* 2–8.

FREUD, S. 1926. *Psychopathology of Everyday Life.* New York: MacMillan Co.

————. 1927. *The Ego and the Id* (1923). London: Hogarth Press.

————. 1950. *The Interpretation of Dreams*. New York: Modern Library.

————. 1954. Project for a scientific psychology. In *Origins of Psychoanalysis: Letters to Wilhelm Fliess, Drafts and Notes, 1887–1902*. New York: Basic Books.

FRIEDMAN, M., and ROSENMAN, RAY H. 1974. *Type A Behavior and Your Heart*. New York: Knopf.

FROMM, E. 1968. *The Revolution of Hope*. New York: Harper & Row.

FULLER, R. B. 1969. *Operating Manual for Spaceship Earth*. New York: Delta Books.

————. 1970. *Utopia or Oblivion*. New York: Bantam Books.

————. 1973. *Earth Inc.* New York: Doubleday.

FUNG, YU-LAN. 1958. *A Short History of Chinese Philosophy*. New York: Macmillan.

GAINOTTI, G. 1969. Reactions "catastrophiques" et manifestations d'indifférence au cours des atteintes cerébrales. *Neuropsychologia*. 7: 195–204.

GALAMBOS, R. 1956. Suppression of auditory nerve activity by stimulation of efferent fibers to cochlea. *J. Neurophysiol.* 19: 424–37.

GALBRAITH, J. K. 1967. *The New Industrial State*. Boston: Houghton Mifflin Co.

GALE, G. 1974. Chew's monadology. *Journal of the History of Ideas*. 35 (April–June, 1974): 339–48.

GALIN, D. 1974. Implications for psychiatry of left and right cerebral specialization. *Arch. Gen. Psychiatry*. 31: 572–83.

————, and ORNSTEIN, R. 1972. Lateral specialization of cognitive mode: an EEG study. *Psychophysiology*. 9: 412–18.

————. 1974. Individual differences in cognitive style: I. Reflective eye movements. *Neuropsychologia*. 12: 367–76.

GANNON, L., and STERNBACH, R. A. 1971. Alpha enhancement as a treatment for pain: a case study. In *Biofeedback and*

Self Control, ed. J. Stoyva, et al. Chicago: Aldine, Atherton.

GARDNER, E. 1968. *Fundamentals of Neurology.* Philadelphia: W. B. Saunders Co.

GAZZANIGA, M. S. 1970. *The Bisected Brain.* New York: Appleton-Century-Crofts.

————. 1971. Changing hemisphere dominance by changing reward probability in split-brain monkeys. *Exp. Neurol.* 33: 412–19.

————, and HILLYARD, S. A. 1971. Language and speech capacity of the right hemisphere. *Neuropsychologia.* 9: 273–80.

GLOBUS, GORDON G. 1973*a.* Unexpected symmetries in the 'World Knot.' *Science,* 180 (4091).

————. 1973*b.* Consciousness and brain. *Arch. Gen. Psychiatry.* 29: 153–77.

GOERTZEL, V., and GOERTZEL, M. G. 1962. *Cradles of Imminence.* Boston: Little, Brown & Co.

GOLEMAN, DANIEL. 1975. Meditation and consciousness: an Asian approach to mental health. *Am. J. Psychotherapy.* 41–54.

GOODWIN, B. C. 1973. Mathematical metaphor in development. *Nature.* 242: 207.

GORDON, H., and SPERRY, R. W. 1969. Lateralization of olfactory perception in the surgically separated hemispheres of man. *Neuropsychologia.* 7: 111–120.

GORDON, W. J. 1961. *Synectics.* New York: Harper & Row.

GOVINDA, L. A. 1969. Logic and symbol in the multi-dimensional conception of the universe. *Main Currents.* 25: 59–62.

————. 1974*a.* *Foundations of Tibetan Mysticism.* New York: Samuel Weiser.

————. 1974*b.* *The Psychological Attitude of Early Buddhist Philosophy.* New York: Samuel Weiser.

GRANIT, R. 1955. Centrifugal and antidromic effects on the ganglion cells of the retina. *J. Neurophysiology.* 1: 388–411.

GREELEY, A. and MCCREADY, W. 1975. Are we a nation of mystics? *New York Times Magazine,* January 26, 1975.

GREEN, A. 1974. Brainwave training, imagery, creativity and integrative experiences. *Proceedings of the Biofeedback Research Society,* Denver.

GREEN, E., and GREEN, A. 1971. How to make use of the field of mind theory. In *Varieties of Healing Experience.* Los Altos, Cal.: Academy of Parapsychology and Medicine.

GREEN, E. E., GREEN, A. M., and WALTERS, E. D. 1970. Voluntary control of internal states: psychological and physiological. *Journal of Transpersonal Psychology.* 2 (Part 1): 1–26.

————. 1971. Biofeedback for mind-body regulation: healing and creativity. Paper delivered at symposium on "The Varieties of Healing Experience." De Anza College, Cupertino, California.

GREEN, E. E., FERGUSON, J., GREEN, A., and WALTER, D. 1970. Voluntary control of internal states. Unpublished manuscript. Menninger Foundation.

GREGORY, R. L. 1967. *Eye and Brain.* London: Hutchinson.

GROF, STANISLAV. 1972. Varieties of transpersonal experiences: observations from LSD psychotherapy. *J. Trans. Psychol.* 4 (1): 45–80.

GROTJOHN, M. 1960. Ego identity and the fear of death and dying. *J. Hillside Hosp.* 9: 147.

GUENTHER, H. V., and KAWAMURA, L. S. 1975. *Mind in Buddhist Psychology.* Berkeley: Dharma Publishing.

GUTHRIE, W. K. C. 1969. *A History of Greek Philosophy.* Cambridge, Eng.: Cambridge Univ. Press.

HALL, M. N., HALL, G. C., and LAVOIE, P. 1968. Studies of psychological functions in patients with unilateral or bilateral-midline brain lesions. Paper presented at the 7th International Congress of Rorschach and Other Projective Techniques, London, August, 1968.

HALLIDAY, A. M., DAVISON, K., and BROWN, M. W., ET AL.

1968. Comparison of effects on depression and memory of bilateral ECT and unilateral ECT to the dominant and non-dominant hemisphere. *Br. J. Psychiatry.* 114: 997–1012.

HARMAN, W. W. 1975. The societal implications and social impact of psi phenomena. Address to the Eighteenth Annual Convention of the Parapsychological Association, Santa Barbara, Cal., August 22, 1975.

HAYES, W. 1971. Molecular genetics: an introductory background. In *The Social Impact of Modern Biology,* ed. W. Fuller, London: Routledge & Kegan Paul.

HÉCAEN, H. 1962. Clinical symptomatology in right and left hemispheric lesions. In *Interhemispheric Relations and Cerebral Dominance,* ed. V. B. Mountcastle. Baltimore: Johns Hopkins Press.

———, and AJURIAGUERRA, J. 1964. *Lefthandedness.* New York: Grune & Stratton.

HEILBRONER, R. L. 1960. *The Future as History.* New York: Harper & Row.

———. 1967. Do machines make history? *Technology and Culture.* 8 (3).

HEISENBERG, WERNER. 1958. *Physics and Philosophy.* New York: Harper Torchbooks.

———. 1971. *Physics and Beyond.* New York: Harper & Row.

———. 1973. Smithsonian presentation in memory of Copernicus. *Science News.* 103 (May 5).

———. 1974. *Across the Frontier.* New York: Harper & Row.

HERNANDEZ-PEON, R. 1963. Neurophysiological mechanisms of wakefulness and sleep. Paper presented at the International Congress of Psychology. Washington, D.C.

HERRIGEL, E. 1971. *Zen in the Art of Archery.* New York: Vintage Books.

HESS, W. R. 1957. *Functional Organization of the Diencephalon.* New York: Grune & Stratton.

HILGARD, E. 1965. *Hypnotic Susceptibility.* New York: Harcourt, Brace & World.

HILL, D. 1952. EEG in episodic psychiatric and psychopathic behavior. *EEG Clin. Neurol.* 4: 419.

HOFF, E. C., KELL, J. F., and CARROLL, M. N. 1963. Effects of cortical stimulation and lesions on cardiovascular function. *Physiol. Rev.* 43: 68–114.

HOFFER, A., and OSMOND, H. 1967. *The Hallucinogens*. New York: Academic Press.

HOFFER, E. 1951. *The True Believer*. New York: Harper & Row.

HOLLOWAY, F. A., and PARSONS, O. A. 1969. Unilateral brain damage and bilateral skin conductance levels in humans. *Psychophysiology*. 6: 138–48.

HOLMES, T. H., and MASUDA, M. 1970. Life change and illness susceptibility. Paper presented as part of Symposium on Separation and Depression: Clinical and Research Aspects, at the Annual Meeting of the American Association for the Advancement of Science. Chicago, December, 1970.

HOLMES, T. H., and RAHE, R. H. 1967a. Schedule of recent experience (SRE). University of Washington School of Medicine, Department of Psychiatry.

————. 1967b. The social readjustment rating scale. *J. Psychosomatic Res.* 11: 213–18.

HOLMES, T. S., and HOLMES, T. H. 1970. Short-term intrusions into the life style routine. *J. Psychosomatic Res.* 14: 121–32.

HOMMES, O. R., and PANHUYSEN, L. H. H. M. 1970. Bilateral intracarotid Amytal injection. *Psychiatr. Neurol. Neurochir.* 73: 447–59.

————. 1971. Depression and cerebral dominance. *Psychiatr. Neurol. Neurochir.* 74: 259–70.

HORD, DAVID, and BARBER, JOSEPH. 1971. Alpha control: effectiveness of two kinds of feedback. *Psychonomic Science.* 25 (3): 151–54.

HOROWITZ, M. J. 1972. Modes of representation of thought. *J. Am. Psychoanal. Assoc.* 20: 793–819.

HOUSTON, J. 1975. Putting the first man on earth. *Saturday Review*, February 22, 1975.

HOYLE, F. 1955. *Frontiers of Astronomy*. New York: Harper & Row.

————. 1960. *The Nature of the Universe.* New York: Harper & Row.

HUBBARD, L. R. 1951. *Science of Survival: Prediction of Human Behavior.* Sussex, England: The Publications Organization.

————. 1954. *The Creation of Human Ability.* Los Angeles: American Saint Hill Organization.

HUME, R. E. 1934. *The Thirteen Principal Upanishads.* New York: Oxford Univ. Press.

HUMPHREY, M. E., and ZANGWILL, O. L. 1951. Cessation of dreaming after brain injury. *J. Neurol. Neurosurg. Psychiatry.* 14: 322–25.

HUNTER, R. 1967. On the experience of nearly dying. *Am. J. Psychiatry.* 124: 84–88.

HUTCHINS, R. M. 1968. *The Learning Society.* New York: Praeger.

HUXLEY, A. 1945. *The Perennial Philosophy.* New York: Harper & Brothers.

HUXLEY, J. 1947. *Touchstone for Ethics.* New York: Harper & Brothers.

————. 1963. The future of man: evolutionary aspects. In *Man and His Future,* ed. G. Wolstenholme. Boston: Little, Brown & Co.

————. 1968. Preface to *Runaway World: A Symposium on Man and His Future,* ed. E. Leach. Oxford, Eng.: Oxford Univ. Press.

IBERALL, A. 1972. *Toward General Science of Viable Systems.* New York: McGraw-Hill.

INKELES, A. 1960. Industrial man. *Amer. J. Sociology.* 66 (July, 1960).

————. 1969. Making men modern: on the causes and consequences of individual change in six developing countries. *Amer. J. Sociology.* 75 (2).

JAEGER, W. 1965. *Paideia: The Ideals of Greek Culture.* 2nd ed. Oxford, Eng.: Oxford Univ. Press.

JAIN, MISHRILAL, and JAIN, KAMAL, M. 1973. The science of yoga: a study in perspective. *Perspectives in Biology & Medicine.* (Autumn, 1973): 93–102.

JAMES, WILLIAM. 1935. *The Varieties of Religious Experience.* New York: Longmans, Green & Co.

JARVIS, H. F. 1953. Episodic rage, theta rhythms and obsession. *J. Mental Sci.* 99: 253–56.

JEANS, J. H. 1937. *The Mysterious Universe.* Cambridge, Eng.: Cambridge Univ. Press.

———. 1951. *The Growth of Physical Science.* Cambridge, Eng.: Cambridge Univ. Press.

JOHNSON, C. 1966. *Revolutionary Change.* Boston: Little, Brown & Co.

JOHNSON, J. D., and GAZZANIGA, M. S. 1971. Reversal behavior in split-brain monkeys. *Physiol. Behav.* 6: 707–09.

JOHNSON, LAVERNE C. 1970. A psychophysiology for all states. *Psychophysiology.* 6: 501–16.

JOHNSON, R. 1957. *Nurslings of Immortality.* New York: Harper & Brothers.

JOHNSSON, A., ET AL. 1972. A feedback model for biological rhythms. I. Mathematical description and basic properties of the model. *J. Theor. Biol.* 36: 153–74.

KAHN, H., and BRIGGS, B. BRUCE. 1972. *Things to Come.* New York: Macmillan.

KAHN, H., and WEINER, A. 1967. *The Year 2000: A Framework for Speculation on the Next Thirty-Three Years.* New York: Macmillan.

KAMIYA, JOE. 1968. Conscious control of brain waves. *Psychology Today.* 1: 57–60.

———. 1969. Operant control of the EEG Alpha rhythm and some of its reported effects on consciousness. In *Altered States of Consciousness,* ed. C. Tart. New York: John Wiley.

———., ed. 1971. *Biofeedback and Self Control.* An Aldine

reader on the regulation of bodily processes and consciousness. Chicago: Aldine, Atherton. DNLM: WL 102 K156.

KAPITZA, P. L. 1962. The future of science. *Bulletin of the Atomic Scientists.* 18 (April, 1962): 3–7.

KAPLEAU, P. 1967. *Three Pillars of Zen.* Boston: Beacon Press.

KARLSSON, H. G., ET AL. 1972. A feedback model for biological rhythms. II. Comparisons with experimental results, especially on the petal thythm of Kalanchae. *J. Theor. Biol.* 36: 175–94.

KASAMATSU, A., and KIRAI, T. 1966a. Studies of EEG's of expert Zen meditators. *Folia Psychiatrica Neurologica Japonica.* 28: 315.

———. 1966b. An electroencephalographic study on Zen meditation. *Folia Psychiatrica Neurologica Japonica.* 20: 315–36. Reprinted in Tart (1969).

KASTENBAUM, R. 1965. The realm of death: an emerging area in psychological research. *J. Human Relations.* 13: 538–52.

———, and AISENBERG, R. 1972. *The Psychology of Death.* New York: Springer Verlag.

KENNARD, M. A. 1953. The EEG in psychological disorders, a review. *Psychosomatic Medicine.* 15: 95–115.

———, and SCHWARTZMAN, A. E. 1956. A longitudinal study of changes in EEG frequency patterns as related to psychological changes. *J. Nerv. Ment. Dis.* 124: 8–20.

KENNETT, J. 1972. *Selling Water by the River.* New York: Vintage Books.

KEYNES, G., ed. 1969. *Blake: Complete Writings.* New York: Oxford Univ. Press.

KIEFER, DURAND. 1971. EEG alpha feedback and subjective states of consciousness: subject's introspective overview. *Psychologia: An International Journal of Psychology in the Orient.* 14 (1): 3–14.

KINSBOURNE, M. 1970. The cerebral basis of lateral asymmetries in attention. *Acta Psychologica.* 33. In *Attention and Performance III,* ed. A. F. Saunders, pp. 193–201. Amsterdam: North Holland Publishing Co.

————. 1972. Eye and head turning indicates cerebral lateralization. *Science*. 176: 539–41.

KIRK, G. S. 1970. *Heraclitus: The Cosmic Fragments*. Cambridge, Eng.: Cambridge Univ. Press.

KLEIN, G. S. 1959. Consciousness in psychoanalytic theory. *J. Am. Psychoanal. Assoc*. 7: 5–34.

KLEITMAN, N., and DEMENT, W. C. 1957. The relation of eye movements during sleep to dream activity: an objective study of dreaming. *J. Exp. Psychol*. 53: 339.

KNOTT, J. R. 1965. EEGs in psychopathic personality and in murderers. In *Applications of EEG in Psychiatry: A Symposium,* ed. W. P. Wilson. Durham, N. C.: Duke Univ. Press.

KOESTLER, A. 1968. *The Ghost in the Machine*. New York: Macmillan.

————. 1972. *The Roots of Consciousness*. New York: Random House.

KOHLBERG, L. 1969. Stage and sequence: the cognitive-developmental approach to socialization. In *Handbook of Socialization Theory and Research,* ed. D. Goslin. New York: Rand McNally.

KOGA, Y., and AKISHIGE, Y. 1970. Psychological study on Zen and counseling. In *Psychological Studies on Zen,* ed. Y. Akishige. Tokyo: Zen Institute of Komazawa University.

KORZYBSKI, A. 1958. *Science and Sanity*. Lakeville, Conn.: The International Non-Aristotelean Library.

KOZYREV, N. A. 1968. Possibility of experimental study of the properties of time. Washington, D.C.: Joint Publications Research Service. No. 45238. May 2, 1968.

KREITMAN, N., and SHAW, J. C. 1965. Experimental enhancement of alpha activity. *EEG and Clinical Neurophysiology*. 18: 147–55.

KRIPPNER, S. 1967. The ten commandments that block creativity. *Gifted Child Quart*. Autumn, 1967, pp. 144–56.

————. 1969. The psychedelic state, the hypnotic trance, and the creative act. In *Altered States of Consciousness,* ed. C. Tart. New York: John Wiley & Sons.

————, and HUGHES, 1970. *Psychology Today.*

KRIPPNER, S., and MEACHAM, W. 1968. Consciousness and the creative process. *Gifted Child Quart.* Autumn, 1968.

KRISHNAMURTI, J. 1969. *Freedom from the Known.* New York: Harper & Row.

KRUEGER, A. P. 1973. Preliminary consideration of the biological significance of air ions. In *The Nature of Human Consciousness,* ed. R. Ornstein. San Francisco: W. H. Freeman.

KUBIE, L. 1958 *Neurotic Distortion of the Creative Process.* Lawrence, Kan.: Univ. of Kansas Press.

KUHN, THOMAS. 1962. *The Structure of Scientific Revolutions.* Chicago: Univ. of Chicago Press.

LANSDELL, D. H. 1952. *Nature.*

LAO TZU. Ca. sixth century B. C. *Tao Te Ching.* Translated by Ch'u Ta-Kao. New York: Samuel Weiser, 1973. Translated by Gia-Fu Feng and Jane English. New York: Vintage Books, 1972.

LASHLEY, K. S. 1929. *Brain Mechanisms and Intelligence.* Chicago: Univ. of Chicago Press.

LASZLO, E. 1972a. *The Systems View of the World.* New York: Braziller.

————. 1972b. *Introduction to Systems Philosophy.* New York: Gordon & Breach.

LAWRENCE, JODY. 1972. *Alpha Brain Waves.* Los Angeles: Nash. DNLM: WL 102 L421a.

LAWTON, R., and TRENT, P. 1972. *The Image Makers.* New York: McGraw-Hill.

LEE, D. 1950. Codifications of reality: lineal and nonlineal. *Psychosom. Med.* 12: 89–97.

LEGGETT, T. A. 1972. *A First Zen Reader.* Rutland, Vermont: C. E. Tuttle.

LESHAN, L. 1969a. Physicists and mystics: similarities in world view. *J. Transpersonal Psych.* 1 (2).

————. 1969b. *Toward a General Theory of the Paranormal.* New York: Parapsychology Foundation.

LESTER, D. 1967. Experimental and correlational studies in the fear of death. *Psychol. Bull.* 67: 27–36.

LEVY, J. 1969. Possible basis for the evolution of lateral specialization of the human brain. *Nature.* 224: 614–15.

———. 1970. *Information Processing and Higher Psychological Functions in the Disconnected Hemispheres of Human Commissurotomy Patients.* Thesis, California Institute of Technology.

———, NEBES, R., and SPERRY, R. W. 1971. Expressive language in the surgically separated minor hemisphere. *Cortex.* 7: 49–58.

LEVY, J., TREVARTHEN, C., and SPERRY, R. W. 1972. Perception of bilateral chimeric figures following hemispheric deconnexion. *Brain.* 95: 61–78.

LEX, BARBARA W. 1974. Voodoo death: new thoughts on an old explanation. *Am. Anthropol.* 76: 818–23.

LIFTON, ROBERT JAY. 1968. Adaptation and value development: self-process in protean man. In *The Development and Acquisition of Values,* report of a conference. National Institute of Child Health and Human Development. Washington, D. C. 15–17 May, 1968.

——— and OLSON, ERIC. 1974. *Living and Dying.* New York: Praeger.

LILLY, J. C. 1972a. *The Human Biocomputer.* New York: Julian Press.

———. 1972b. *The Center of the Cyclone.* New York: Julian Press.

LIVINGSTON, R. B. 1959. Central control of receptors and sensory transmission systems. In *Handbook of Physiology-Neurophysiology,* ed. H. W. Magoun, pp. 741–60. 1st ed. Washington, D.C.: American Physiological Society.

LONEGRAN, B. 1957. *Insight: A Study of Human Understanding.* London: Longmans.

LORENS, S. A., and DARROW, C. W. 1962. Eye movements, EEG, GSR, and EKG during mental multiplication. *EEG and Clinical Neurophysiology.* 14: 739–46.

LORENZ, K. 1966. *On Aggression*. New York: Harcourt, Brace & World.

LOVEJOY, A. O. 1936. *The Great Chain of Being*. New York: Harper & Brothers.

LOVELL, A. C. B. 1959. *The Individual and the Universe*. New York: Harper.

————. 1967. *Our Present Knowledge of the Universe*. Cambridge, Mass.: Harvard Univ. Press.

LUBORSKY, L., and SHEURIN, H. 1956. Dreams and day residues: a study of the Poetzl observation. *Bulletin of the Menninger Clinic*. 20: 135–48.

LUCE, G. 1971. *Biological Rhythm in Human and Animal Physiology*. New York: Dover Books.

LUCKMANN, B. 1970. The small life-worlds of modern man. *Social Res*. 37 (4).

LUTHE, W. 1963. Autogenic training: method, research and application in medicine. *Amer. J. Psychotherapy*. 17: 174–95. Reprinted in Tart (1969).

LYNCH, J. J., ET AL. 1971. On the mechanisms of the feedback control of human brain wave activity. *J. Nerv. Ment. Dis*. 153: 205–17.

McADAM, D. W., and WHITAKER, H. A. 1971. Language production: electroencephalographic localization in the normal human brain. *Science*. 172: 499–502.

McBAIN, W. N. 1970. Quasi-sensory communication: an investigation using semantic matching and accentuated effect. *J. Personality and Social Psych*. 14: 281–91.

McCLURE, C. M. 1959. Cardiac arrest through volition. *California Medicine*. 90: 440–41.

McKEE, G., HUMPHREY, B., and McADAM, D. 1973. Scaled lateralization of alpha activity during linguistic and musical tasks. *Psychophysiology*. 10: 441–43.

McKEEVER, W. F., and HULING, M. 1970. Left cerebral hemisphere superiority in tachistoscopic word recognition performance. *Percept. Mot. Skills*. 30: 763–66.

MCKELLAR, P., and SIMPSON, L. 1954. Between wakefulness and sleep. *Brit. J. Psychol.* 45: 266–76.

MACLEAN, P. 1962. New findings relevant to the evolution of psychosexual functions of the brain. *J. Nerv. Ment. Dis.* 135: 289–301.

MAHARISHI MAHESH YOGI, trans. *Bhagavad Gita.* Chapters 1–6. With commentary. Baltimore: Penguin Books, 1973.

MARGENAU, H. 1950. *The Nature of Physical Reality.* New York: McGraw-Hill.

———. 1963. Philosophy of physical science in the twentieth century. In *The Evolution of Science,* ed. G. S. Metraux and F. Crouzet. New York: Mentor Books.

———. 1966. ESP in the framework of modern science. *Amer. Soc. Psychical Res.* 60 (3).

MARKLEY, O. W., et al. 1974. Changing images of man. Report No. 4, Center for the Study of Social Policy, SRL, Menlo Park, California.

MARTIN, P. W. 1955. *Experiment in Depth.* London: Routledge & Kegan Paul.

MARUYAMA, M. 1960. Morphogenesis and morphostasis. *Methodos.* 12 (48).

———. 1963. The second cybernetics: deviation-amplifying mutual causal processes. *Amer. Scientist.* 51 (2): 164–79.

———. 1967. The Navaho philosophy: an esthetic ethic of mutuality. *Mental Hygiene.* 51 (2): 242–49.

MASCARO, J., trans. *Bhagavad Gita.* Baltimore: Penguin Books, 1970.

———., trans. *The Dhammapada.* Baltimore: Penguin Books, 1973.

MASLOW, A. 1962. *Toward a Psychology of Being.* New York: Van Nostrand Reinhold.

MASTERS, R. E., and HOUSTON, J. 1966. *Varieties of Psychedelic Experience.* New York: Holt, Rinehart & Winston.

MATSUMOTO, H. 1970. A psychological study of the relation between respiratory function and emotion. In *Psychological*

Studies on Zen, ed. Y. Akishige. Tokyo: Zen Institute of Komazawa University.

MAUPIN, E. W. 1965. Individual differences in response to a Zen meditation exercise. *J. Consulting Psychol.* 29: 139–43.

MAY, R. 1966. *Psychology and the Human Dilemma.* New York: Van Nostrand Reinhold.

MEAD, M. 1957. Toward more vivid utopias. *Science.* 126 (3280): 95–961.

————. 1964. *Continuities in Cultural Evolution.* New Haven, Conn.: Yale Univ. Press.

————, and PAUL BYERS. 1968. *The Small Conference.* New York: Humanities Press.

MEHRA, J., ED. 1973. *The Physicist's Conception of Nature.* Dordrecht, Holland: D. Reidel.

MEISSNER, W. W. 1958. Affective responses to psychoanalytic death symbols. *J. Abnorm. Soc. Psychol.* 56: 295–99.

METZNER, R. 1968. On the evolutionary significance of psychedelics. *Main Currents.* 25 (1).

MEYER, D. R. 1972. Access to engrams. *American Psychologist.* 27: 124–33.

MEYER, R. J., and HAGGERTY, R. J. 1962. Streptococcal infections in families. *Pediatrics.* 29: 539–49.

MIKURIYA, T. H., PELLETIER, K. R., and GLADMAN, A. E. 1976a. Unstable sub-beta EEG with beta tracking failure in psychiatric dysfunction. *Proceedings of the Biofeedback Society of California.* San Diego.

————. 1976b. Spasmodic acute and chronic dysrhythmic subbeta EEG: psychiatric implications. *Proceedings of the Biofeedback Research Society.* Denver.

MILLER, E. 1971. Handedness and the pattern of human ability. *Br. J. Psychol.* 62: 111–12.

MILLER, N. E. 1971. Learned modifications of autonomic functions: a review and some new data. In *Biofeedback and Self Control 1970,* ed. T. X. Barber, et al. Chicago: Aldine, Atherton.

MILNER, B. 1967. Cited by Rossi, G. F., and Rosadini, G. R. Experimental analysis of cerebral dominance in man. In *Brain Mechanisms Underlying Speech and Language,* ed. D. H. Millikan and F. L. Darley, p. 177 ff. New York: Grune & Stratton.

MIURA, I., and FULLER-SASAKI, R. 1965. *The Zen Koan.* New York: Harcourt, Brace & World.

MONOD, J. 1971. *Chance and Necessity.* New York: Random House.

MORRELL, L. K., and SALAMY, J. G. 1971. Hemispheric asymmetry of electrocortical responses to speech stimuli. *Science.* 174: 164–66.

MOUNTCASTLE, V. B., ED. 1962. *Interhemispheric Relations and Cerebral Dominance.* Baltimore: Johns Hopkins.

MULHOLLAND, T. B. 1969. Feedback method: a new look at functional EEG. *Electroenceph. Clin. Neurophysiol.* 27: 688.

———, and PEPER, ERIK. 1971. Occipital alpha and accomodative vergence, pursuit tracking, and fast eye movements. *Psychophysiology.* 8 (5): 556–75.

MUMFORD, L. 1956. *The Transformations of Man.* New York: Harper & Brothers.

MUNDY-CASTLE, A. C. 1957. The EEG and mental activity. *EEG and Clinical Neurophysiology.* 9: 643–55.

MURPHY, MICHAEL. 1972. *Golf in the Kingdom.* New York: Delta.

MURTI, T. R. V. 1955. *The Central Philosophy of Buddhism.* London: Allen & Unwin.

MUSÈS, C. 1972. Working with the hypernumber idea. In *Consciousness and Reality: The Human Pivot Point,* ed. C. Musès and A. M. Young. New York: Outerbridge & Lazard.

———, and YOUNG, A. M., EDS. 1972. *Consciousness and Reality: The Human Pivot Point.* New York: Outerbridge & Lazard.

MYERS, F. W. H. 1903. *Human Personality and Its Survival of Bodily Death.* New York: Longmans, Green & Co.

288 Bibliography

NEBES, R. 1971a. Handedness and the perception of the part-whole relationship. *Cortex.* 7: 350–56.

———. 1971b. Superiority of the minor hemisphere in commissurotomized man for perception of part-whole relations. *Cortex.* 7: 333–49.

NEEDHAM, J. 1956. *Science and Civilization in China.* Vol. 2. Cambridge, Eng.: Cambridge Univ. Press.

NEIHARDT, JOHN G. 1961. *Black Elk Speaks: Being the life story of a holy man of the Oglala Sioux, as told through John G. Neihardt (Flaming Rainbow).* Lincoln, Nebraska: Univ. of Nebraska Press.

NOYES, RUSSELL, JR., and KLETTI, ROY. 1976. When you think you're going to die. *Behavior Today,* February 16, 1976, p. 5.

OATES, J. C. 1972. New heaven and earth. *Saturday Review,* November 4, 1972.

OKUMA, T., KOGU, E., IKEDA, K., and SUGIYAMA, H. 1957. The EEG of yoga and Zen practitioners. *Electroencephalography and Clinical Neurophysiology.* Supplement 9, p. 51.

OPPENHEIMER, J. R. 1954 *Science and the Common Understanding.* New York: Oxford Univ. Press.

ORNE, M. 1959. The nature of hypnosis: artifact and essence. *J. Social and Ab. Psych.* 58: 277–99.

ORNSTEIN, R. E. 1972. *The Psychology of Consciousness.* San Francisco: W. H. Freeman.

OSBORNE, SALLY R. 1972. Autoregulation of phase relations between left and right occipital brain potentials through the use of immediate biological feedback. *Dissertation Abstracts International.* 32 (8-B): 4901.

OSTRANDER, S., and SCHROEDER, L. 1970. *Psychic Discoveries Behind the Iron Curtain.* New York: Prentice Hall.

OSWALD, I. 1957. The EEG, visual imagery and attention. *Quarterly Journal of Experimental Psychology.* 9: 113–18.

OUSPENSKY, P. D. 1934. *A New Model of the Universe.* New York: Knopf.

PATANJALI. 1953. *How to Know God: The Yoga Aphorisms of Patanjali*. Translated with a commentary by Swami Prabhavananda and C. Isherwood. New York: Harper & Brothers.

PATTISON, E. M. 1967. The experience of dying. *Am. J. Psychotherapy*. 21 (1): 32–43.

PEARCE, J. C. 1971. *The Crack in the Cosmic Egg*. New York: Julian Press.

PELLETIER, K. R. 1974*a*. Altered attention deployment in meditation. In *The Psychobiology of Transcendental Meditation,* ed. D. Kanellakos and J. Lukas. Reading, Mass.: W. A. Benjamin Press.

————. 1974*b*. Influence of transcendental meditation upon autokinetic perception. *Journal of Perceptual and Motor Skills*. 39: 1031–34.

————. 1974*c*. Neurological, psychophysiological, and clinical differentiation of the alpha and theta altered states of consciousness. *Dissertation Abstracts International*. 35/1, 74–14, 806.

————. 1974*d*. Neurological, psychophysiological, and clinical parameters of alpha, theta, and the voluntary control of bleeding and pain. *Proceedings of the Biofeedback Research Society*. Denver.

————. 1974*e*. Psychophysiological parameters of the voluntary control of blood flow and pain. In *The Psychobiology of Transcendental Meditation,* ed. D. Kanellakos and J. Lukas. Reading, Mass.: W. A. Benjamin Press.

————. 1975*a*. Diagnosis, procedure, and phenomenology of clinical biofeedback. *Proceedings of the Biofeedback Research Society*. Denver.

————. 1975*b*. Diagnostic and treatment protocols for clinical biofeedback. *Journal of Biofeedback,* Fall/Winter, 1975. 2 (4).

————. 1975*c*. I shall feel no pain and bleed no blood. In *Psychology and Life,* ed. P. G. Zimbardo and F. L. Ruch. Glenview, Ill.: Scott, Foresman & Co.

————. 1975*d*. Mind as healer, mind as slayer. *Lifelong Learning* Berkeley: University of California Press.

290 Bibliography

————. 1975e. Neurological substrates of consciousness: Implications for psychosomatic medicine. *Journal of Altered States of Consciousness.* 2 (1).

————. 1975f. Theory and applications of clinical biofeedback. *Journal of Contemporary Psychotherapy.* 7 (1).

————. 1976a. Applications of meditative exercises in enhancing clinical biofeedback outcome. *Proceedings of the Biofeedback Research Society.* Denver.

————. 1976b. Holistic applications of clinical biofeedback and meditation. *Journal of Holistic Health.* 1.

————. 1976c. Increased perceptual acuity following transcendental meditation. In *Scientific Research on Transcendental Meditation: Collected Papers,* ed. L. Domash, J. Farrow, and D. Orme-Johnson. Los Angeles: Maharishi International Univ. Press.

————. 1976d. *Psychosomatic Medicine.* Announcement of the Gladman Psychosomatic Medicine Center, Berkeley.

————. 1976e. What to tell your patients when they ask about biofeedback. *Extension Division Catalog,* University of California School of Medicine, Los Angeles.

————. "Mind as Healer, Mind as Slayer." *Psychology Today.* February, 1977.

————. 1977. *Mind as Healer, Mind as Slayer: A Holistic Approach to Overcoming Stress.* New York: Delacorte Press.

————, and GARFIELD, C. 1976. *Consciousness: East and West.* New York: Harper & Row.

PELLETIER, K. R., and PEPER, E. 1974. The chutzpah factor in psychophysiological parameters of altered states of consciousness. *Proceedings of the Biofeedback Research Society.* Denver.

————. 1977a. The chutzpah factor in altered states of consciousness. *Journal of Humanistic Psychology.* 17 (1). Reprinted in *Transpersonal Education,* ed. C. G. Hendricks. Englewood Cliffs, N.J.: Prentice-Hall.

————. 1977b. "Developing a biofeedback model: alpha EEG as a means for pain control." *The International Journal of Clinical and Experimental Hypnosis.* XXV, 4, 361–371.

PELLETIER, K. R., GLADMAN, A. E., and MIKURIYA, T. H. 1976. Clinical protocols: professional group specializing in psychosomatic medicine. Berkeley: Autogenic Systems.

PENFIELD, WILDER. 1976. *The Mystery of the Mind.* Princeton, N. J.: Princeton Univ. Press.

PEPER, ERIK. 1970. Feedback regulation of the alpha electroencephalogram activity through control of the internal and external parameters. *Kybernetik.* 7 (3): 107–12.

———. 1971a. Comment on feedback training of parietal-occipital alpha asymmetry in normal human subjects. *Kybernetik.* 9: 156–58.

———. 1971b. Reduction of efferent motor commands during alpha feedback as a facilitator of EEG alpha and a precondition for changes in consciousness. *Kybernetik.* 9: 226–31.

———. 1973. Biofeedback as a core technique in clinical therapies. Paper presented at the 81st Annual Convention of the American Psychological Association, Montreal.

PERLS, F. S. 1969. *Gestalt Therapy Verbatim.* Lafayette, California: Real People Press.

PERRY, J. W. 1962. Reconstitutive process in the psychopathology of the self. *Ann. N. Y. Acad. Sci.* 96: 853–76.

PIETSCH, PAUL. 1972. Shuffle brain. *Harper's Magazine,* May, 1972.

PINES, MAYA. 1973. *The Brain Changers: Scientists and the New Mind Control.* New York: Harcourt Brace Jovanovich.

PLATO, *Timaeus.* Translated by R. G. Bury. London: Loeb Classical Library, 1929.

POETZL, O. 1960. The relation between experimentally induced dream images and indirect vision. *Psychological Issues.* 2 (3).

POLAK, F. 1973. *The Image of the Future.* Translated and abridged by E. Boulding. San Francisco: Jossey-Bass. Original Dutch edition, 1951.

POLANYI, K. 1944. *The Great Transformation.* New York: Holt.

POLANYI, M. 1958. *Personal Knowledge*. New York: Harper & Row.

———. 1966. *The Tacit Dimension*. London: Routledge & Kegan Paul.

POLLEN, DANIEL A., and TRACHTENBERG, MICHAEL, C. 1972. Alpha rhythm and eye movements in eidetic imagery. *Nature*. 237: 109.

PRESMAN, A. S. 1970. *Electromagnetic Fields and Life*. New York: Plenum Press.

PRIBRAM, K. H. 1962. The neuropsychology of Sigmund Freud. In *Experimental Foundations for Clinical Psychology*, ed. A. J. Bachrach. New York: Basic Books.

———. 1971. *Languages of the Brain: Experimental Paradoxes and Principles in Neuropsychology*. Englewood Cliffs, N. J.: Prentice-Hall.

———. 1974. Holonomy and structure in the organization of perception. Preprint from the Department of Psychology, Stanford University. Stanford, California.

PRINCE, R. 1971. Interest disorders. *Journal for the Study of Consciousness*. 4:62–82.

QUARTON, G. 1967. Deliberate efforts to control human behavior and modify personality. *Daedalus*. 96 (3).

QUIGLEY, C. 1961. *Evolution of Civilizations*. New York: Macmillan.

RADHAKRISHNAN, S. 1958. *Indian Philosophy*. New York: Macmillan.

RAHE, R. H. 1969. Life crisis and health change. In *Psychotropic Drug Response: Advance in Prediction*. Springfield, Ill.: C. C. Thomas.

———. 1973. Life-change measurement as a predictor of illness. *Proceedings of the Royal Society of Medicine*. 61: 1124–26.

———, ET AL. 1964. Social stress and illness onset. *J. Psychosom. Res*. 8: 35–44.

RAKSTIS, T. J. 1968. Helping cancer victims come back. *Today's Health*. 46: 40–41.

RAPAPORT, D. 1967. States of consciousness: a psychopathological and psychodynamic view. In *Collected Papers of David Rapaport,* ed. M. M. Gill., pp. 385–404. New York: Basic Books.

RASHKIS, H. A. 1952. Systemic stress as an inhibitor of experimental tumors in Swiss mice. *Science*. 116: 169–71.

REICH, CHARLES, A. 1970. *The Greening of America*. New York: Random House.

REINHOLD, H. A., ED. 1944. *The Soul Afire: Revelations of the Mystics*. Meridian Books. Reprinted 1960.

RHINE, L. E. 1961. *Hidden Channels of the Mind*. New York: W. Sloane Assoc.

––––––. 1970. *Mind over Matter*. New York: Macmillan.

RHUDICK, P., and DIBNER, A. 1961. Age, personality, and health correlates of death concerns in normal aged individuals. *Journal of Gerontology*. 16: 44–49.

RICHTER, C. P. 1957. On the phenomenon of sudden death in animals and man. *Psychosomatic Medicine*. 19: 191–98.

RICKETT, W. A., trans. 1965. *Kuan-Tzu*. Hong Kong: Hong Kong Univ. Press.

RIZZOLATTI, G., UMILTA, C., and BERLUCCHI, G. 1971. Opposite superiorities of the right and left cerebral hemispheres in discriminative reaction time to physiognomical and alphabetical material. *Brain*. 94: 431–42.

RORVIK, D. M. 1970. Brain waves. *Look*. 34: 88–95.

––––––. 1973. The Theta Experience. *Saturday Review: Sciences*. 1 (4): 46–51.

ROSEN, DAVID H. 1975. Suicide survivors: a follow-up study of persons who survived jumping from the Golden Gate and San Francisco–Oakland Bay Bridges. *Western Journal of Medicine*. 137: 289–94.

ROSENTHAL, ROBERT. 1966. *Experimenter Effects in Behavioral Research*. New York: Appleton-Century-Crofts.

ROSS, N. W. 1966. *Three Ways of Asian Wisdom*. New York: Simon & Schuster.

Rossi, G. F., and Rosadini, G. R. 1967. Experimental analysis of cerebral dominance in man. In *Brain Mechanisms Underlying Speech and Language,* ed. D. H. Millikan and F. L. Darley, pp. 167–84. New York: Grune & Stratton.

Roszak, Theodore. 1974. Science and its public: the changing relationship. *Daedalus.* Summer.

Rothenberg, Albert. 1971. The process of Janusian thinking in creativity. *Arch. Gen. Psychiatry.* 24: 195–295.

Ruffini, R. 1973. Neutron Stars and Black Holes in Our Galaxy. *Trans. N.Y. Acad. Sci.* 35.

Russell, B. 1945. *History of Western Philosophy.* New York: Simon & Schuster.

Sachs, M. 1969. Space time and elementary interactions in relativity. *Physics Today.* 22: 51–60.

Salk, J. 1972. *Man Unfolding.* New York: Harper & Row.

———. 1973. *The Survival of the Wisest.* New York: Harper & Row.

Sargent, J. D., Green, E. E., and Walters, E. D. 1973. Preliminary report on the use of autogenic feedback techniques in the treatment of migraine and tension headaches. *Psychosomatic Medicine.* 35 (3): 129–35.

Satyanarayanamurthi, G. V., and Sastry, P. B. 1958. A preliminary scientific investigation into some of the unusual physiological manifestations acquired as a result of yogic practices in India. *Wiener Zeitschrift Für Nervenheilkunde.* 15: 239–49.

Saunders, M. G., and Zubek, J. P. 1967. EEG changes in perceptual and ·sensory deprivation. *Electroencephalography and Clinical Neurophysiology.* Supplement 25, pp. 246–56.

Schacter, S. 1964. The interaction of cognitive and physiological determinants of emotional states. In *Advances in Experimental Social Psychology,* ed. L. Berkowitz. Vol. 1. New York: Academic Press.

Schaefer, S., et al. 1973. Operant control of autonomic functions: biofeedback bibliography. *Percept. Mot. Skills.* 36: 863–75.

SCHILPP, P. A., ED. 1949. *Albert Einstein: Philosopher-Scientist*. The Library of Living Philosophers. Evanston, Ill.: Open Court Publishing Co.

SCHLEGEL, R. 1972. *Inquiry into Science*. New York: Doubleday.

SCHMEIDLER, GERTRUDE, and LEWIS, LARRY. 1971. Mood changes after alpha feedback training. *Perceptual and Motor Skills*. 32 (3): 709–10.

SCHWAB, J. J. 1970. Comprehensive medicine and the concurrence of physical and mental illness. *Psychosomatics*. II (6): 591–95.

SCHWARTZ, G., DAVIDSON, R. J., MAER, F., ET AL. 1973. Patterns of hemispheric dominance in musical, emotional, verbal and spatial tasks. Read before the Society for Psychophysiological Research, New Orleans, 1973.

SCHWARTZ, G. E., DAVIDSON, R. J., MAER, F., and BROMFIELD, E. 1974. *Psychophysiology*. 11 (2): 227.

SCHWARZ, JACK. 1977. *The Path of Action*. New York: E. P. Dutton.

SCIAMA, D. W. 1959. *The Unity of the Universe*. London: Faber & Faber.

SELIGMAN, D. 1969. What they believe: a Fortune survey. *Fortune*, January, 1969.

SELYE, H. 1950. *The Physiology and Pathology of Exposure to Stress*. Montreal: Acta.

———. 1956. *The Stress of Life*. New York: McGraw-Hill.

———. 1974. *Stress Without Distress*. Philadelphia and New York: J. P. Lippincott Co.

SEMMES, J. 1968. Hemispheric specialization: a possible clue to mechanism. *Neuropsychologia*. 6: 11–26.

SHAPIRO, DEANE H., JR., and ZIFFERBLATT, STEVEN M. 1976. Zen meditation and behavioral self-control: similarities, differences, and clinical applications. *American Psychologist*. 519–32.

SHAPIRO, D., TURSKY, B., and SCHWARTZ, G. E. 1970. Differentiation of heart rate and systolic blood pressure in man by operant conditioning. In *Biofeedback and Self Control*, ed. T. X. Barber. Chicago: Aldine, Atherton.

SHARPLESS, S., and JASPER, H. H. 1956. Habituation of the arousal reaction. *Brain*. 79: 655–80.

SHERRINGTON, SIR CHARLES. 1947. *The Integrative Action of the Nervous System*. Cambridge, Eng.: Cambridge Univ. Press.

SHEVRIN, H. 1973. Brain wave correlates of subliminal stimulation, unconscious attention, primary and secondary process thinking, and repressiveness. *Psychol. Issues*. 8: 56–87.

SILVERMAN, A. J., ADEVAI, G., and McGOUGH, W. E. 1966. Some relationships between handedness and perception. *J. Psychosom. Res*. 10: 151–58.

SIMEONS, A. T. W. 1961. *Man's Presumptuous Brain: An Evolutionary Interpretation of Psychosomatic Disease*. New York: Dutton & Co.

SIMON, H. A. 1957. *Models of Man*. New York: John Wiley & Sons.

SIMONTON, O. C., and SIMONTON, S. 1975. Belief systems and management of the emotional aspects of malignancy. *Journal of Transpersonal Psychology*. 7 (1): 29–48.

SKINNER, B. F. 1971. *Beyond Freedom and Dignity*. New York: Knopf.

SLATER, P. E. 1970. *The Pursuit of Loneliness*. Boston: Beacon Press.

SLATTER, K. H. 1960. Alpha rhythms and mental imagery. *EEG and Clinical Neurophysiology*. 12: 851–59.

SMITH, A. 1966. Speech and other functions after left (dominant) hemispherectomy. *J. Neurol. Neurosurg. Psychiatry*. 29: 467–71.

SPARKS, L. 1962. *Self-Hypnosis*. New York: Grune & Stratton.

SPERRY, R. W. 1965. Mind, brain, and humanist values. In *New Views of the Nature of Man*, ed. J. Platt. Chicago: Univ. of Chicago Press.

————. 1968. Hemisphere deconnection and unity in conscious awareness. *Am. Psychol*. 23: 723–33.

————, GAZZANIGA, M. S., and BOGEN, J. E. 1969. Interhemispheric relationships: the neocortical commissures:
syndromes of hemisphere disconnection. In *Handbook of
Clinical Neurology,* ed. P. J. Vinken and G. W. Bruyn.
Vol. 4. Amsterdam: North Holland Publishing Co.

STACE, W. T. 1960. *The Teachings of the Mystics.* New York:
New American Library.

STAPP, H. P. 1971. S-matrix interpretation of quantum theory.
Physical Review. D3: 1303–20.

STEIN, MARVIN, SCHIAUI, RAUL C., and CAMERINO, MARIA.
1976. Influence of brain and behavior on the immune system. *Science.* 191: 435–40.

STERMAN, M. B. 1974. Neurophysiological and clinical studies
of sensorimotor EEG biofeedback training: some effects on
epilepsy. In *Seminars in Psychiatry,* ed. L. Birk. Vol. 5
(4): pp. 507–25. New York: Grune & Stratton.

————. 1975. Clinical implications of EEG biofeedback training: a critical appraisal. In *Biofeedback: Theory and Research,* ed. Gary E. Schwartz and Jackson Beatty, chapter
18. New York: Academic Press.

————, MACDONALD, L. R., and STONE, R. K. 1974. Biofeedback training of the sensorimotor electroencephalogram
rhythm in man: effects on epilepsy Epilepsia. 15: 395–416.

STENT, G. 1972. Prematurity and uniqueness in scientific discovery. *Sci. Am.* 227: 84–93.

————. 1975. Limits to the scientific understanding of man.
Science. 187: 1052–57.

STEVENS, J. 1959. Emotional activation of the EEG in convulsive disorders. *Journal of Nervous and Mental Disorders.*
128: 339–51.

SUINN, R. M. 1976. Body thinking: psychology for Olympic
champs. *Psychology Today,* July, 1976.

SULLIVAN, H. S. 1953. *The Interpersonal Theory of Psychiatry.*
Edited by H. Perry and M. Gawel. New York: Norton &
Co.

SUZUKI, D. T. 1952. *Studies in the Lankavatara Sutra.* London:
Routledge & Kegan Paul.

————. 1959a. *Zen and Japanese Culture*. New York: Vollingen Series.

————. 1959b. Preface to *Mahayana Buddhism,* by B. L. Suzuki. London: Allen & Unwin.

————. 1963. *Outlines of Mahayana Buddhism.* New York: Schocken Books.

————. 1968a. *The Essence of Buddhism.* Kyoto, Japan: Hozokan.

————. 1968b. *On Indian Mahayana Buddhism.* Edited by E. Conze. New York: Harper & Row.

SWISCHER, L., and HIRSCH, I. J. 1972. Brain damage and the ordering of two temporally successive stimuli. *Neuropsychologia.* 10: 137–52.

SZENT-GYORGI, A. 1960 *Introduction to a Submolecular Biology.* New York: Academia Press.

TARSKI, A. 1944. The semantic conception of truth and the foundations of semantics. *Philosophy and Phenomenological Res.* 14: 359.

TART, C. T. 1967. Psychedelic experiences associated with a novel hypnotic procedure, mutual hypnosis. *Amer. J. Clin. Hypnosis.* 10: 65–78. Reprinted in *Altered States of Consciousness: A Book of Readings,* ed. C. T. Tart, pp. 291–308. New York: John Wiley & Sons.

————. 1970. Transpersonal potentialities of deep hypnosis. *J. Transpersonal Psych.* 2 (I).

————. 1972. State of consciousness and state-specific sciences. *Science.* 176: 1203–10.

————, and DICK L. 1970. Conscious control of dreaming: 1. The posthypnotic dream. *J. Ab. Psych.* 76: 304–15.

TERZIAN, H. 1964. Behavioural and EEG effects of intracarotid Sodium Amytal injections. *Acta Neurochir.* (Wien). 12: 230–40.

THIRRING, W. 1968. *Urbausteine der Materie. Almanach der Osterreichischen Akademie der Wissenschaften.* 118: 153–62. Vienna, Austria.

THOM, R. 1972. *Stabilité Structurelle et Morphogenese.* Reading Mass.: W. A. Benjamin, Inc.

Time, December 11, 1972, p. 43. The greening of the astronauts.

TINBERGEN, NIKOLAS. 1974. Etiology and stress diseases. *Science.* 185: 26.

TOULMIN, S. 1973. Smithsonian presentation in memory of Copernicus. *Science News.* 103.

TOWNES, CHARLES. 1976. The convergence of science and religion. *California Monthly,* February, 1976, pp. 10–19.

TREHUB, A. 1971. The brain as a parallel coherent detector. *Science.* 174: 722.

ULLMAN, M., and KRIPPNER, S. 1970. *Dream Studies and Telepathy: An Experimental Approach.* New York: Parapsychology Foundation.

VARNI, J. G., DOERR, H. O., and FRANKLIN, J. R. 1971. Bilateral differences in skin resistance and vasomotor activity. *Psychophysiology.* 8: 390–400.

VELLA, E. J., BUTLER, S. R., and GLASS, A. 1972. Electrical correlate of right hemisphere function. *Nature.* 236: 125–126.

VICKERS, G. 1970. *Freedom in a Rocking Boat: Changing Values in an Unstable Society.* London: Penguin Press. Reprinted, New York: Pelican Books, 1972.

VIVEKANANDA, S. 1972. *Jnana Yoga.* New York: Ramakrishna-Vivekananda Center.

VON BERTALANFFY, L. 1967. *Robots, Men and Minds.* New York: Braziller.

————. 1971. System, Symbol, and the Image of Man. In *The Interface Between Psychiatry and Anthropology,* ed. I. Gladston, chapter 4. New York: Brunner-Magel.

WADA, J., and RASMUSSEN, T. 1960. Intracarotid injection of Sodium Amytal for the lateralization of cerebral speech dominance. *J. Neurosurg.* 17: 266–82.

300 Bibliography

WADDINGTON, C. H. 1969. The theory of evolution today. In *Beyond Reductionism,* ed. A. Koestler and J. R. Smythies. London: Radius Book/Hutchinson. Reprinted 1972.

WALKER, EVAN HARRIS. 1970. The nature of consciousness. *Mathematical Biosciences.* 7: 131–78.

————. 1974. Consciousness and quantum theory. In *Psychic Exploration: A Challenge for Science,* ed. J. White. New York: G. P. Putnam's Sons.

WALLACE, ANTHONY F. C. 1956. Revitalization movements. *Amer. Anthropologist.* 58: 264–81.

————. 1972. Paradigmatic processes in cultural change. *Amer. Anthropologist.* 74: 467–78.

WALLACE, G. 1926. *The Art of Thought.* New York: Harcourt Brace.

WALLACE, R. K. 1970. Physiological effects of transcendental meditation. *Science.* 167: 1751–54.

————. 1974. *Neurophysiology of Enlightenment: Scientific Research on Transcendental Meditation.* New York: MIU Press.

WALTER, R. D., and YEAGER, C. L. 1956. Visual imagery and electroencephalographic changes. *EEG and Clinical Neurophysiology.* 8: 193–99.

WALTER, W. G. 1963 *The Living Brain.* New York: Norton.

WANG, S. C. 1964. *Neural Control of Sweating.* Madison, Wisconsin: Univ. of Wisconsin Press.

WATERS, FRANK. 1963. *Book of the Hopi.* New York: Ballantine Books.

WATTS, A. W. 1957. *The Way of Zen.* New York: Vintage Books.

————. 1967. *The Book: On the Taboo Against Knowing Who You Are.* New York: Collier.

WEIL, A. 1973. *The Natural Mind.* Boston: Houghton Mifflin.

WEINBERG, S. 1974. Unified theories of elementary-particle interaction. *Scientific American.* 231 (1): 50–59.

WEINER, N. 1954. *The Human Use of Human Beings.* New York: Avon Books.

WEINSTEIN, E. A., and KAHN, R. L. 1955. *Denial of Illness:*

Symbolic and Physiological Aspects. Springfield, Ill.: Charles C. Thomas.

WEISS, P. 1969. The living system. In *Beyond Reductionism,* ed. A Koestler and J. R. Smythies. London: Radius Book/Hutchinson. Reprinted 1972.

WEISSKOPF, V. F. 1972. *Physics in the Twentieth Century, Selected Essays.* Cambridge, Mass.: M.I.T. Press.

WEITZBAUM, J. 1972. The impact of the computer on society. *Science.* 176: 609.

WEITZENHOFFER, A. 1953. *Hypnotism.* New York: John Wiley.

WENGER, M. A., BAGGHI, B. K., and ANAND, B. 1961. Experiments in India on "voluntary" control of the heart and pulse. *Circulation.* 24: 1319–25.

———. 1963. "Voluntary" heart and pulse control by yoga methods. *International Journal of Parapsychology.* 5: 25–41.

WERRE, P. F. 1957. Relations between EEG and psychological data in normal adults. Leiden: Leiden Univ. Press.

WEYL, H. 1949. *Philosophy of Mathematics and Natural Science.* Princeton, N.J.: Princeton Univ. Press.

WHALEN, R. J. 1972. *Catch a Falling Flag.* New York: Houghton, Mifflin.

WHEELER, J. A. 1971. From Mendeleev's atom to the collapsing star. *Trans. N.Y. Acad. Sci.* 33:

———. 1973. Interview in Intellectual Digest, May, 1973.

WHITE, J. 1972. *The Highest State of Consciousness.* Garden City, N.Y.: Doubleday.

WHITE, L. 1967. The historic roots of our ecologic crisis. *Science.* 155 (3767).

WHITE, M. J. 1969. Laterality differences in perception: a review. *Psychol. Bull.* 72: 387–405.

WHITEHEAD, ALFRED NORTH. 1925. *Science and the Modern World.* New York: Macmillan.

———. 1961. *The Interpretation of Science, Selected Essays,* ed. A. H. Johnson. Indianapolis and N.Y.: Bobbs-Merrill.

WHITFIELD, I. C. 1967. *The Auditory Pathway.* Baltimore: Williams & Wilkins.

WIENER, P. P. 1951. *Leibniz—Selections*. New York: Ch. Scribner's Sons.

WIGNER, E. P. 1961. Remarks on the mind-body question. In *The Scientist Speculates,* ed. I. J. Good. London: Heineman.

———. 1970. *Symmetries and Reflections,* Scientific Essays. Cambridge, Mass.: M.I.T. Press.

WILHELM, H. 1964. *Change: Eight Lectures on the I Ching.* New York: Harper Torchbooks.

WILHELM, R. 1967. *The I Ching or Book of Changes.* Princeton, N.J.: Princeton Univ. Press.

———. 1972. *The Secret of the Golden Flower.* London: Routledge & Kegan Paul.

WILLIAMS, M. 1953. Psychophysiological responsiveness to psychological stress in early schizophrenic reaction. *Psychosom. Med.* 15: 456–63.

WITKIN, H. A. 1969. Influencing dream content. In *Dream Psychology and the New Biology of Dreaming,* ed. M. Kramer. Springfield, Ill.: C. C. Thomas.

WOLF, W. 1970. Are we ever reborn? *J. for the Study of Consciousness.* 3 (2).

WOLFF, H. G. 1953a. Changes in vulnerability of tissue: an aspect of man's response to Throat. *The National Institute of Health Annual Lectures.* U.S. Dept. of Health, Education and Welfare, Publication No. 388, pp. 38–71.

———. 1953b. *Stress and Disease.* Edited and revised by Stewart Wolf and Helen Goodell. Second Edition, 1968. Springfield, Ill.: Charles C. Thomas.

WOODRUFF, DIANA S., and BIRREN, JAMES, E. 1972. Biofeedback conditioning of the EEG alpha rhythm in young and old subjects. *Proceedings of the Annual Convention of the American Psychological Association.* 7 (Pt. 2): 673–74.

WOODRUFF, W. 1967. *Impact of Western Man.* New York: St. Martin's Press.

WOODWARD, F. L., ED. and TRANS. 1973. *Some Sayings of the Buddha.* New York: Oxford Univ. Press.

WOOLFOLK, R. L. 1975. Psychophysiological correlates of meditation. *Arch. Gen. Psychiatry.* 32: 1326–33.

YOUNG, ARTHUR M. 1976*a*. *The Reflexive Universe*. New York: Delacorte Press.
———. 1976*b*. *The Geometry of Meaning* New York: Delacorte Press.

ZAIDEL, ERAH, and SPERRY, R. W. 1975. Unsigned, untitled comment in *Behavior Today,* October 13, 1975.
ZANGWILL, O. L. 1967. Speech and the minor hemispheres. *Acta Neurol. Psychiatr. Belg.* 67: 1013–20.
ZIMMER, H. 1972. *Myths and Symbols in Indian Art and Civilization*. Princeton, N.J.: Princeton Univ. Press.

Index

305

complementarity principle, 53–63; creativity theory, 105–6; determinism and, 48–53; and hologram theory, 126–41; hypothetical entities, 51–2; neuronal functions and, 132–41; objectivity vs. projection in, 42–6; uncertainty principle, 14, 33, 49–51, 52, 58, 69, 126, 127, 132, 133, 136, 246–7. *See also* physics
quarks, 14, 52

Rahe, Richard, 198, 199, 200
Rama, Swami, 150–1, 168
reality, 37–9, 128–32
rebirth, 231–6; spiritual, 228–9
Reich, Charles, 19
Reichian analysis, 23
Relativity Theory, 56–8, 241–2, 246, 251–2. *See also* Einstein, Albert
relaxation response, 197, 201–7
relaxation techniques, 70, 88, 204
religion, 63–6, 208, 210, 215, 223, 231, 235–6
repression, 102, 179
reticular activating system (RAS), 76, 77–81, 189
reverie, 168
revitalization, 7, 8
Rosen, David H., 227–8, 229
Rosenthal, Robert, 45
Roszak, Theodore, 18
Rothenberg, Albert, 105, 106
Russell, Bertrand, 107, 138

samadhi, 151–2
Schachter, Stanley, 193
Schedule of Recent Experience Scale (SRE), 198–9
Schoenberg, Arnold, 106–7
Schwarz, Jack, 145–6, 171–5
science: confluence with religion and mysticism, 5–7, 13–14, 63–6; evolution of, 248–57; holistic orientations, 3–4. *See also* scientific inquiry; scientific method
science of consciousness, 16–19, 143, 256–9; evolutionary theory and, 241–8; primary focus of, 19; principle of complementarity, 53–63; Relativity Theory and, 56–8
scientific inquiry: classical, 32–3,

37–9, 48–9; on death, 237–8; Gödel's Theorem and, 46–8, 52; indeterminacy, 131–2; meaning and, 18–19; newly evolving model, 36; objectivity in, 17–18, 39–46; prematurity, 250; and technological innovation, 14–15. *See also* scientific method
scientific method, 64; and altered consciousness, 57–8; isolation of relevant variables, 41–2; "unacceptable" data, 15–16. *See also* scientific inquiry
scientism, 248
Selye, Hans, 71, 183, 188, 194, 200
sex differences, 91, 97–100
Shakyamuni Buddha, 180
Shapiro, Deane H., Jr., 205–6
Shaw, J. C., 161
Shevrin, Howard, 82, 83–5
Simeons, A. T. W., 190–3, 194, 195, 200
Singh, B., 151–3
Skinner, B. F., 34, 256
slow-wave potentials, 123–6, 127, 135
space-time continuum, 56–7, 246, 251
Sperry, Roger, 88–9, 92–3, 94, 100–1, 103–4, 249–50
spontaneous remission, 181, 184
Sri Ramananda, 151
Stent, Gunther S., 141, 250
Sterman, Barry, 75–6, 158
stress and stress disorders, 28–9, 182, 183, 185–201, 218; biochemical response to, 185–8; brain function and, 102, 186–95; meditation to reduce, 203–7. *See also* psychosomatic disorders
Structure of Scientific Revolutions, The (Kuhn), 10, 37, 38
subliminal perception, 80, 81–5
suicide, 227–9
synaptic cleft, 123, 126, 133, 136

Tart, Charles, 8, 254
technology, 13–14, 142
theta activity, 155, 163–71, 172, 173; creativity and, 164, 165–8; psychopathological correlates, 163–4, 165
Thom, R., 130